Costly Grace

Costly Grace

An Evangelical Minister's
Rediscovery of Faith,
Hope, and Love

Rob Schenck

HARPER

An Imprint of HarperCollinsPublishers

Poem by Peter Frick on page 252 excerpted from Dietrich Bonhoeffer Works in English series copyright © Fortress Press; reproduced by permission.

HarperCollins books may be purchased for educational, business, or sales promotional use. For information, please email the Special Markets Department at SPsales@harpercollins.com.

FIRST EDITION

Library of Congress Cataloging-in-Publication Data has been applied for.

ISBN 978-0-06-268793-7

18 19 20 21 22 LSC 10 9 8 7 6 5 4 3 2 1

To Cheryl, an extraordinary woman,
the best life partner imaginable,
without whom this story could never be told.
I love you more deeply and fully than I have ever loved
another human being.

Cheap grace is the mortal enemy of our Church. Our struggle today is for costly grace.

—DIETRICH BONHOEFFER, *THE COST OF DISCIPLESHIP*

Contents

Author's Note

English translations of the Bible vary greatly. Evangelicals typically read from a broad cross section of them. In keeping with our long-established and fluid practice of picking a translation based on the language style or word choice related to a particular passage, I've used a variety of translations in this writing, including the King James Version, New International Version, the English Standard Version, the Revised Standard Version, the New American Standard Version, and others.

Preface

This is my story, or, to be more precise, these are my stories. Three of them, each distinct with a trajectory that then changed course—disrupting my life, thrusting me into the limelight, and complicating the lives of my family members. All of them share an important element: they revolve around my faith in God and my confession of Jesus Christ as Savior and Lord.

I am a born-again Christian and an evangelical minister. I've been a believer for over forty years and ordained for thirty-five. For the last two decades I've served as a missionary to top elected and appointed officials in Washington, D.C., including members of Congress, White House personnel, and federal judges. Whenever I meet new people, I often watch split-second deliberations flicker across their faces. Some worry I will try to convert them or preach to them about their own beliefs or the evil in their souls (or their voting histories). Sometimes I see a flash of anger, or an initial openness give way to an impenetrable wall of resistance to anything I might say.

I've also seen faces light up with warmth and eagerness to hear my message. The nature of their curiosity is sometimes sacred, sometimes the opposite. Some hope I might impart wisdom about a gospel passage, but others beg me to share some terrible insider story about those they perceive to be our enemies—the liberals and the Democrats, the atheists and the abortionists, the champions of gay rights and transgender bathrooms—so that they can add some telling, personal details to what they already know from Fox News, Rush Limbaugh, and, sometimes, from the pulpit during Sunday services. If this is what they're looking for from me these days, they'll be disappointed by my response.

Mine is not a story of faith discovered and then abandoned—a familiar trope. No, I'm determined to always be an evangelical, now and until the day I die. The gospel, the *evangel*, the Good News of God's generous and permanent love for all of humanity, is at the heart of what I believe. I remain joyfully and with great conviction a believer in this *evangel*.

Like most Christians, my road to faith was fraught with mixed motives, imperfect desire, and a shallow understanding of the full implications of what immersion in religious life entails. When I fully surrendered to the Lord, my life changed course irrevocably—it will forever remain the most significant day of my life. In my first conversion, I encountered an uncluttered, straightforward, what-you-see-is-what-you-get Jesus. He was the rabbi who taught a compassionate and moral way of living in his Sermon on the Mount. ("Blessed are those who hunger and thirst for righteousness, for they shall be satisfied.") This Jesus called people to love God and to love one another. ("Blessed are the merciful, for they shall receive mercy.") He welcomed everyone, including the worst of sinners, to join him on the path to paradise. ("Blessed are the poor in spirit, for theirs is the kingdom of heaven.") He was patient, forgiving, peaceful, and utterly selfless. And he was even more: a model for a way to live a life of goodness. He was the Son of God, and his resurrection offered me and fellow believers the power to overcome human weakness and proclivity toward sin and replace it with the sincere effort to strive for good. Jesus' message moved me emotionally, it filled a deep spiritual void in my heart, and it fed and sustained me intellectually. With it came a surrogate family marked with warmth, love, acceptance, and deep bonds of friendship.

With time, though, I nearly lost track of this first Jesus. I would pray in His name and invoke His teachings publicly and privately, but I became spiritually disoriented and, in many ways, isolated. During my second life, I would listen to and eagerly follow the politicized gospel preached by other, insistent voices from the political arena, talk radio, and an audience craving movement champions. I distorted the words or muffled the voice of Jesus, too often preferring instead the sound of my own. A looming shadow cast by outsized political celebrities clouded my vision so that I could no longer see Jesus as He truly was and is. Instead, I had entered a kind of hall of mirrors with my own reflection and those of other players striding with purpose into the highest reaches of political power. As I joined them, I left behind many of those with whom I began my journey. My world shrank from a vast extended family to one that was small, and insular, and politically radical—even as we presented ourselves as the champions of conservatism.

For more than thirty years, I espoused and embodied the type of "born-again" evangelical Christianity that had become almost synonymous with a right-wing and increasingly aggressive Republican Party. What was once a simple, gratifying spiritual community defined by Jesus' command to love God and neighbor and to care for the sick, the lonely, the poor, and the forgotten had been nearly lost and certainly compromised by the political posturing and sparring of the last decades. I often played an important role in that gamesmanship and in the destructive transformation of what was once a beautiful thing.

As Saint Paul traveled to Damascus, you could say he had it easy. His journey was interrupted by a blinding light and Jesus spoke directly to him. God was no less determined to reorient my work, but did so incrementally. Slowly, inexorably, through unexpected messengers, I was forced to stop ignoring my arrogance, my ambition, and the often cynical actions of my community. When I began to listen with an open heart to everyone—including those I had considered my "enemies"—I began to understand that I, and my community, had committed a grievous sin: we distorted the true gospel of our Lord for our immediate purposes. But these inchoate feelings found their crucible only when I rediscovered the life and writings of Dietrich Bonhoeffer, a German theologian and evangelical pastor who was executed in a Nazi concentration camp for his opposition to Adolf Hitler. When I reread his work and then undertook a pilgrimage following his life and ministry, I found a posthumous spiritual mentor who could lead me out of my confusion and back on the path toward the Christ I had met decades earlier.

Later, my doctoral work focused on Bonhoeffer's theological insights. I found I could not master the German necessary for that level of research, so instead I looked at the evangelical church during the time in which he lived. What I discovered shocked me but also completely reorganized my thinking. I saw in those times a reflection of our own. My thesis was simple: for American evangelicals, the lines between theology and politics have become blurred, eroding the boundaries that distinguish the spiritual from the temporal, generating confusion among many believers about their Christian and political identities, exposing them to the temptation of political idolatry. What had happened to the German Christians was happening to us.

My rediscovery of Bonhoeffer brought me back to an appreciation of the true meaning of the gospel. It also led to a rebirth of love and commitment in my marriage and with my children and a reconfiguration of my public mission. But there were inevitable, sadly necessary losses. My relationship to a community I once held dear was strained almost to the breaking point by political calculations that seemed profoundly compromised.

Mine has been an odyssey of hope found, then lost, but rediscovered. In recounting my modern-day pilgrimage, during a time of great spiritual pain and national discord, I hope to give others reason to believe—maybe for the first time, or, after faith has been lost, to believe again.

Bonhoeffer taught me that a minister must be engaged fully with the world, and I have been especially blessed to have enjoyed a life crowded with a fascinating array of people, some of whom have touched my word positively, and others in ways much less so. I write with no judgment of them here—my judgment is directed internally. These stories are not intended to impugn, insult, or disparage others, because I believe, with soul-deep conviction, that we are *all* sinners saved by God's Amazing Grace. I cannot expect more or better of others than I can of myself. I am deeply aware of my own flaws: my pride, my ambition, and my capacity to rationalize actions I know, deep in my heart, are wrong. A basic fact of our humanity is that we are all capable of the very worst of human behaviors. As one of my early mentors, a Lutheran pastor, once said, "Everybody has a little good and a little bad. Don't ever forget that."

I haven't. And in these pages, I will share my reckoning with both.

Part I

My First Conversion

In ordinary life we hardly realize that we receive a great deal more than we give, and that it is only with gratitude that life becomes rich. It is very easy to overestimate the importance of our own achievements in comparison to what we owe others.

—DIETRICH BONHOEFFER,
LETTERS AND PAPERS FROM PRISON

I

Coming to Jesus

Ll our young lives my identical twin brother, Paul, and I
had searched for a place to belong. We were two Jewish
kids who knew no other religious identity but, at the same
time, were no longer practicing the faith in which we had been raised.
Marge, our mother, was a convert and our father, Hank, had lost interest in continuing our religious education when the social and financial
demands of temple membership exceeded what he thought was fair.
And so our bar mitzvah preparations ended abruptly.

Our hometown of twelve thousand, Grand Island, New York, was
literally an island, smack dab in the middle of the Niagara River, just
three miles upstream from the famous falls. When I rode my bike along
West River Road, I could see Ontario, Canada, and when I hitchhiked
to a friend's house on the East River, I would look across to the Buffalo
suburbs of Kenmore and Tonawanda. We were the youngest of four,
our two sisters, from our mother's first marriage, were six and eight
years older. We all loved each other but our ages, different families of
origin, and respective cultural experiences—they had started out in
life as Christians, my brother and I as Jews—not to mention the unique
bond that is twinship, left Paul and me in our own world.

So many times in my life, Paul was the catalyst for momentous
change. And none of the biggest moments—not the years of ministry,
not the arrests for our acts of conscience in anti-abortion protests, not
the move to Washington, D.C., or the work with elected officials, the

publicity, or the politics—would have happened if Paul had not forged a friendship with a Methodist minister's son, Charlie Hepler. Charlie was an intense, withdrawn, and troubled boy, but Paul drew him out in long conversations about God, about the Bible, about Christianity and prayer. My brother would come home and share those conversations with me in the basement room we claimed as our private space. I listened with genuine interest and curiosity, but also skepticism—even worry. I could not ignore all the stories about the Manson Family murders, or how Hare Krishna devotees had left secure middle-class lives to wear strange robes and sell flowers in airports and on sidewalks. It was a time when weird cults ensnared vulnerable young people and turned them into zombies.

My brother was a levelheaded guy, so all this talk about Christianity felt unsettling to both my Jewish and secular sensibilities. Our father was not a pious man, but his ethnic Jewish identity was strong and predicated as much in family tradition as in suspiciously viewing any majority religious group as potential persecutors. For me, all Christians were pretty much alike, and I knew nothing about Methodists, much less their founder John Wesley, who emphasized not the busy, endlessly rationalizing mind but touching the heart of the believer.

As Paul talked about Jesus, I remembered when, as a six-year-old boy, I went to play at the house of a Portuguese-Catholic neighbor. In my little friend's bedroom hung a crucifix, the image of a bloodied man, with jutting ribs and a crown of thorns, dangling from nails. I was transfixed by it, yet frightened into a sleepless and fitful night. Years later, when I was a pot-smoking thirteen-year-old, I went to the Buffalo Memorial Auditorium and encountered the man on the cross again— this time earnest but still tragic—from a very different perspective in the rock opera *Jesus Christ Superstar*.

The musical was consistent with who we were back then—too young to have been involved in the counterculture of the sixties, but just old enough to indulge in its lingering messages and music and challenges to authority. Our father set the tone and the direction—more accurately the lack of direction—for our lives. He subscribed to the "hands-off" school of parenting with spasms of explosive rage. In general, our early adolescence was remarkably unsupervised. This comported with the way Dad grew up in the thirties and forties, with a working mother and a chronically ill father who was often hospitalized. For us, though, coming of age during the tempestuous post-Vietnam era meant exposure to the youth culture of the day, but without the existential stakes of being drafted. We protested the bombing of Cambodia, Nixon, and napalm. Jesus as countercultural rebel fit nicely into those times. We challenged everything, our hair was long, and we wore army fatigue jackets and provocative T-shirts. Our bedroom was festooned with beads and plastered with iridescent posters, including one of Popeye and Olive Oyl having sex—all bathed in the glow of a black light and the haze of marijuana smoke. In those days the life of Christ was not completely alien to me, but the Christian religion Paul was exploring seemed a bridge too far. And yet, slowly, I began to venture across it. At least to see what might be on the other side.

One day Paul told me Charlie had invited us to go to church with him. Not his father's prestigious church, Trinity United Methodist—a large, established institution, located prominently in the center of the Island—but the Emmanuel Evangelical United Brethren. This group, which had recently merged with the Methodists, had colonial-era German roots. Emmanuel, known among locals as the *other* Methodist church, had a relatively young minister and a slightly bohemian vibe, and Charlie liked the motley group of young people who gathered there. We joined him for the Friday-night prayer meeting.

Charlie escorted us into the simple sanctuary that reminded me of our childhood temple, Beth El, in Niagara Falls. A prayer service was under way and Pastor Fred Dixon came down off the platform to be with the people, a stark contrast with our rabbi's remote behavior. Emmanuel felt more like being in somebody's living room than in a religious ritual. I looked around at the pews: older men and women sat with young parents of small children, and there were many teenagers, most a few years older than Paul and me. It was the unseen presence, though, that affected me. My brother and I sensed something more than simple human companionship in that place—a presence outside and above the people collected there. I would later call it "the Spirit of God," but I had no such language then. Whatever it was, I was transported to a new realm, one that was permeated with love and an overwhelming, palpable, and almost visible energy.

After the service, Charlie led us to the adjoining fellowship hall, where about fifteen kids were sitting on the floor in a circle. They looked like us: boys with shoulder-length hair, T-shirts, torn-up jeans, and weathered army jackets. Two older girls strummed guitars and led the group in singing as Paul, Charlie, and I found spots in the circle. I was unsure about being a Jewish kid in a Christian church. I found out only later that everyone was delighted Charlie had managed to bring the two *Jewish* Schenck boys to the meeting; they had never spent time with Jews before. To show us how much they accepted us, one of the girls told us the Jewish people were "the apple of God's eye." We had grown up with regular infusions of the "Chosen People" narrative but never imagined that, for these Christians, Jews would have a special place in God's plan for the world. Christians had always been portrayed as anti-Semites. To have our Jewishness celebrated, rather than shunned, came as a gratifying surprise.

When the group sat on the floor, leaning against each other, swaying back and forth to the music, I tentatively joined them as they sang, "I've got peace like a river / I've got peace like a river / I've got peace like a river in my soul." Some of them had their eyes closed; others looked at each other and exchanged smiles. We all rocked gently in the candlelight, and gradually I got the hang of the chorus. I didn't expect to be moved or to feel as if I had caught a glimpse of something I had longed for. But in that room, for the first time in my life, I knew a profound feeling of comfort and connection as peace flowed like a river in my own restless, troubled, adolescent soul.

★★★

Paul and I returned to the Friday-night meetings, but not because I had come to a personal belief in God—not yet. We have always been seekers, and we were looking for something more meaningful than the cultural and religious netherworld we inhabited at the time. Untethered to a synagogue or religious study, classic rebels without causes, we experienced what I now realize was spiritual hunger. We read the Hindu Vedas, books about the search for extraterrestrial life, and what was known as the Aquarian Gospel—an early-twentieth-century manuscript that was a potent mix of astrology, Christianity, and philosophy. We went to meetings at Emmanuel because we liked the kids who were there, the feeling of community, the introduction to Jesus—it all felt harmonious. It was a new kind of family.

Charlie told us a special speaker was going to lead a combined Lenten service at Trinity Methodist, his father's church. I had no idea what Lent was but knew it came around the time of Passover, which somehow made it less alien. The fact that Dr. Peter Bolt would be coming all the way from England was a big deal in our small town. Plus, I had never been inside a formal Methodist church and I was curious. I envisioned there would be hooded monks intoning Latin prayers, but Charlie reassured us it would be a lot like Emmanuel. The rest of our Friday-night group was going and Paul and I didn't want to be left out, so we accepted Charlie's invitation. Before the event, my brother and I planned our strategy. We worried the ushers might throw us out if they discovered we were Jewish. What would we say? Argue or just get out as quickly as possible? We decided we would leave peacefully.

I was a nervous wreck, but the people were warm and loving, accepting and welcoming, just as the young people at Emmanuel were on Friday nights. And once again I felt a presence in the sanctuary. We were instantly at home and our sense of comfort and safety only increased as the service wore on. No guitars this time, but instead a strenuous organ nearly drowned out the voices of the congregants. Then Reverend Bolt preached the sermon and invited us to "meet here the living Lord Jesus Christ." I wanted to respond, but I hesitated as I thought of my father's disapproval. Our bedtime stories were often about the Holocaust and the crimes against humanity, mostly against Jews, that had been perpetrated by Christians. Part and parcel of this was his emphasis on not believing the tenets of Christianity, because he saw them as being intrinsically hostile toward Jews. (That didn't stop him from falling in love and deciding to marry my mother, who was a Christian. But she had to agree to convert.) Now Reverend Bolt was encouraging us to step forward and embrace those Christian beliefs—and change our identity in the process. The implications were enormous.

As Reverend Bolt waved people forward, the organ played, first softly and then gradually building to a crescendo that reflected the experience in my soul. As I saw others leave their pews, it was as if an external power was forcing me to join them. I recognized more fully than I had ever before that Christianity, in all its grandeur and simplicity, was the true and even ultimate belief. Paul and I glanced at one another, then simultaneously rose and made our way to the aisle.

Here I was, an already awkward sixteen-year-old male, bending my knees for the first time in my life to pray in public. Yet I did it almost automatically, feeling barely self-conscious. Paul was right beside me. "Dear God, I admit I am a sinner in need of your saving," I repeated after Reverend Bolt. "I confess my sin and trust in Jesus alone as my

Savior. I pledge to follow Christ as my Lord. Thank you for your great gift of salvation. Send your Holy Spirit to help me live for You all the days of my life. In Jesus' name. Amen."

Some at the altar were crying. Others looked profoundly relieved. I don't know what I looked like, but Paul's face betrayed a simple happiness that I imagine might have also been on my own. A lifetime of weight had lifted from my shoulders, and I experienced a satisfaction I had never known—not in temple, not in a marijuana high, not during sex with a girlfriend, not at a concert. Nowhere had I known the peace that I knew at that moment, in my soul, psyche, body. As I returned to my pew, some who had remained seated were smiling approvingly as we passed. The service closed as we sang:

It is joy unspeakable and full of glory,
Full of glory, full of glory;
It is joy unspeakable and full of glory,
Oh, the half has never yet been told.

I felt every word.

As Paul and I left the church, we met our friends from Emmanuel who had been sitting on the floor in Trinity's expansive vestibule. They had sent a spy in to report on whether we had responded to the altar call, and when it was confirmed we had, there were lots of "Praise the Lord"s. They had wondered if this would be the night we would be saved.

In fact, it was.

When we joined up with our group, smiling and awash in the afterglow of our official and, for evangelicals, crucial public profession of faith, they effusively congratulated us on what we had done. I felt instantly better—spiritually, morally, and even socially. Now I belonged: to God and to the community that had so warmly welcomed, accepted, even affirmed me. Peace was present in that group that I had never experienced at home, in school, or anywhere else. There was friendship and there was music. Our soundtrack was the soaring organ music and the intimate strumming of a guitar while youthful voices sang. Everything about these kids and their churches fed my ravenous soul. I was happy in a way I had never before experienced.

Something about the gospel and the Christian religious experience made sense to me, both intellectually and emotionally. Perhaps this was evidence of my Jewish background: we learned it was our responsibility to wrestle with God and spiritual messages in an active way—as Jacob wrestled with the angel. All that I had learned so far came together. I needed to only look at the positive impact Jesus had made on the lives of those I had come to know, and I wanted the same for me.

At the end of the night, Paul went off with one of our new spiritual companions, and I headed home alone. All my senses heightened in new and extraordinary ways. I looked up at the stars and was struck by the sheer magnificence of God's creation. I felt so completely transformed, I assumed that it would be evident to everyone—strangers on the street, my classmates, my sisters, and of course my parents. Perhaps they would be impressed by my joy and conviction. At some point during that walk home, I realized that part of my responsibility as a new Christian was to bear witness to my conversion. And the place to start was at home.

2
Faith of Our Fathers

When I walked through our front door, I began to ascend the stairs to make the obligatory check-in with my parents. But the night of the service at Trinity, I paused and reflected on what had occurred. As much as Paul and I had changed that momentous evening, all the external points of reference in our lives remained the same. This was still my house, my parents were still my parents, our religious identity had been Jewish. But now, that last certainty had changed.

A wrought-iron railing separated the living room area from the descending staircase, and through it I could see my mother reclining on her La-Z-Boy as she did every night, comfortably watching her favorite TV shows, occasionally helping Dad out with some paperwork for his business. There, Dad sat in his own special chair, adjacent to hers. The gravity of my announcement now made me anxious—my emotions teetered between excitement and dread.

I wanted to tell my parents what had happened to Paul and me that evening, and about the joy of being a part of this beautiful community, the rich world that had opened up as we accepted Jesus as our Savior. But I also knew how completely it upended our cherished family narrative. The one in which my father, Hank, the good Jew, fell in love with Marjorie Wright, a gentile widow with two daughters, in the laundry room of a town-house complex where they lived across the street from each other. It included the trials they had been through, the family conflict before Mom converted, the Jewish identity he had managed to forge for all of us. We knew how to say the prayers, we celebrated the holidays, we stayed home for Rosh Hashanah and fasted on Yom Kippur. We were pretty much on par with most nominal Jews.

The prospect that Mom and Dad could ever succeed as a couple was daunting. When they met, Mom had been widowed for two years—her alcoholic husband had shot himself with a rifle in the attic of their small home, leaving her with two little girls. To add still another level of pathos, Mom suffered from polio as a child and always walked with the help of a cane.

If my mother's handicap was physical, Hank Schenck's was social. He was shy and awkward, but nonetheless approached Marge as she struggled with her basket of laundry. Gallant in his own way, he helped her carry it. Eventually he would make sure they did laundry on the same days so he could see her. He finally summoned the courage to ask her out. My father's family had hoped that their only surviving son, whose extroverted older brother, an Air Force captain, had been killed in a plane crash in Korea, would continue the Schenck name. But they had never dreamed he would choose a disabled, widowed mother of two who was also a shiksa.

When Dad announced his engagement, the family threatened to boycott the wedding unless Marge, a baptized Catholic who had been raised as an Episcopalian, converted to Judaism. Mom had long since left her religion behind and had no objection to their demands. A very understanding and accommodating Reform rabbi was enlisted. He was willing to be flexible about the rigors of Jewish conversion but required my mother to promise the children would be raised Jewish. She agreed, and my parents exchanged vows under a chuppah, the traditional wedding canopy, and seemed to embody a romantic love-conquers-all kind of tale.

But, over time, the touching story of their falling in love and overcoming obstacles gave way to another reality. Both my parents were given to bouts of depression that left them deeply angry—with themselves, with each other, and often with us kids. I can remember many loud and menacing outbursts, my father enraged and threatening, my mother silent but tormented. Money was always a problem—the usual version of never enough. On the night of my conversion, the scene I was about to disrupt in our living room was a calm one—a rare break from years of emotional tumult during most of my childhood and adolescence.

The financial worries were only a part of a much deeper dysfunction that organized our lives. Mom often pulled me aside to demand, "Where's your father?" Dad was usually in the garage tinkering with his massive collection of electrical paraphernalia, a hobby he began as a communications engineer in the Air Force that would later turn into a small business installing phone systems. The garage was his domain, a place where he could gain necessary solitude and a sense of control. But, for Mom, Dad's absences were the harbinger of permanent, catastrophic loss. "I wanna know if he's alive," she would repeat, as if the trauma of her first husband's violent death never left her.

I was scared by her intensity and learned to chalk it up to her quirky personality. But there was more. When Paul and I were around nine years old, Mom suddenly disappeared for what seemed like a terribly long time. Dad and my sisters would only say Mom was in the hospital. When she came home, the powerful medication she was given left her vague and spaced out. At dinner one night, when Dad was working late, she insisted on cutting everyone's badly undercooked strip steaks. She was disoriented and mumbling incoherently. She repeatedly plunged the blade toward the meat on our plates but missed by inches. The dining room table was permanently scarred. I was terrified. My oldest sister, Kathy, gently took the knife and finished serving the dinner.

Mom's extreme moods calmed down as we grew up; perhaps she

was on medication, perhaps having young twin boys worsened her condition, perhaps she just mellowed with age. No one could have imagined the kind of pain and torment the docile middle-aged couple had endured and inflicted when looking at them, sitting in the lamp-light peacefully, watching *The Rockford Files*. I was too familiar with my father's rages and my mother's depressions, and I dreaded trigger-ing either with the news I was about to share. And yet the happiness I felt was so great, the transformation so profound, I couldn't contain myself—despite the fact it would introduce such a potentially volatile revelation into this hard-won tranquility.

I slowly ascended the stairs and walked into the living room. When Mom asked me the pro forma parental question of where I had been, I told her I had gone to Trinity Church. This got her attention less for the religious identity than for its prestige in our town. This was the church of the upper classes, the businessmen and the prominent citizens. These were not the kind of people with whom my parents naturally so-cialized. I could have said that I had gone golfing at the country club and elicited the same reaction. Here was the moment when I could have derailed the conversation, sparing both them and me. But my ex-perience had been too consequential to handle with our usual family approach of passivity and evasion. I decided to try to explain, announc-ing that a visiting British minister had invited us to make Jesus Christ our Lord and Savior and I had accepted the invitation. I had been born again, I said.

Dad put down his paper with a snap and glowered at me. I knew that look. It was usually the prelude to an explosion of rage, and I steeled myself for what was coming. We may not have been religious Jews—at home we ate pork and shrimp, food considered *treyf* or forbidden by observant members of our religion—but there was never any question of our religious identity. In that moment, as I faced my father, I thought of the wartime scrapbook he had kept as a teenager.

When we were small, Paul and I would sit on our dad's knees at our dining room table, the book open in front of us as he slowly turned the pages. Carefully cut newspaper and magazine clippings, especially those involving aerial bombings over Europe, were pasted on the thick pages.

But the record of the heroism of our troops was also a record of tragedy: black-and-white photos of mass graves, human bodies piled atop ash heaps, haunted faces peering out from behind barbed-wire fences, the striped uniforms that looked like sinister and humiliating pajamas, the fragile mountains of discarded eyeglasses. The man to whom I had just announced my conversion had spent a lot of time schooling his two young sons in the collective iconography of the Holocaust. Our childhood imaginations could not fathom what these ghastly scenes were, so our father explained. "This is an example of man's inhumanity to man," he would say. "The Nazis were the most evil people who ever held power, more vile even than the Egyptians who had enslaved our Jewish people. They singled out the Jews, our own people, for extermination. Your generation must never let this happen again," he said, closing the book. "This is what happens when good people do nothing."

And, he told us, the good people who did nothing were Christians.

Now, years later, my father was being told his son had just become a Christian. He was stunned by the certainty of my response. This struck at the core of who he was and who he had raised his sons to be. This skinny kid, six months shy of his sixteenth birthday, had presented him with a fact that challenged his basic expectation that his sons would keep the faith, marry Jewish women, father his Jewish grandchildren, and maintain the traditions of the Schenck family. I wanted to explain that my commitment meant belonging. It meant a new, accepting family, a theology that promised redemption. It meant the presence of this remarkable man, Jesus Christ, in every breathing moment of my days. How could I put all this into words? I was speechless and embarrassed.

"It means Jesus," I said haltingly as my father kept asking what it meant to be saved. I became more and more inarticulate. Finally, Dad couldn't restrain himself. He stormed down the stairs to his garage workshop, his safe retreat when family tensions became too much. My mother had watched this unfold with expressions of curiosity and worry on her face. It was her turn. She asked me why I thought I needed to do this.

Why did I *need* it? I couldn't answer that. What I did know was that I *wanted* it more than I had ever wanted anything in my life. At that point I was too exhausted to explain. The extremes of emotions buffeting me ranged from the deep joy of my time at church to the pain of this confrontation. The conversation ended, at least for that night. Paul didn't come home until my parents were sound asleep. He avoided facing the assault that I experienced as the messenger.

Paul and I were, as always, a united front, which didn't help matters. Dad's anger and sense of betrayal was doubled. This rebellion was too personal. How would he ever explain his sons' defections to Aunt Nikki and her husband, Uncle Al, the cultural pillars of our family, or to his mother, our Nana, and the rest of the Schenck clan? Paul and I held firm, even reveling in what we decided were storms of religious persecution that swirled around us. When we brought the stories of our father's anger to our new friends, they only reinforced our resolve, telling us to stand strong against the devil's attempts to crush our faith. We learned not to shy away from using our father's rejection to enhance our status. After all, none of these believers from Christian families ever had to face religious persecution in their own homes.

When Paul and I announced we were going to be baptized "by full immersion" in the Niagara River, my father realized he needed to deploy the biggest guns in his arsenal. He demanded that before we did this, Paul and I had to see a Hasidic rabbi at the Lubavitcher Chabad House outreach center. "Chabadniks," a derogatory nickname my own family used to describe these "backward Jews" of Eastern European ancestry, were known for their strict adherence to religious law and by their peculiar dress—the men with their long side curls, impressive pointed beards, and prayer shawl tassels flopping from their waists.

Previously, Dad had had no use for these supposed troglodytes. Now they might provide a necessary religious constraint on his two sons whose inappropriate fervor had dangerously metastasized. Paul and I saw the impending encounter with the modern-day Pharisees as yet another opportunity to face an oppressor and emerge even stronger in our testimony of the gospel. So together the three of us drove to Main Street in Buffalo. Dad spent some of the drive continuing his efforts to persuade us to abandon our newfound faith and the rest in agitated silence. We finally arrived and were met by Rabbi Heschel Greenberg.

He welcomed the three of us into a small synagogue. We sat surrounded by stacks of prayer books and other Judaica, and then he asked what brought us to Christianity. We had rehearsed this moment, and Paul began by talking about the biblical prophesies foreshadowing the Messiah. My job was to explain how Jesus aligned perfectly with these predictions. Then it was Rabbi Greenberg's turn. He told us flatly that Christians believe that Jesus was the Messiah but this was not the case. He explained that according to Sacred Scripture, the Messiah would restore the throne of David, rebuild the Temple, and gather the exiles to create the political and spiritual redemption of the Jewish people by bringing them back to Jerusalem. The Messiah was unlikely to perform signs or wonders, but he must be a descendant of David—which Jesus was not.

Rabbi Greenberg went on to challenge the whole notion of conversion. Didn't we have any appreciation for the terrible role of conversion in the history of the Jews, when our people suffered and died as the result of Christian efforts to change their beliefs? We listened respectfully but refused to budge. He then tried the personal tack and probed the pain we were inflicting on our parents. He asked Dad about the kind of Jewish home he had created for us, only to discover that Mom was of gentile birth, which was bad enough, but that she had also undergone a Reform rite of conversion—not an Orthodox one—rendering it "illegitimate" and of no effect. Because the Jewish religion is matrilineal, our mother's Christian birth compromised our Jewish identity. He looked at my father reproachfully for not having shared this crucial bit of information. Disgusted, he deemed my father's twins goyim and gave up.

So did our father. Our visit to the rabbi had exhausted all the resources of his opposition. During the ride home from Buffalo, he was silent, staring ahead, a defeated man. He realized that no argument, no anger, no ultimatums, could change us, and after that he became even more remote. When we defied his plea not to be baptized, instead enthusiastically undergoing immersion by church leaders in the Niagara River, he resolved himself to having lost his sons. My mother was loyal to my father, and a cold wall of silence went up between us and our parents.

3
End Times

During the first summer after our conversion, Paul and I jumped into a cramped Ford Fairlane piloted by the daughter of a prominent family of Emmanuel Church. A recent high school graduate headed for college in the fall, she represented one of the responsible "elders" of our Christian tribe. We were headed for Jesus '74, an outdoor Christian rock music festival held at a big farm in rural Mercer, Pennsylvania. A farmer organized the event that brought together top-flight Christian musicians for the annual three-day festival. This was to be *our* Woodstock, with all sorts of Christian denominations—Baptists, Catholics, Mennonites, Assemblies of God, Presbyterians, Methodists, and even non-Christians who might wander in for the music but leave saved by Jesus.

We arrived on a gorgeous summer day, thrilled to be a part of something big and important and cool—and spiritual. Young families camped alongside wild twenty-somethings, toddlers with dirty faces staggered around taking first steps in the crowd, and a few people of our parents' generation were there. But overwhelmingly there were thousands and thousands of kids our age, nearly all of them white and middle class. For the next three days we sat on blankets, slept in sleeping bags in our tents, feasted on peanut butter and jelly sandwiches, and roasted marshmallows over the fire pit. We stood up and cheered and danced when early Christian rock-and-roll pioneer Larry Norman appeared on stage with his electric guitar and wearing a long green coat with a serpentine tail.

"Why should the devil have all the good music?" he shouted, throwing his head back as his long blond hair streamed behind him. We all went hoarse screaming our approval. When Phil Keaggy walked onstage—the John Sebastian of our world—he dazzled us with the simplicity of his acoustic guitar, his fingers tripping up and down the frets as he sang the lyrical, joyful song "What a Day," about the glorious return of Jesus Christ to reclaim his own and take us all to heaven. Nothing moved us like Andraé Crouch, though. The black gospel singer who later turned pop artist, with his sideburns swooping down his cheeks, sat at the piano while the Disciples, his backup band and singers—women with enormous Afros and men wearing tight vests and shirts—provided harmony as he belted out his top hit, "I Don't Know Why Jesus Loves Me."

One afternoon at the festival, I found myself alone with Cheryl Smith, the girl I had noticed at Emmanuel the first night I attended service there. She was a smart, shy, and very pretty flute player in the Grand Island Senior High School band. With her blond hair and coy smile, she made it difficult for me to focus on God. After one particularly glorious afternoon of music, we washed each other's hair under the stand-alone spigot that was our only source of water for the weekend, and by the time our heads were dry, I could imagine sharing my life with her. I only knew a bit about Cheryl's family story: her house had burned down a year earlier, her parents were divorced, which was unusual in our town, and—unlike many other mothers on the Island— her mom worked outside the home. In a strange way, these unconventional facts of her life made her seem more accessible to me. We were both marginal people in different ways: Cheryl because of her unusual family circumstances, and me because of the unconventional strains in my own family.

I had learned about her journey of faith from a time of sharing at one of our youth circles. She told us that after an initial introduction to the message of Christ while watching a televised sermon at home one night, she attended a youth group at the big Trinity Church. Cheryl's coming to Christ was not at an altar. For her, the moment came when she returned home that night and, once in her bedroom, got on her knees and prayed, "Jesus, come into my heart." Cheryl's father, like mine, was unimpressed with her life-changing conversion. We both laughed ruefully, in the emotional solidarity of children who had seemingly surpassed their parents in understanding the profound. Seventy-two hours before, I had left our house in Grand Island filled with anticipation for the music and for the freedom. I returned with both—and, as a bonus, a huge crush on Cheryl Smith.

Paul and I began the school year in the fall of 1975 drastically changed from the pot-smoking smart alecks our classmates might have remembered from our freshman year. Back then, as in most schools at the time, our culture was dichotomized between the "jocks" and "freaks." If we were part of any group during freshman and sophomore years, Paul and I were with the freaks. My hair was as long as most of the girls'. I wore jeans every day and smoked both cigarettes and weed—although I never indulged in alcohol, the inebriant of choice for football players and other athletes. But now Paul and I were as holy in our faith as we had been righteous in our rebellion—but much happier. Even though most of the external parameters of our lives did not change—school, work, and home life—the way we functioned within them was transformed. One night Paul and I smashed our huge collection of rock-and-roll albums, purging the satanic strains from our lives. None of my friends had expected me to convert, much less to become an outspoken, dedicated, holy-living "Jesus freak." I got lots of skeptical looks when I passed out gospel tracts, encouraging them to read and experience the joy of coming to Jesus. One lunch hour, another recently "saved" kid stood up on a cafeteria table to share a message he said he was receiving from God. The room was in shock. Then Paul stood up to provide the exegesis to what our classmate had shared. I began to counsel young people who came to the table for spiritual care.

As this went on, the students in the cafeteria, many of them my friends, sat in stunned silence. The vice principal asked us to stop, but we had hit our stride, with no intention of interfering with the work of the Spirit who we knew had inspired us. We were not on the tables for long, but afterward a few kids who would have never talked to us in the past approached to ask questions. One girl was crying and talked about the guilt she experienced after having had an abortion. I had not thought much about abortion, although I knew what it was: a final escape from a big mistake. I would have imagined that relief and not guilt would be the resulting emotion. I tried to talk to her about the love of Jesus, how forgiving He was and how she should turn to Him for comfort during times of pain, but I am not sure that what I said made much of an impression. We were unprepared for all this, to say the least.

One day, Mr. Anker, my industrial arts instructor, noticed I was carrying a shiny, new, green-vinyl-covered *Living Bible*. He stopped me after class and said I looked like a man of the cloth. He suggested that I should consider the ministry as a possible profession. I blushed but felt myself stand a bit straighter. The idea had occurred to me before that moment, but his offhand remark validated what had been just a daydream. I began to think seriously about preaching as a calling.

I was a restless kid and eager to get started with my life, especially since I had lost sixteen irreplaceable years as a nonbeliever while the world was rocketing toward the end of the world. At the time, Paul, Cheryl, and our friends at Emmanuel were all reading Hal Lindsay's *Late Great Planet Earth*, subtitled *A Penetrating Look at Incredible Prophecies Involving This Generation*. It painted a bleak picture of an out-of-control youth culture ravaged by promiscuity and drugs, an increase in natural catastrophes, a revival of satanic witchcraft, and the looming threat of cataclysmic war in the Middle East. All portended the apocalyptic appearance of an Antichrist, whose presence preceded the return of Jesus Christ to earth to reign in righteousness over His people. But not before we, the "saved," would be sucked into the air by way of a secret "rapture," during which Christians rescued by Christ were lifted to heaven, their sudden disappearance confusing and worrying those who were "left behind." I did not want to be among them.

The End Times seemed upon us on a global scale. We watched Palestinian terrorists murder Israeli athletes in Munich; Black Panthers had gunned down a California judge they had kidnapped while he presided from the bench. The Weather Underground, a militant network of American radicals, bombed the Pentagon. All this, plus some of the first public displays of homosexuality on screen and in parades, was evidence to us that the world was going to hell. One of the first Christian songs I heard as a new believer, and one that eased me across the cultural threshold from sinful acid rock to heavenly Christian rock, was Larry Norman's rapture-themed "I Wish We'd All Been Ready," in which he articulated all our fears and worries about being unprepared for the impending End Times.

The knowledge that our days were numbered informed every aspect of my life. Even though we hadn't yet graduated from high school, time was running out for Cheryl and me to get married and have kids. I also wanted to enjoy what limited life I had on this earth—and get something done for the Lord. I knew the parable of the talents from the gospel of Matthew, in which Jesus told the story of a man who entrusts his three servants with specific amounts of money—or "talents"—while he takes a long journey. When he returns, the man asks each servant for an accounting of what they've done with his capital. Two of them report strong returns on their investments of his money, but one buried his talent in the ground, afraid to risk losing it. The two who took the risk and reaped a reward are commended as "good and faithful servants." But the fearful one is denounced, then warned: "To everyone who has will more be given, and he will have an abundance. But from the one who has not, even what he has will be taken away."

The idea of getting nothing accomplished for the Lord before He returned and held me to account preoccupied me. I needed to get going. So it was that during those last two years of high school, Paul and I helped establish a coffeehouse outreach ministry called the Maranatha Christian Center, named for the biblical term meaning "come quickly," which refers to the longing of early Christians for the return of Jesus Christ. Open only nights and weekends, it was an early version of a pop-up café, with complimentary hot and cold beverages and snacks. Teens from our hometown would sit at bistro tables and talk about spiritual matters with trained counselors. The objective was to win souls to Christ, but we tried to do it gently, by making friends and not overtly pushing an agenda. We would witness, which is to say we would talk about how we found Jesus, to drop-ins who came by for free refreshments. More than once I participated in an exorcism to cast out the demons of drug addiction and promiscuity. We were responding to the alienated zeitgeist of the seventies, offering a place where adolescent cultural rebels, latchkey kids, and children of what seemed like an epidemic of divorce could find instant friendship and connection from caring peers and "elders" who also served as surrogate parents.

One afternoon in the fall of our senior year, the adult leaders of Maranatha, now looking more and more like a real congregation, asked me to share my story at one of their first special services. It was held on a Friday night and included Holy Communion. When the big day arrived, I spent the hours before the service in a complete and accelerating panic—so anxious, at one point, that I almost threw up. That evening my mouth was dry, my hands were shaking, and my stomach was in knots. I mounted the podium and looked down at my carefully prepared remarks. Since I was speaking as a convert, I brought to bear my Jewish background and described how Communion reflects the Passover meal, or seder.

Liturgical churches—Catholic, Episcopal, and Orthodox—make this comparison all the time, but evangelicals don't. I spoke about Jesus as a Jew celebrating the Feast of the Unleavened Bread, but also as our Savior, who had embraced all people, Jew and gentile. It was an eye-popping revelation for the collection of Christian neophytes and small-town Methodists gathered in the borrowed Presbyterian sanctuary. They had never before considered the ways in which Judaism and Christianity were intertwined, and not just historically but also theologically and in terms of salvation. The feedback I got was overwhelmingly positive: those who attended were eager to learn more details about Christianity that would deepen their faith. For the first time I experienced the satisfaction that comes with an appreciative audience. When it was over, some of the men among the church leadership suggested I might have "a call of God on my life," hinting at a possible ministerial future. My hope that one day I would become a minister was becoming a reality faster than I had imagined.

The message I wanted to carry to the multitudes was simple: human beings were separated from God because of our sin. The problem went all the way back to Adam and Eve in the Garden of Eden, when God told them they could eat from every tree except the tree of the knowledge of good and evil. They ignored the divine command and willfully took of the fruit of that forbidden tree, thinking they could determine for themselves what was right and wrong and ignore God's moral law. The result was "the fall," when mankind became alienated from its creator and was doomed to eternal damnation. Every generation since has carried that same sin in their hearts, perpetuating the problem.

At first, God gave his law in the Old Testament as a set of rules and required sacrifices to set human beings straight, but that failed to do the trick. So God, in his love for humanity, provided the perfect sacrifice his law demanded in the person of Jesus Christ, who came preaching the gospel, or "evangel," the *good news* that reunion with God was possible by way of his voluntary death on the cross. The prerequisite to accessing this salvation from damnation is first believing in Jesus' atoning death and resurrection, making Him the Lord, or boss, of one's life—putting Him in charge, following and obeying His commands, and praying for His guidance. Reading the Bible was absolutely necessary to understand these things and benefit from them. God, the Bible, prayer, obedience, and telling others how they could be saved from hell was all of a piece—it constituted saving faith. This is what I believed, what I had experienced, and what I wanted to tell the world. The best way to do it would be as a pastor, an evangelist, or a Bible teacher, but I still wasn't sure that's what I wanted to do. I simply wanted to share the joy of knowing Jesus and all the wonderful things I was learning from the Bible. Now that I felt I knew God personally and what he wanted from mankind, I was obligated to communicate that truth to every person I encountered. But how I would do that was still uncertain.

Paul and I graduated with Cheryl and Paul's girlfriend Becky in the class of 1976. Becky was a bold, outspoken tomboy, whose parents were well-loved Bible teachers in our new world. A propitious year, and not only because it was the bicentennial—an evangelical Southern Baptist peanut farmer from Georgia was running for president. We would turn eighteen that year, all of us before November, just in time to cast our first presidential ballots for Jimmy Carter, whose unabashed "born-again" Christianity had never been seen before in American politics. His candidacy brought the realization that we were part of a formidable voting block of some fifty million born-again Christians in the United States. We had until then felt like a powerless, disfavored, disenfranchised minority, but that would now change. Carter was also a Democrat, as was my father, which meant he was for the poor, the "little guy." All of this seemed exactly what Jesus had wanted from each of us. Carter didn't need to convince any of us that he was able to run the country; we just wanted one of our own in the highest office in the land. His faith was all the qualification he needed.

It was also during this time that, validated by the elders of my new church, my conviction grew that ministry was, indeed, God's will for my life. When I first broached the subject of pursuing the ministry with my pastor, Fred Dixon, he suggested seminary—which would have required an undergraduate degree—but college was out of the question. Not only could my family not afford it, but it represented capitulation to a social demand my father resented. He had dropped out of college after his older brother's death, and no one else in the immediate Schenck universe was college educated. They were self-made men, some even quite wealthy. You launched yourself into the working world, used your brains and brawn, and made something of yourself. Nobody needed a piece of paper on the wall to accomplish any of that.

Dad had inculcated this ethic in Paul and me, and we approached our new ministerial careers in the same way he approached his phone business. We would be entrepreneurial men of the cloth, starting our own religious enterprises, hunting down and securing funders, relying not on ancient liturgies and millennia-old conventions but on our own wits and business acumen. We imagined ourselves to be old-fashioned itinerant ministers, preaching, teaching, baptizing, commissioning, even ordaining clergy all over the country, on the fly, just like the first apostles.

Cheryl and I talked about marriage, but she planned to go to college. I was impatient—I wanted to start my ministry with her by my side immediately. I worried that her leaving for school would break the momentum we had started. I promised her she could continue her studies if we got married, but her mother was upset that her daughter would be getting married so young and worried that Cheryl would never be self-sufficient without a college education.

The ministry became my top priority, but I needed to support my family and be the head of the household. I imagined Cheryl and I would travel around the country for a while, or maybe serve in a pastorate as I established my reputation as a clergyman and preacher. We would eventually settle and raise our family. I would always work, and work hard, while Cheryl would remain at home and raise our children. Our community reinforced this interpretation of how a family should be structured, especially in the face of societal pressures emanating from the women's movement that threatened the hierarchy of the household as we knew it. Marriage was a "calling" and something sacred. Your mate was "God's match for you." Like Eve to Adam, Cheryl would be my "helpmeet," the caretaker of our family's needs, while, in turn, I would provide the sustenance. I was to "love her as Christ loves the church." She would submit to me as I submitted to Christ—that was what the Bible taught.

Paul and Becky were following the same path, and our parents were surprisingly supportive of the marriages of their two eighteen-year-old sons to two eighteen-year-old girls. At the time, I was working at a retail electronics store, making just enough to pay for my gas and a few other things, but I was sure I could do better in short order and earn enough to rent a small apartment. Paul had already been accepted at Elim Bible Institute, in Lima, New York, a school founded in 1924 to train Christ-centered, spiritually empowered leaders who would carry the gospel into the world to prepare us for the End Times. He had secured the sponsorship of a church, which would cover his tuition and expenses, and would attend in the fall. As soon as I could bank enough to take care of Cheryl and me, I planned to go there as well. Elim was a nonaccredited, private religious academy, so Paul and I would not obtain formal degrees there, but it would qualify us for ministerial ordination.

In the fall of '76, as I was wondering exactly what my next steps needed to be, Reverend David Brett, a professor of "personal evangelism" at Elim, came to our coffeehouse as a guest speaker. He spoke to us about his work with Teen Challenge, the worldwide network of church-sponsored rehabilitation centers for recovering drug addicts founded by David Wilkerson, a legendary figure in our world and author of the bestseller *The Cross and the Switchblade,* about his work in New York City and his success in bringing Puerto Rican gang members to Christ. Brett had worked with Wilkerson in early-sixties Greenwich Village, where they had pioneered the coffeehouse outreach model of evangelism that we used as the pattern for our Maranatha Center, which that night was packed for his appearance.

Reverend Brett brought a single, autographed copy of Wilkerson's book, and he gave me the prized volume. It became my other Bible. I devoured it in a week and referred to it constantly. At last I had found the direction I longed for; each page revealed answers to questions about how I was going to conduct my calling. I wanted to be one of those Christians who plunged deep into the margins of American life, carrying the message into ghettos and to do my part in hastening the evangelization of the world—a prerequisite for the return of Christ, which I believed was imminent.

With Dave's encouragement, I visited a Teen Challenge center in the nearby city of Rochester, to see if there were any opportunities for me to get started in the kind of hands-on work I was picturing. When I arrived at two side-by-side, decrepit Victorian houses in a dangerous inner-city neighborhood, I instantly knew this was where I belonged. The door opened and a short, stocky African-American man wearing a clerical collar poked his head out, probably assuming I was another junkie in need of shelter. Instead I told him I was applying for a job. He gave me a big smile and introduced himself as the director, Reverend Herb Severin. After a few minutes of friendly conversation and an instant interview, I became the center's new van driver. Chauffeuring a bunch of junkies around may not have been the glamorous preaching life I had imagined, but I humbly accepted.

I quit my job at the electronics store and told my parents, Paul, and Cheryl that I'd be moving into a residential center for heroin addicts. My parents were in shock. Cheryl was excited but concerned about a long-distance relationship. Paul was thrilled I'd be an hour closer to him at Elim. Cheryl and I hastened our plans for marriage so she could join me in short order, and soon I was settled in my new room, a former storage area under the staircase at the Teen Challenge house.

When I arrived in that late autumn of 1976, about a dozen young men, most of them Puerto Ricans from Brooklyn, were living at the facility in Rochester. One day, about a week after I started driving the center's van, Adalberto, a recovering addict and resident counselor, suggested that I preach in the chapel during services the next day. I was taken aback. In my mind, this was true ministry of the Word, and I was intimidated—I had only ever given that one Friday sermon to our fledgling Maranatha congregation in the rented sanctuary. But I was thrilled at the opportunity. The next day my Teen Challenge congregation consisted of a dozen bedraggled and indifferent residents seated on a hodgepodge of worn-out chairs, but I approached my assignment as if it were in the pulpit of Westminster Abbey. I was a hit with the crowd, and our director began to organize preaching opportunities for me in area churches that supported our work. I can remember looking down at my hands on one of those occasions, with my fingers clamped so tightly to the pulpit's side panels that my knuckles had turned white. But I was growing as a preacher, hitting my stride, and knew that I was getting through to people.

Meanwhile, back home in Grand Island, our wedding preparations were gaining momentum. Cheryl was in anguish about disappointing her mother, who, not surprisingly, still wanted her in college instead of married to me and living among drug addicts. But Cheryl knew what she wanted, so she borrowed a wedding dress from a close friend, arranged to use the Presbyterian church and its modest fellowship hall for our ceremony, and organized a cake-and-punch reception. To honor my father, we had a formal Jewish-Christian affair with dual officiants. Cheryl joined me beneath the *chuppah* and during a brief ceremony we recited our vows. I turned to Cheryl and said, "I will love you, comfort you, honor you, cherish you, and keep you, forsaking all others. Clinging only to you, as long as we both shall live." She repeated the same to me. And then we kissed.

"Ladies and gentlemen, I would like to present for the first time, Mr. and Mrs. Robert Schenck."

Until death do us part, we were one.

4

Pastor and Father

In the spring of 1977, I brought my new wife home to my two-bedroom apartment in the Teen Challenge house in Rochester. We shared a bathroom with the office staff, and residents would regularly shout to me through our bedroom window. At Teen Challenge, I became a kind of circuit-riding, weekend gospel warrior. Cheryl and I often hit the road together, bundling our residents into a van to take them to a different church within a few hours' drive, where I would either preach the sermon or simply take a few minutes in the service to raise some money to support our work. Occasionally I would ask one of the recovering addicts to testify or tell his story of finding freedom from drugs and crime through faith in Christ, and maybe sing a gospel song, which many of our more gregarious types just loved to do. I gained confidence as a preacher, even though I had not yet received credentials to be an official minister. Most denominations require ministerial candidates to possess a master of divinity degree, but all I had were a few nonaccredited Elim courses and undergraduate Bible correspondence courses. After a few months, I was already restless. I wanted badly to be ordained, but the path to my goal was uncertain.

As would often happen in my life, there was a providential intervention. Reverend Paul Johansson, Elim's vice president and an officer on its credentialing committee, agreed to interview me. He had gotten to know Paul during his time at Elim. And it turned out Reverend Johansson was also an identical twin, whose brother, a pastor in New

York City, was named Rob. Twins by the same name sure left me feeling comfortable with him. In a long phone interview with "Paul Jo," as he was affectionately known, I discussed my coming to Jesus and how my faith had developed and what my intentions were for serving Christ as a minister. Paul had said similar things when he went through the same vetting. Reverend Johansson knew my brother and my mentor, Tommy Reid, and he said that gave him confidence in me. I talked about my work with Teen Challenge and the joy and commitment I felt in sharing the good news of the gospel.

He told me—as he had told Paul—he would normally not recommend someone so young and with so little training for a ministerial license, the first step toward ordination, but he would make the exception in my brother's and my case because he saw promise. He warned me, though, that he would be paying close attention to what I did, saying that, in an old house, cracks in the basement are nothing to worry about, but that is not so in new construction. In his estimation I was a new house, and he would be looking for cracks in my foundation.

Preparation for the ministry is intellectually rigorous, demanding a mastery of Old and New Testament literature, hermeneutics (or the science of Bible interpretation), the history of ancient Israel and the Christian church, biblical languages—Hebrew, Greek, and Latin—and comprehensive surveys of theology, Christian counseling, and even church educational administration. Over the three years I studied, my favorite course was Christian Discipleship, or how to live like Jesus. By the time Cheryl and I celebrated my twenty-first birthday, I was carrying a "license to preach," giving me the title of "Reverend." I had opened new Teen Challenge Centers in Syracuse and Buffalo and been promoted to executive director of the Upstate New York system, Empire State Teen Challenge.

It was an idyllic time for us, as broke and busy as we were. There were plenty of harrowing moments, like the time one of our residents came after me with a garden hoe. (Thankfully he missed me.) More than one confessed to having committed murder, and one told me he had repeatedly raped his own daughter. Notwithstanding such shocking revelations, and the risk that came with living beside these guys, I felt I was truly living the life of a minister, ministering to the least among us. It was a challenge at times to find the image of Christ in a strung-out, thieving, lying addict, but those were exactly the kind of people Jesus most wanted us to love and bring into our hearts. Even so, we had to take care of ourselves, and the close call with the garden hoe, followed by a menacing threat against Cheryl by a neighbor with a bowie knife, persuaded me we should leave our heroin addicts and move to our own place.

We eventually settled into a $125-a-month apartment on a leafy street in the suburb of East Rochester—and felt like we were in the lap of luxury. Then, in the fall of 1978, another prayer was answered when Cheryl's pregnancy test showed positive. Since the moment I met Cheryl, she had imagined herself as a happy mom. She loved children and volunteered to work with them wherever we were—in church nurseries and Sunday schools, in backyard vacation Bible clubs, and with Down syndrome kids at summer camp. And my joy was increased, because in becoming parents we were not only doing something emotionally gratifying, but literally fulfilling God's first commandment, to "be fruitful and multiply." I had been taught from the first days of my Christian faith that a father's role and responsibilities reflect the job description of our Heavenly Father more fully than even that of a preacher.

Whatever difficulties my own parents might have had, I was sure Cheryl and I would avoid them. We understood what it meant to be a "Christian family," and we knew where to look to unlock the secrets to a happy home. After all, our entire world was organized to support Christian family life. We joined about fifty others at a small country church where some of the women sported "chapel bonnets," in obedience to Saint Paul's command for women to pray with their heads covered. They offered each other everything from recipes and tips on shopping bargains to informal Christian marriage counseling. The men worked hard to be the providers their wives and families deserved and the Lord expected. As the time grew nearer for the birth of our first child, they gave us a baby shower, and along with the onesies and washcloths and bibs were a few books on Christian family life.

One of the most important volumes was by celebrity Baptist pastor Tim LaHaye and his wife, Beverly. Eventually he would write the massively successful Left Behind series of novels focusing on the End Times, but before he wrote these blockbusters, he and his wife were the authors of a series of highly influential books on Christian marriage and family life.

The Act of Marriage: The Beauty of Sexual Love was a sensation in the evangelical community and useful for two relative innocents. I had had my escapades with teenage sex before I came to faith in Christ, but they were hardly sophisticated or mutually satisfying. Now that I was a responsible, married Christian man, I was, like most evangelicals, consigned to the role of disapproving observer of the sexual revolution. The LaHayes' book gave us permission to be active participants, but not the promiscuous or licentious version that nonbelievers practiced. In fifteen chapters, ranging from "The Sanctity of Sex" to "Practical Answers to Common Questions," they explored the beauties and the specifics of sexual acts in a Christian marriage. The LaHayes left us able to feel God's grace while having a healthy, robust intimate life in which intercourse was not just for procreation but also for a full expression of the miracle of God's creation in the love between a man and a woman. (Not to mention the best insurance policy of all to prevent wandering eyes.)

Another must-read for parents was *Dare to Discipline,* the all-time most popular evangelical source on child-rearing by pediatric psychologist and radio personality Dr. James Dobson, a superstar in our evangelical world. He was the Benjamin Spock of our culture, and you were not only a good parent for following his instruction, you were an educated and informed parent. We learned from reading Dobson how much children needed discipline and how necessary it was if they were to respect their parents. Dobson was clear that parents had a responsibility to discipline kids, and that meant a spanking now and then was not just appropriate but necessary. Reading and carefully following Dobson meant you were an earnest Christian parent who saw your duty as a calling from God. I just needed to look back on my own upbringing, those wild days in our early teens when our parents seemed to have disappeared, to realize how helpful it would have been for us if our parents had "dared to discipline."

Cheryl's and my experiences with dysfunctional homes had left us determined not to blow it as parents and to do better with our kids than our parents had done with us. We not only read the books, we took every church-sponsored parenting workshop, seminar, and retreat available—and there were many. We lived by the ethic that the best parenting advice of all could be found in the Bible, which spoke clearly to how we could be the best mother and father. Scripture laid out a perfect parenting method: firm discipline matched with tough but abundant love, regular and careful instruction in the faith, and precise behavioral boundaries. We were sure that in all this we would be almost guaranteed nearly perfect Christian children.

In a way, we saw our task as reclaiming human civilization. By "training up a child in the way he should go," as one Bible verse put it, we would preserve as much as we could of a God-fearing society in the present while we set up a godly generation to take the reins of culture in the future. Our kids would be the leaders of tomorrow—in the church, civil society, education, business, the arts and entertainment, and, of course, politics—and they would bring their stalwart Christian convictions and way of life with them into those spheres of influence. Not only was parenting a source of great happiness for Cheryl and me, it was also an essential component of God's strategic mission.

Given all this support, I threw myself into preparations for fatherhood and, at twenty-one, felt more than mature enough to be a dad: I had prayed about it, read about it, heard plenty of sermons on it, preached a sermon or two on it, talked with peers about it, counseled parents on it, and studied what the Bible said about fatherhood. On a more practical level, I went to Lamaze childbirth classes with Cheryl, learned breathing techniques and how to apply effleurage, and coached her in focusing, panting, and blowing.

But none of that could have prepared me for the day that Cheryl went into labor. I was preaching in a church forty-five minutes from our hospital, and I was coming to my last point when I saw Cheryl in the front row, her eyes wide-open, pointing to her big belly. I've never finished a sermon so quickly! We raced to the hospital, where we spent the next fifteen hours. A little after six a.m. Anna Lynn arrived at 9.3 pounds. This was as close as I would ever come to being present at the creation, and I felt the radiance of pure love: God's love, mine for Cheryl, and our love for this marvelous new person. Three weeks into Anna's new life, Cheryl and I took her to a nearby David Wilkerson Crusade, where the man who inspired my ministry venture dedicated my daughter to the Lord. Evangelicals do not baptize infants, because baptism is seen as an informed act of the conscious will. We do, however, literally, lift a new child up to the Lord, as the biblical Hannah did with her son Samuel and as was done with Jesus in the Temple. Wilkerson did that with Anna, praying God's richest blessing on her and us.

For Cheryl, to be Anna's mother and my wife was a full-time job, one she took to with contentment and commitment. Her college dreams had long been eclipsed by our busy life and marriage, and she found that serving our family was fulfilling. I was an eager and involved dad, but given all my work and the necessity of keeping up with my studies in order to be credentialed as a minister, I struggled to be present like many of my male contemporaries. On top of very demanding ministry work that required my crisscrossing the state, tending to our three Teen Challenge Centers, and preaching many weekends at different churches, I was also engrossed in my schoolwork. Somehow we kept it all in balance. As usual, it seemed as if my life and Paul's ran on parallel tracks. He, too, had become a new father, with a baby girl of his own, Leah Naomi, who would grow up to be like a sister to her cousin Anna.

By the time Paul's and my ordination exams were scheduled, we had migrated from the Elim Fellowship to the Assemblies of God, a much larger but similarly Pentecostal body that owned and operated Teen Challenge. Paul had also become our Buffalo director. It had not really been a choice. The denominational office had contacted both of us to announce that if we expected to keep our jobs, we needed to carry their ministerial credentials—not Elim's. The process we had been through with Elim was compatible enough with the new denomination that they simply replaced our Elim license cards with theirs. That gave both of us access to the much more prestigious Assemblies of God pulpits for guest preaching, and the substantial network of clergy, institutions, and benefits—such as continuing education, clergy-specific publications, and even a sophisticated retirement program—offered to its thirty thousand registered clergy. Paul and I kept up relationships with colleagues at Elim and in virtually every major Christian denomination, but the Assemblies of God now took precedence over all of them.

During my studies, I saw much more clearly my options. Ministers are trained to follow one of three possible trajectories: a pastor, caring for a flock; an evangelist, proclaiming the gospel under tents, in theaters, arenas, even on sidewalks; or a missionary, setting up beachheads for evangelization in far-off places around the globe. You can't be "evangelical" without being "mission oriented," whether that mission was in the neighborhood church or the African bush. "Mission" is an essential component of the evangelical ethos and I soon realized this was where I would channel my energies. I just wasn't sure at that point what it would look like, since there was a huge barrier between me and ordination, the final step in achieving full ministerial status. That barrier was also known as final exams.

Those immune to test anxiety will never fully comprehend the sheer terror I experience when faced with exams. I could imagine no greater blow or humiliation than to be tested and fail. Cheryl would try to remind me that this was not something that happened very frequently, but her reassurance was irrelevant.

The Assemblies of God ordination examination was broken into two intimidating sections: a long, comprehensive written portion, followed by an oral exam conducted by a tribunal of church elders interrogating me on every aspect of the Bible and church teaching. I would be taking the written part in the office of my presbyter, a local pastor who served as a kind of "bishop" for a geographic region. The clouds of despair and anxiety parted just a bit to let in some light when I learned I could bring my Bible and any notes it might contain. If evangelicals are known for anything, it is for our active engagement with our Bibles. We are enthusiastic notetakers and commentators, marking up our Bibles with marginalia, highlighting whole paragraphs in different colors, and even taping extra paper to pages so we can write more. It wasn't uncommon for me to hear people pulling pens out of their pockets and purses and riffling pages as I announced my sermon text. For most evangelicals, a thoroughly annotated Bible is the sure sign of a serious Christian.

The main portion of the written exam would surround the core beliefs of our church—what are called "the Sixteen Fundamental Truths." Each of the precepts would be based on specific Bible verses. I created a system with codes that matched the primary verse to the numbered "Truth." I was confident I could memorize at least those initial references. I then scribbled cramped citations for related texts near the numbered one so I could follow a thread, and jammed still other notes in the adjoining margins. I passed the written exam with a 97 percent.

But the worst was still to come: the oral exam, in which no assistance from crib notes was permitted. I repeated to myself that I was not alone, God would be with me, and I prayed desperately. I was told Cheryl would be required to sit with me and I felt a sense of relief. Prospective ministerial spouses are very important players in the ordination process. After all, a wife was expected to be her husband's biggest supporter, booster, prayer partner, sounding board, shoulder to cry on, protector, defender, and all-around assistant. Cheryl was up to the task, but she had no idea when we drove to the state offices of the Assemblies of God, just north of Syracuse, how much scrutiny she would be under. The examiners were determined to discover if she had the comportment and commitment to be a properly supportive clergy spouse and a model for others.

Colleagues and friends who had been through the exams would roll their eyes at the mention of "the Oral" and say with resignation, "I'll pray for you, brother." In my world, this was the equivalent of an oral defense of a PhD dissertation—where you either succeeded and could pursue your chosen profession, or failed and had to start over or abandon your dreams. Now it was my turn—or rather *our* turn, because Cheryl would be treated as an extension of me. It was an odd way to approach the task, as this was not the way we truly lived, or the way we related to each other. We were mostly equal partners. We needed one another and supported each other, and sometimes we would share affectionate exasperation with many of the most rigid aspects of our church's dogma about women's subordination to men. But I was feeling drawn into the dominant male church culture as well, and in events like this, no matter what our quotidian lives might have looked like, Cheryl was technically my subordinate. She never regarded herself as that to me, but she understood I was to be the head of our household. And, as a young mother, she knew her principal responsibility was child-rearing. No matter what we thought of it, that's what the Bible commanded.

We entered the district presbytery building; I was drenched with sweat and felt nauseated. The executive, general, and sectional presbyters—about thirty older, experienced pastors from across the state—were going to ask me some one hundred questions, each in turn, over the course of two hours. The group included a few caustic New Yorkers, ratcheting up the likelihood of humiliation in my mind. I was too young, I thought. How presumptuous of me to have assumed I was ready to take on this monumental responsibility. We sat silently outside the conference room door. After about twenty minutes of anxiously waiting, we were invited into the formal chamber, arranged much like a court hearing room, with long tables configured in a U, a phalanx of mostly graying ministers in crisply pressed shirts, their thick, dark ties accenting pin-striped three-piece suits. Cheryl and I were shown to two chairs at a small table nestled at the top of the U. The district superintendent, Almon Bartholomew ("Brother B."), the quintessential proper Protestant minister, began speaking slowly with precise, almost exaggerated diction: "Brother and Sister Schenck, thank you for joining us here today. This is your ordination interview. Let us pray."

I don't remember his prayer, because I was too busy begging God for mercy. Cheryl gave my damp hand a squeeze, and the questioning began, moving up and down the tables until almost every minister had his chance at me. I felt pummeled by what I thought were relentlessly hostile questions. When one of the inquisitors noted my "youthful age," I took it as a signal that there was no chance for me to succeed. The inquiry turned to Cheryl, and she was asked how she saw my calling. She replied that she trusted in God and would support me and the ministry God had given to me as my wife and Anna's mother. I was very proud of her, knowing how difficult it must have been for her to speak facing a roomful of middle-aged, graying leaders who held my future in their hands. The questioners returned to me until Brother B. dismissed us, saying that they planned to pray over my fate.

Painfully long minutes passed and finally we were invited back in. I was resigned to failure, but when I saw the smile on Brother B.'s face, it was obvious I had passed. Before announcing their decision, he had one final admonition, warning me that bearing the permanent title of "Reverend" meant I would be judged differently from others, in everything that I did, from the movies I attended to the clothes that I wore. He asked if I would be ready for such scrutiny. When I replied I would, he offered his congratulations and opened his Bible to read to me 1 Timothy 4:1–10:

> The Spirit clearly says that in later times some will abandon the faith and follow deceiving spirits and things taught by demons. Such teachings come through hypocritical liars, whose consciences have been seared as with a hot iron. They forbid people to marry and order them to abstain from certain foods, which God created to be received with thanksgiving by those who believe and who know the truth. For everything God created is good, and nothing is to be rejected if it is received with thanksgiving, because it is consecrated by the word of God and prayer.
>
> If you point these things out to the brothers and sisters, you will be a good minister of Christ Jesus, nourished on the truths of the faith and of the good teaching that you have followed. Have nothing to do with godless myths and old wives' tales; rather, train yourself to be godly. For physical training is of some value, but godliness has value for all things, holding promise for both

the present life and the life to come. This is a trustworthy saying that deserves full acceptance. That is why we labor and strive, because we have put our hope in the living God, who is the Savior of all people, and especially of those who believe.

The words seemed so personally directed to me that I had goose bumps as he read them.

5

Missionary Evangelist

During the time that I was studying to be ordained and endured the written and oral exams, I left Teen Challenge and accepted a conventional position as an assistant pastor in a quiet suburban congregation, Webster Assembly of God, just outside of Rochester, New York. Intellectually, I appreciated the importance of this kind of pastoral work: weddings, baptisms, comforting grieving families, and Christian education of children were the warp and woof of church life. But for me it was a struggle. I celebrated the presence of so many people eager to find and serve Jesus in the heart of middle-class America, but I was troubled by the sense that my presence there did not make much of a difference in the world. There would always be ministers for congregations such as these. They would never feel abandoned or neglected. I knew that if I weren't there, there were a dozen other newly minted clergy eager to leap at the opportunity to serve. No sooner had I started than I wanted out.

My professional unhappiness was in dramatic contrast to the ease and contentment I felt in my personal life. I was the dad to an adorable toddler daughter, and Cheryl and I were still in the honeymoon period of our marriage. We were both fully invested in congregational life. Cheryl became friends with many of the women of the church. She developed children's Bible study programs, helped other young mothers navigate the world of new babies, and used her musical skills to coach me in one of my unlikely duties, leading congregational singing.

But in the end I simply missed a more difficult and demanding flock. I was intent on getting back into much more demanding work. My Teen Challenge life was what I considered real ministry work: seeing souls changed by the power of God and the love of his people. I saw Christ in the faces of those who were reviled by society—the modern-day Samaritans, the prostitutes, the poor in spirit. In the Webster church, I felt like I was treading water; my job was to comfort the comfortable, to educate those who already were well schooled in scripture, to engage with people I could easily number among my friends. I didn't feel I was using my calling to the fullest, and looked for opportunities to reenter inner-city ministry.

Feeling almost irrelevant was deeply disconcerting to me, especially while momentous and important changes were taking place all around me. The whirlwind of social upheaval in the early eighties, marked by widespread access to abortion, gay rights marches, rampant divorce, and assisted suicide movements, was considered by our religious community to violate all the most sacred premises of the teachings of Jesus Christ. Every one of these social movements, it seemed to me, could be contradicted by a relevant biblical passage. When I first arrived at Webster in 1980, I was familiar with Reverend Jerry Falwell. He had recently founded the Moral Majority, an organization leading a campaign to galvanize American Christians against what Falwell had identified as the dual evils of the time: the creeping socialism of the welfare state and overwhelming moral degeneracy. He argued persuasively that from its very inception the United States was a Christian nation, but those values could only be sustained by strong leaders. He urged us to channel the old-time religion into a force to oppose the anti-Christian Equal Rights Amendment, feminism, and the burgeoning gay rights movement and, heralding back to the Great Awakening in the nineteenth century, urged the country to embark on a revival of religion.

When I first voted for a Republican presidential candidate in the fall of 1980, I knew I was one of millions of evangelicals who felt reassured that Ronald Reagan understood our values and shared our vision to make America once more a "shining city on a hill." That metaphor resonanted with me and nearly every Christian I knew. It was a reference to Jesus' words from the Sermon on the Mount: "Ye are the light of the world. A city that is set on a hill cannot be hid."

To further demonstrate how things were going to change, within the first week of his inauguration, Reagan invited Falwell and several other ministers to the White House. All the issues we found so worrisome at last appeared to face opposition in a government embodied by our new president. It seemed the fulfillment of what Christian broadcaster Pat Robertson observed when he calculated that at the moment Protestants and Catholics realized they were fed up with the status quo and voted in concert, we would be able to gain political ascendancy and finally run the country properly.

Falwell convinced me that Bible-believing Christians—particularly ministers like me—had avoided involvement in political debates for much too long, an argument that comported seamlessly with the urgency of the Last Days narrative that continued to motivate so much of my work. If I were to be true to my faith, my convictions and belief could not be confined to Sundays, or even within a traditional pastor's portfolio that made me feel so constrained.

I felt I was living two lives, fervently trying to discern my next steps while doing all that I needed to do at Webster. And, much to our joy, we discovered Cheryl was pregnant again. This time, though, I had my heart set on a boy. I took enormous pleasure in my daughter and saw great promise in her future. But a son would provide an heir—not to a fortune I knew would never be mine, but to my calling. My boy would be a man of God, a minister of the Word, the inheritor of my ministry. In my world, the "mantle" of a father's ministry was often passed on to the son. The colonial firebrand Jonathan Edwards had Jonathan the Younger, the contemporary healing evangelist Oral Roberts had his son Richard, the venerable Billy Graham had his Franklin. When the sonographer confirmed the presence of a little boy, I thanked God. What I didn't know then was that all my presumptions about this baby boy's adult life would plant the seeds for the greatest rupture in our family. I couldn't see that then; the specter of his arrival was bathed in blithe bliss.

Meanwhile, my original clerical sponsor, Reverend Paul Johansson, had offered me an off-hours teaching opportunity at Elim's satellite campus, located in Orchard Park, near our hometown in Buffalo. We commuted back and forth together, and the hour-long drive with him became an opportunity for me to benefit from his pastoral guidance. I confided in him my dissatisfaction with suburban church work. He asked if I had ever considered doing something other than staff pastoring. I replied, almost impatiently, as if the answer should have been obvious: of course I had, and would like to try my hand at something else. He told me that his twin brother in New York was looking for someone to run an urban internship program for Elim students and he wondered if I might be interested.

Training aspiring ministers in inner-city evangelism in New York City? I could feel the surge of energy that had eluded me for a year. The mere thought of entering the major leagues of ministry in one of the world's great urban centers, and of working for the twin brother to the vice president of my alma mater—Pastor Rob Johansson at Long Island City's Community Gospel Church—left me ecstatic. "Pastor Rob," as Paul Jo's brother was called, invited me to New York for an in-person interview. He explained that my position would be to develop a curriculum and a fieldwork program for college interns in urban cross-cultural ministry. It was exactly the kind of substantive challenge I was longing for. When I returned home to announce I had gotten the job,

Cheryl seemed pleased we would have an adventure in the big city. But she was in her eighth month of pregnancy, surrounded by supportive women in the congregation, and this opportunity meant she would be leaving a sedate and predictable life for all the uncertainty of the intimidating Big Apple.

I told Pastor Rob we would have to delay our arrival until after the birth of our next child. Cheryl went into labor on a hot July evening in 1981. Thinking we had plenty of time, I puttered around before packing her up for the twenty-minute drive to Highland Hospital, but our son had other ideas. We had barely parked the car before he was born. We named him Matthew, because in Hebrew *Matti-yahu* means Gift of God. Our family felt complete.

In the breathless heat of August, we drove to Queens in a rented Ryder truck loaded with our two small children and all our earthly possessions. Once there, the custodian led us to an upstairs staff apartment just over the six-hundred-seat sanctuary, which he assured us was completely private except on baptismal Sundays. As with most evangelical churches, this one kept a full baptismal tank, a kind of hybrid bathtub and wading pool, at the ready for immersing new converts. The tank was elevated above the heads of the congregants so it could be clearly seen by everyone in attendance, and this particular tank happened to be located on the opposite side of our bathroom wall. We had privacy Monday through Saturday, but on baptismal Sundays, there was a parade of robed candidates trooping through our bathroom to gain entrance to the tank, where they were fully submerged, returning dripping wet through our apartment.

Pastor Johansson was very unlike his twin brother. Where Paul Johansson was warm and approachable, Rob could be imperious, critical, not very clear about his expectations, but emphatic about his disappointments. Still, I dug in and laid the groundwork for what would eventually become the New York School of Urban Ministry. Our mission was to host and train college students to work in city ministry, and then to connect them with churches throughout the metropolitan area. As part of my orientation to this new position and environment, I met pastors from across the city and built a network of people from many different communities. This was my kind of work: interacting with an economically and racially diverse population and reaching out to the homeless in city shelters, the poor in soup kitchens, the recovering addicts in rehab centers, and others who suffered, from Hell's Kitchen to Harlem. But much as I liked a lot of the work, being so far from home was tough, and things were even harder for Cheryl and the kids. She was alone for much of the day with an infant and an active little girl, in a big and complicated city where she knew no one. The women at church were friendly in that sort of brusque, New York way, and this was a busy urban parish, not the small-town community she had known so well. Cheryl was nothing if not resourceful, but I knew she missed her family and all the support that smaller, slower churches had afforded us.

Meanwhile, back home near Buffalo, my brother, Paul, had left Teen Challenge and was developing his own church. Though in its very early stages, with Tommy Reid's help, the nascent collection of members had already purchased a building—a former Orthodox Jewish funeral home—and transformed it into a chapel that sat about 150 people. The morning and evening Sunday services were filled, and Paul needed help he could trust to continue the expansion, so he asked if I would return and work with him. He knew my New York assignment was a struggle and imposed a special hardship on Cheryl. We talked it over, agreed it was time to go home, and accepted Paul's invitation.

He and I, along with our wives, knelt at the altar during the state-wide meeting of the Assemblies of God. The executive presbyters and the district officers, about fifteen men in all, gradually moved along the altar rail in a cluster, on the opposite side from where we and other candidates knelt, and laid their hands on each ordinand's head and shoulders, setting us apart "for the work of the ministry." Once more, God had brought me to the altar rail and changed my life. At the conclusion of the ritual, Brother B. read the remainder of that passage from I Timothy he had read to me in the conference room:

> Don't let anyone look down on you because you are young, but
> set an example for the believers in speech, in conduct, in love,
> in faith and in purity. Until I come, devote yourself to the public
> reading of Scripture, to preaching and to teaching. Do not neglect
> your gift, which was given you through prophecy when the body
> of elders laid their hands on you.
> Be diligent in these matters; give yourself wholly to them, so that
> everyone may see your progress. Watch your life and doctrine
> closely. Persevere in them, because if you do, you will save both
> yourself and your hearers.

Powerful emotions threatened to overwhelm me; I was perilously close to crying. When I got up from that kneeling pad, I was officially an ordained minister. I had become what God meant me to be.

Our parents attended the ceremony that day. Dad may have struggled with his sons' adopted religion and vocation inwardly, but he managed to be proud of our accomplishments and show up when it mattered. In that way Dad was always two people in one. He had a very cosmopolitan side, an adjective he loved to use about himself and other people he found very interesting. But there was the provincial Dad, too. It was a struggle that wouldn't end until the very last days of his life. For me, his dual nature was both appealing and maddening. Still, in this moment, it allowed us to bridge the divide that was caused by Paul's and my conversions eight years earlier.

At a celebratory dinner afterward, Cheryl gave me a leather-bound "minister's manual," a volume that provides a new clergyman with instruction on comportment, dress, work habits, general Bible verses as guides, service outlines for weddings, funerals, baby dedications, Communion, baptism—all the rules and suggestions necessary to carry out my work and fully inhabit my new identity. Inscribed on the first page was this message:

To my husband,
    In whom I delight as I watch God develop all that he has for you. As I begin to realize the magnitude of the calling on your life, I start to understand the responsibility of my life. To be the one whom God has chosen to join you with your life entirely. I pray I will always be the "crown of my husband." There is no other man that I honor, respect, or love more than you.
Love, Cheryl

I emerged from that day a few inches taller, feeling a sense of great accomplishment and sober responsibility. With this title came a legal status: I could now solemnize marriages, gain entry to hospitals and prisons, and even opt out of the Social Security system. From one hour to the next, I was entitled to almost instantaneous and universal respect from the general public. Back then, opinion polls found clergy to be among the most admired professions. I felt more consequential, more confident, and more secure than I ever had in my life, fully prepared to undertake this calling for the rest of my life. I had found a noble way to serve God, my family, and all of humanity. I knew I would need to be watchful so that the sin of pride would be kept in check.

Despite the thrill of the work, the managerial style of Paul Johansson, the expense, and the isolation for Cheryl made leaving New York a relief. But I was presented with a new test in working so close to my twin brother. As Paul had preceded me toward a Christian life, so, too, was he leading me now into a new phase of my ministry—being part of building a brand-new church. Our relationship was never defined by Paul as the pioneer and me as the follower. We were both too headstrong, and we weren't just brothers but identical twins. It's hard to describe what it's like to share your DNA with another person, but at times I couldn't detect where I stopped and Paul began. Growing up, we wore each other's clothes, slept in the same bedroom, never kept a secret from each other, and went just about everywhere together. We thought so much alike that we nearly completed each other's sentences.

We were far from identical in our leadership styles and how we saw the world. Paul's moral compass has never been as flexible as mine. I have always been more relaxed about life, I don't take things quite as seriously. He's more certain of himself and about his convictions and less eager to laugh, or see the humor or the irony in a situation. Even as assertive as he could be—and he says the same about me—we have always seen each other as equals. But now, he was technically my superior, which meant that a new power dynamic had been superimposed on our relationship. I felt the tension immediately when Cheryl and I arrived back in Buffalo. After we got settled, I went to Paul's office to talk about our plans. As the head of the church, he had the largest office, and he sat behind his impressive desk while I sat facing him, as all his employees did. We both tried to ignore the elephant in the room and pretended as if nothing had changed between us.

Paul knew about my goal of being a missionary and he proposed I become minister of missions and evangelism for the newly established New Covenant Tabernacle. Such a post would include evaluating prospective missionary projects for the church to support financially and with volunteer help. It would also include fund-raising for those projects and hosting missionaries on "furlough," a period of respite from their arduous fields of endeavor. Some churches even took on "resident missionaries," who would live in temporary quarters provided by the congregation and assist the church's outreach in various ways. Managing all that would be part of my portfolio.

In most evangelical churches, it is an exciting day when a missionary comes to tell a story about the conversion of the unsaved, the pagans, or even the "heathen." The missionary's work visiting churches and (in those days) showing slides from their work in the field is critical to their success in raising financial support, typically in the form of monthly pledges. But it is more than that. A missionary's "deputation" visit is an opportunity for everyone to vicariously move toward obeying the "Great Commission," Christ's mandate to "Go into all the world and proclaim the gospel to the whole creation," which had to occur before Jesus would return to set up his thousand-year righteous kingdom on earth.

During those first few days, Paul felt the need to assert his authority, and I was in the grip of a similar need to assert the fact that he had no authority over me. For me, this was unsustainable. We would have brief arguments over trivial matters and then return home, where Becky and Cheryl listened patiently as we complained about our respective twin. After a few days of fraternal tug-of-war, we sat down and figured out a plan. I assured him I was not interested in pastoral work—preaching, baptisms, burials, weddings, counseling, family work. That was all his domain. I said I wanted to be a true missionary, taking the gospel into desperate communities. I told him I missed my Teen Challenge junkies. We decided my work would be external. "Paul is in-house, Rob is out-house," we joked. I didn't want to report to him, but I wanted to support his ministry and his church. The solution was to create my own organization with its own board of directors so I wouldn't be reporting to Paul. The result was a fully autonomous nonprofit religious corporation called New Covenant Evangelical Ministries, or NCEM.

I took on oversight of the church's missions department, vetting prospective candidates for short-term missionary assignments—sometimes being deployed for a few weeks or as much as a few years. They might be sent to work at a home for unwed mothers in South Carolina, or in a hospital in war-torn Lebanon. In addition to hosting the missionaries' visits to our church pulpit, I traveled to some forty countries, returning to our congregation's annual convention with firsthand reports on what I had seen and experienced. All of this was typical work for a minister of missions, but I had also added my own twist: I was doing missionary work myself—preaching to the masses in other places, enlisting short-term volunteers to assist existing missionary enterprises, and training "nationals," or indigenous church leaders. Paul went along with all this, and my denominational authorities eventually approved of the innovation, registering me officially as a "missionary evangelist." The tension with Paul had broken, and I had secured my dream job.

My ecstasy was short-lived. One night after Matthew had turned a year old, he appeared uncomfortable, alternating between listlessness and agitation. Cheryl thought he had a cold and nursed him once more before putting him to bed. But he didn't wake up normally the next morning, and when Cheryl picked him up, he was unresponsive, his forehead on fire. After a brief visit to the pediatrician, we raced to the emergency room at Buffalo Children's Hospital in downtown Buffalo. Along the way, Matthew had repeated seizures. He was whisked into intensive care immediately upon arrival. After just a few hours we were told he had bacterial meningitis, a terrifying infection of the membrane around the brain.

It was agonizing to witness our little boy moaning and squirming, with intravenous needles stuck into the bottoms of his feet and a tube down his nose. Cheryl and I took turns keeping vigil at his bedside and prayers were sent up throughout our community. Until Matthew's illness, I had been an intrepid warrior for Christ's kingdom, but at this point I collapsed. One night, when I was home taking care of Anna, I dropped to my knees in distress. I wasn't just scared; I was terrified— and angry at God. Instead of folding my hands and closing my eyes, I clenched my fists and fixed my eyes on the ceiling, and then I yelled, "Why the hell would you do this to me? What do you want from me? Take everything, but don't take my child. Oh, God, don't take my child." I started to cry. It was catharsis, prayer, and sacrilege bundled together. This wouldn't be the only time I let God have it.

Most people think of ministers as faith filled and dutifully obe- dient, no matter their circumstances, but that wasn't my experience, nor would it be for most of the men of God I would come to know and work with throughout my career. We all have breaking points, and clergy are no exception. Like Moses, who lost his temper over the rebellious Israelites and smote the rock, rather than speak to it as God had instructed, I would lose my patience more than once, sin- ning in the process. One well-known evangelist friend who landed in the hospital due to exhaustion recounted to me how he lay in his bed moaning, "Why, God? Why? I'm doing everything you told me to do, and I end up here?" Then he said he heard a voice from heaven thun- der, "My servant, you're full of shit." It was his rather unconventional way of describing both his moment of reckoning and his irreverent humanity.

After a week, Matthew's temperature abated and his playfulness returned. But I was still too furious at God to thank him for the good news. No matter how long it's been since a child has recovered from a life-threatening experience, the possibility of his or her death haunts you for the rest of your life. God had been merciful to us in this instance—despite my impertinence—but a much bigger test of faith was right around the corner.

Back when Cheryl was pregnant with Anna, she had felt a lump in her neck, which turned out to be a suspicious growth on her thyroid gland. She had a biopsy done and the results were uncertain, but because of her age it was assumed to be benign. Her doctor advised that it be removed, but there was no rush. But by September 1982, two months after we moved back to Buffalo, the lump in Cheryl's neck had grown so large, her physician recommended its removal as soon as possible. It wasn't an easy decision to make: the operation was daunting, and we had no health insurance. I was the sole provider, and we were living off scant and unpredictable donations and the occasional $100 honorarium from a preaching engagement. In those days we could barely make our $250-a-month mortgage payment, and we were already deeply in debt after Matthew's hospitalization. We knew this surgery would only add more red ink. But there was no question Cheryl needed the procedure, and within weeks she was checked into Buffalo's beloved Sisters of Charity Hospital.

The evening of her operation, I sat alone, praying and fidgeting in a waiting area for two hours before the surgeon came out of the operating room and beckoned me to a private consulting booth. He told me they had discovered a malignancy and it had spread to the lymph system, and arterial and muscle tissue was affected. The operation was going to be much more complicated than we had initially thought.

I was shell-shocked. The doctor, in his bloodied scrubs, had just told me my wife—my best friend, my most intimate companion, my partner in ministry, the mother of my two small children—had cancer, and that it was extensive. The dreaded disease had come way too early: we had just turned twenty-four. I immediately called Cheryl's mom, Virginia, Paul, my parents, my sisters, and Pastor Tommy Reid; they all came quickly to the hospital. My impulse was to pray; my mother-in-law and my dad were not naturally sympathetic to the ritual, but they acquiesced and bowed their heads with the rest of us as I asked the Lord to help us and to restore Cheryl to health. When Pastor Reid arrived, he was allowed access to Cheryl even before I saw her, to anoint her with oil and to pray the New Testament prayer of faith, for God to save the sick, that I had recited so many times for others.

On the outside, I was assuring everyone that God was with us, just as he had been with Matthew, and we knew he answered prayers. On the inside, though, I was trembling, desolate, and almost ill, now with the anguish of losing Cheryl and being left alone to raise two kids without her. When she came to, swathed in bandaging that framed her face like a rugby helmet with an oversized chin guard, I loved her more than I ever had. I prayed for her, caressed her brow, answered her anxious questions about the diagnosis and about the kids, and endlessly fed her ice chips. Soon after, she was placed in isolation so she could swallow a radioactive isotope to bombard residual cancer cells. It proved successful and she was released to recover at home. My challenge became finding a way to pay the outstanding $60,000 bill, a gigantic sum of money, considering my entire income that year was less than $25,000. The surgeon mercifully cut his bill in half, and family and friends contributed toward reducing the balance. It would take me years to pay it off, but no amount of money mattered as much as Cheryl's life. We were so grateful, and—unlike the way I had acted when Matthew was hospitalized—I turned to God with humble, contrite gratitude for his grace in sparing her.

In the weeks that followed the operation, the rhythms of our life returned to something akin to normal. Cheryl slowly recovered her strength, while Matthew's residual seizures were controlled by an anti-epileptic drug. Anna had started preschool and was loving it. As for me, I held my first service as an independent evangelist in a ballroom at the Hilton Hotel in Rochester, and persuaded Cheryl to share her testimony of how God restored her after her difficult struggle with cancer. The dramatic incision from her carotid artery to her collarbone was barely healed when I called her to the platform, but she spoke eloquently about our family's ordeal.

I threw myself into creating the ministry of my dreams, secure that Cheryl would be fully supported within the church community of New Covenant. We traveled together when the kids were small. For the next four years I traversed the United States and the world, preaching in cities from Gretna, Louisiana, to Halifax, Nova Scotia, from Spokane, Washington, to Orlando, Florida, as well as London, Stuttgart, Mexico City, and even Jerusalem. Sometimes I was alone and sometimes with a dozen or more short-term mission team members in tow, and on occasion my family.

One of the most fruitful trips I took during those first years as a traveling missionary preacher was to a church-sponsored hospital in Marjayoun, Lebanon, at the height of the civil war there. When I returned, this sortie was the subject of my first newsletter, which I called *Covenant Magazine.* Our visit to Lebanon and Israel was filled with the prayerful intentions of so many people. Repeatedly the question of peace had come up amidst the fighting. I wrote, "When you set foot on the soil of a land where hundreds of thousands have lost their lives—where children have grown up in bomb shelters—you quickly realize man's impotence in solving the world's problems." No matter how desperate the problems were, no matter how intractable the conflicts appeared to be, peace was possible because "God's creation still belongs to Him. The devil is the squatter . . . [whose] days are numbered."

During those times, I ministered in churches throughout the U.S., Canada, Europe, and the U.K., interspersed with teaching tours of the Holy Land. Using the Bible as a guide for pilgrim tourists, I would take groups of mostly middle-aged couples through Jerusalem, Bethlehem, to the Sea of Galilee, and other sites of religious significance. When I traveled all over the U.S., visiting churches and preaching, the collections raised tens of thousands of dollars for missionary projects all over the world. When there were mission conventions at the church, I was the master of ceremonies and the host for scores of missionaries on deputation. In the process, I polished my bona fides as a missionary myself, and as an evangelist, which positioned me well for leadership in the wider evangelical arena. I was an ambitious young man, eager to make my mark as a preacher and as someone who "won souls"—that is, someone who brought people to Christ much in the way that the luminaries in the field such as Billy Graham did. In the particular evangelical universe I inhabited, "soul winning" was the most important work anyone could do.

All that hard work paid off. Within a few years I moved from the fringes of American evangelicalism into the center of the establishment. I attended all the right conferences, struck up friendships with all the right players, and sent checks for all the right projects. I also volunteered for boards, committees, and commissions of groups like the National Association of Evangelicals, meeting and talking with some of the biggest names in American, British, and European circles. Billy Graham held worldwide conferences for missionary evangelists, and in 1983, I applied for a scholarship to attend one in Holland. My friends and mentors told me that such assistance only went to the evangelists coming from third world countries, not those who were in comfortable congregations in upstate New York. When the acceptance letter arrived, I felt as if I had been admitted to Harvard.

Evangelicalism has always been built around personalities, from Martin Luther and John Calvin in the sixteenth century to the Wesley brothers in the eighteenth, to Charles Finney and Charles Spurgeon in the nineteenth, and Billy Sunday and Billy Graham in the twentieth. Most members of our constellation of superstars would be joining Graham and nearly four thousand others in the RAI Amsterdam Convention Centre in the Netherlands. We heard from Dr. Paul Yonggi Cho, the founding pastor of Yoido Full Gospel Church in Seoul, South Korea, the world's largest evangelical congregation, with more than sixty thousand service-goers every Sunday; Pat Robertson of the Christian Broadcasting Network; and dozens of lesser-known lights from other parts of the world.

One of the speakers was the television evangelist Robert Schuller, the epitome of the mega-church pastor, who had opened the giant Crystal Cathedral in his headquarters town of Garden Grove, California. Schuller preached the gospel of prosperity. To him, Jesus was the ultimate exemplar of the power of positive thinking. With his slogan, "Find a need and fill it, find a hurt and heal it," Schuller's church drew ten thousand people to its membership rolls and attracted an estimated thirty million television viewers from around the world each week for its Sunday services. Millions more watched Schuller's weekly show, *Hour of Power*—including, surprisingly, my father.

By now my father had softened about his sons' conversions as he watched both of us gain prominence, success, and happiness in our Christian work. In his attempts to connect with our new lives, Dad tentatively explored a bit of the Christian world on television; Pat Robertson and Billy Graham were too much for him, but Robert Schuller's practicality conformed nicely to Dad's own fragile and thwarted ambitions as a businessman. Schuller also insisted the best route to Christ did not require a conversion, which was an approach that made many evangelicals mistrust him, but one that appealed to Dad. In Amsterdam, after I had stood in line for what seemed an eternity, I finally met Schuller and called Dad to tell him—another plank in the bridge across our still uncomfortable religious and emotional divide. It was nice to share this point of interest with my father, and it left me with a longing for much more.

While I was traveling the globe, back in Buffalo, Paul expanded our church's facilities, purchasing an abandoned elementary school and mapping out a plan for a ten-thousand-square-foot sanctuary. Tommy Reid arranged for the dedication ceremony to be led by Dr. Cho. We had started to attract attention and respect; fellow pastors sought us out, and Christian and secular media began to write about us. We were even included in a cover story for the Sunday magazine of the *Buffalo News* with the provocative title "Jews by Heritage, Christians by Faith."

6

Los Pepenadores

In the spring of 1983, after I was back in Buffalo a little over a year, I made my first trip to Mexico City to preach at one of the largest evangelical churches in Latin America, Centro de Fe, Esperanza y Amor—the Center of Faith, Hope & Love. I had been invited by Danny Ost—a larger-than-life missionary. He had literally blanketed Mexico with the evangelical gospel message over a ten-year period from the mid-sixties to the mid-seventies by criss-crossing the country in his Cesna 182 single-engine airplane, dropping millions of pamphlets to the cities, towns, and hamlets below. In 1971, Ost had opened his first center in the northern city of Monterrey. By the time I got there, 250 such centers were scattered throughout the country. The largest, a converted warehouse, was located in the capital. The first Sunday I was there, I preached nine services beginning at nine in the morning and ending at nine at night—all to packed houses.

The next morning I was met at my hotel by Reverend Freddy Gonzales, another American missionary I knew from my old Teen Challenge days. Freddy was one of our star graduates who had not only conquered his addiction to heroin but went on to complete Bible college and become ordained and commissioned as a missionary pastor. He always called me Roberto, which warmed my heart. That morning Freddy invited me to join him on what he referred to as "a tour of hell."

We jumped in a rickety old station wagon and began a dizzying trip north until we reached Cuautitlán; it was a separate municipality, but without any clear boundary, it became part of the urban sprawl of Mexico City. As Freddy chattered about the unique challenges of ministry in this part of the world—dealing with massive poverty and illiteracy, corrupt politicians and police officials—he abruptly turned the car off the road and onto an unpaved dirt path marked by cavernous potholes. We were jostled so violently I had to hold on to keep my head from hitting the side window.

This, he told me, was the road to hell.

Within a few minutes we pulled up over a bern, and Freddy brought us to a sudden, angled stop. I looked out over a landscape unlike any I had seen before. A massive expanse of garbage extended from one end of the horizon to the other, a rainbow of rotting food, paper, twisted metal, bottles, cans, glasses, cloth, and anything else that could possibly be discarded by human beings. Freddy told me to get out of the car and when I did, the full effect of the place hit me. A wall of stench triggered my gag reflex. Flies buzzed around our faces and landed in our hair, on our brows and lips.

Freddy said that we were in "the land of Baal-zebub," referring to the Philistine idol mentioned in the Bible and known as "Lord of the Flies," often used interchangeably with Satan. Freddy led me down a perilous hill of loose trash, my footing giving way every few steps. At one point I fell, and got up to find myself plastered with an oozing, fetid cream of some kind. I wondered why he had brought me here. When I sheepishly asked, he pointed into the distance.

I could barely make out the signs of other human beings in the ruined, rotting landscape. But I could see dozens of battered trucks, like a well-ordered assembly line, dumping their loads before making a U-turn to go back down one of the makeshift roads. As the vehicles moved, they revealed small clusters of men, women, and mostly children, bent over and picking through the mountains of refuse as if they were harvesting crops. Freddy told me they were known as the *pepenadores*. They lived there and worked the piles during the day like slaves. Nightfall brought new horrors from the men who paid the bosses of the *pepenadores* to sexually abuse the women and children.

My mind reeled. There was nothing to say. I stood with Freddy and stared into this abyss of human suffering. He had told me it was hell, and he was right. I was standing in the middle of massive, seething, human-generated wreckage and waste. There were no flames, but there was smoke, from what I later learned were subterranean fires fueled by methane gas. It brought to my mind the Lake of Fire in the book of Revelation. Freddy persisted and told me I could not walk away from this scene of anguish without doing something about it.

I thought I had seen poverty among the homeless in New York, but that day my entire frame of reference shifted when I faced the shocking destitution in Mexico. I was reminded of the proverb "Do not withhold good from those who deserve it, when it is in your power to act. Do not say to your neighbor, 'Come back later, I'll give it to you tomorrow,' when you now have it with you." Desperate as I was to flee, Freddy was right. I couldn't walk away from this.

The *pepenadores* are the untouchables of Mexican society. Some are simply homeless; others are fugitives from the law. For them, the garbage is their whole ecosystem; they live in, on, and off the trash. They make their homes out of it, scavenge for food in it, unearth their clothing from it, and make money by sorting it for *los jefes*, the bosses, who run the syndicates that control the waste-processing industry. Tens of millions of pesos from the value of recycled materials are at stake, most of it ending up in the pockets of politicians.

It seemed at first too big a problem to tackle, but Freddy had a vision: These people could never escape from their lives in the dumps, so it was up to us to bring some measure of civilization to them. He knew that he could build a school, a clinic, and, of course, a church, but he needed my help.

When I left Mexico after that visit and returned to our comfortable home in our quiet suburban neighborhood, I couldn't shake the memory of the people in the dumps. They would invade my thoughts at every turn—when I got a whiff of day-old trash, when I saw one of my children reaching to the ground to pick up a ball, when a garbage truck barreled by our house. I would go to sleep at night imagining the soiled face of a toddler, in a stained and threadbare dress, with no shoes on her feet, or a pregnant woman carrying a backbreaking load of cans and glasses on her shoulders.

My first job was to figure out a way to build a mission church in the garbage dumps, just as we would have done in any remote community that did not have a place to worship. That the location was not the streets of New York, or the bush in Africa, but atop piles of rotting refuse didn't matter. The presence of God is everywhere. Freddy proposed a combination church, school, and food distribution center he and his compatriots wanted to call La Casa de Pan, the House of Bread. I began recruiting cash, supplies, and volunteers from our community. Within a few months I was back in the garbage piles as our team of *gringos cristianos* laid a cinder-block foundation while breathing the putrid air of the *basurero*.

I knew God had brought me there to challenge my faith and to offer me a beautiful opportunity to act on it. In Mexico, God's work and His will seemed to offer constant and often unexpected gifts. I felt especially close to Christ while working in these forgotten and ignored places of human suffering. Jesus said, "It is not the healthy who need a doctor, but the sick." These people were literally and figuratively very sick. They needed our care. I was also mindful of Jesus' parable of the sheep and the goats, when he told the story of how the king would sit on his throne and invite into heaven all those who gave him food when he was hungry, drink when he was thirsty, and clothing to cover his nakedness. When his subjects asked quizzically when they had done that for him, he answered, "Truly I tell you, whatever you did for one of the least of these brothers and sisters of mine, you did for me." Then he warned the others who had failed to take care of the needy, "Depart from me, you who are cursed, into the eternal fire prepared for the devil and his angels. For I was hungry and you gave me nothing to eat, I was thirsty and you gave me nothing to drink, I was a stranger and you did not invite me in, I needed clothes and you did not clothe me, I was sick and in prison and you did not look after me." The work we were doing among the *pepenadores* was serious ministry with consequences that would endure into eternity.

Over the next five years, I expanded our enlistment of volunteers from all over the United States and Canada. We began small, sending a doctor, a dentist, and a nurse, but within a few years, we dispatched dozens of medical, dental, health, and hygiene professionals to La Casa de Pan and many similar sites around the metropolitan area. We deployed mobile medical units, worked with Mexican congregations that adopted abandoned children from the dumps, and eventually opened a local office and hired Mexican staff to maintain the program between visits from U.S.-based personnel.

These were the most fulfilling years of my missionary work. I felt I was really making a difference in the world not just spiritually, as souls were saved, but in every other way, too. We helped people to find freedom from their indentured servitude, brought scrutiny to bear on a horribly corrupt system, and mobilized civil society in a place that desperately needed the kind of perpetual help that only locals could ultimately provide. I often think I should have spent the rest of my life doing this kind of Christian humanitarian work. Back then, it seemed, God had other plans.

7

Our President, Our Prophet

By 1980 the great hope we had felt with the election of fellow evangelical President Jimmy Carter four years earlier had given way to a pervasive sense of his failed promise. We could not ignore the spectacle of the hostages taken in Iran and, closer to home, the long lines at the gas stations, the terrible economy, the general sense of political and social stagnation, and, worst of all, the strengthening of the Soviet Union. As evangelicals we felt desperate to bring America back from this looming catastrophe, which meant we had to get involved before the country was taken over by the radical left. During the Cold War there was a direct relation between the weakening of the United States and the strengthening of the atheistic Soviet Union, and there was no greater harbinger of the dreaded End Times than this godless empire that was the world's greatest persecutor of Christians.

Reagan had revived the popular theme of godless communism, but evangelicals were among the original architects of disdain and even dread of the Soviet Union and Red China. In 1949, Billy Graham declared, "Communism is inspired, directed, and motivated by the Devil himself. America is at a crossroads. Will we turn to the left-wingers and atheists, or will we turn to the right and embrace the cross?" If Satan had a political affiliation, it had to be with the revolutionary left. Fifteen years later, during Barry Goldwater's failed presidential bid in 1964, Reagan had taken to the campaign trail, decrying the so-called capitulation of liberals in the face of communist aggression. His images mixed the spiritual with the political even then. "We are being asked to buy our safety from the threat of 'the bomb' by selling into permanent slavery our fellow human beings enslaved behind the Iron Curtain . . ." he said. "If we are to believe that nothing is worth the dying, when did this begin? Should Moses have told the children of Israel to live in slavery rather than dare the wilderness? Should Christ have refused the Cross? Should the patriots at Concord Bridge have refused to fire the shot heard 'round the world? Are we to believe that all the martyrs of history died in vain?"*

Reagan's narrative had not changed much in the sixteen years from that rousing oratory to his 1980 presidential campaign. We celebrated a politician who, at long last, spoke the truth. Here was someone who was clear about our ultimate dependence on the Almighty and who got it right by seeing that the church and not the state should have the last word. Reagan finally called a spade a spade: Soviet atheism was the greatest menace ever faced by mankind. We knew that this "evil empire" threatened not only our lives but our right to worship Almighty God. The only members of our community who did not support Reagan were the blue-collar factory workers, most of whom were the children of immigrants and staunch union members, and many filled the pews of New Covenant Tabernacle. These victims of Buffalo's crumbling steel industry were stuck in a catch-22: like us, they didn't agree with the secular drift fostered by their own Democratic Party, but if they voted for Reagan, they would hurt the unions that protected their jobs. We felt sorry for them but were confident that, with Reagan gaining ground, our country was finally getting back on track. "If we ever forget that we are One Nation Under God," Reagan memorably observed, "then we will be a nation gone under."

---

* Ronald Reagan, "Address on Behalf of Senator Barry Goldwater: A Time for Choosing," October 27, 1964, the American Presidency Project.

Evangelicals had played a decisive role in getting Reagan elected, and we were determined to flex that newfound muscle by demanding our politicians pay attention to our dislike of homosexual rights, women's rights, and smutty lyrics, and urging them to bring prayer back to public schools and morality back into the public conversation. Our political power was local, and we were learning how to use it.

Within five years Paul's church had become the largest Assembly of God congregation north of the city, with both an elementary and a high school. I had gained some modest fame from my global missionary work, and together we had carved out a place in the broader community of national evangelical leaders. We were young; we were twins; we were "Jewish Believers" and had attracted some media attention, and with that came more and more invitations to participate in large-scale events like the huge General Council of the Assemblies of God, where we participated in debates in front of twenty-five thousand delegates. We also joined several influential organizations, including the National Association of Evangelicals, which was enjoying massive exposure and influence in the wake of Reagan's 1980 victory.

In March of 1983, Fred Dixon, our early pastor and now a member of my support staff, joined me in attending the annual convention of the NAE held in Orlando, Florida. In theory we went for the workshops as much as anything, but the real reason we were there was to attend Reagan's speech on Tuesday afternoon. He was the first president to ever address a body of evangelicals. In spite of Jimmy Carter's unabashed self-identification as a "born-again Christian," we considered Reagan to be the first president to take us seriously. He not only deserved our respect and loyalty but commanded it. Fred and I were two of the first to enter the ballroom at the Sheraton Towers, and we nailed seats in the fourth row, close enough to feel the stage lights. There it was: the official slate-blue-topped podium with the majestic Seal of the

President of the United States hanging on the front. I had never been so close to presidential power, and I was in awe. I had heard people speak of Reagan's "aura" and, in spite of the fact that such an emanation was a pagan superstition, I was sure I was sensing it in that room that day, even before the man had entered.

The platform filled with smiling officials, many of whom I knew personally. The NAE president, Arthur Evans Gay Jr., an Illinois pastor I had only recently come to know, introduced the president, noting that our NAE community deeply appreciated and valued his love for the truth of the Bible and his commitment to its great moral values. The standing ovation lasted a full thirty seconds before we obeyed Reagan's gestures to sit down and let him speak. The only African-American on the crowded dais was the infamous John M. Perkins, a rare civil rights leader in our circles, who had organized voter registration in Mississippi in the sixties. He was a remarkable man who had moved to California and set up a large ministry there. I noticed that he smiled but did not clap, only joining in politely—and tepidly—at the conclusion. It gave me momentary pause. I was aware that the division between the Republican Party and African-Americans was deepening during this period. Reagan's eagerness to cut the federal budget meant many in that community, who were dependent on federal programs, suffered. Added to that were the fissures in the evangelical community—where black churches were typically more progressive, and the white churches leaned conservative. Reverend Perkins was an outlier in that community, and by keeping his hands in his lap during the applause lines, he signaled his distance from the rest of us. That bothered me, but I pushed past it.

There were many reasons most of us were so excited—and relieved—to hear Reagan speak that day. First, it validated us. As powerful as we had become in the public square—swamping the airwaves with ever-expanding media enterprises, spawning *Billboard* chart-topping music hits, scoring major headlines in national newspapers and magazines, and even sporting a Christian theme park rivaling Disneyland—we just couldn't shake our inferiority complex. We had historically lacked the economic and social status of the Episcopalians, the ubiquity of Roman Catholics, the prestige of Presbyterians. No matter how many imposing evangelical church buildings dotted the landscape, no matter how many of us had accumulated significant wealth, in our minds we were still the outsiders, the people on the margins, the churches on the wrong side of the tracks. But with Reagan we had upset the apple cart and turned the world on its head. We had brought about a major political victory, not just for the presidency, but in the Senate, where, with our help, the Republicans had regained control after twenty-five years.

But there was another reason to celebrate that day, perhaps a much more important one. We evangelicals had a mandate to do whatever we could to preserve the basic pillars of a Christianized civilization. We were stewards of the culture, and it was eroding under our feet. Homosexuals were demanding public acceptance, Bible reading and prayer were forbidden in schools, obscene language and images could be seen on broadcast television, and masturbation had even become the theme of songs at the top of the pop charts. It gave us hope and reassurance to have a leader who was determined to maintain what was Christian and godly.

We would continue to help Ronald Reagan achieve his objectives in any way possible, even if they weren't specifically a part of our religious agenda. We needed to keep him in power as long as we could. At the time of his speech, a debate was raging in Congress over a "nuclear freeze," a proposal presented by Senator Ted Kennedy and one of our own, Senator Mark Hatfield (a Baptist), that would have prevented the deployment of U.S. missiles in Europe. The idea was gaining momentum within Congress and among grassroots groups, but conservatives were overwhelmingly opposed. I only learned later, when I had made friends in Congress, that the day before the Orlando event, the president invited a group of influential Republican leaders and sympathetic members of Congress to the White House to discuss the problem. They urged the president to use his bully pulpit to bring this issue to the voters. Right after that meeting, President Reagan tweaked the speech he would deliver to us the next day.*

"The American experiment in democracy rests on this insight," he said, when we finally stopped applauding. "Its discovery was the great triumph of our Founding Fathers, voiced by William Penn when he said, 'If we will not be governed by God, we must be governed by tyrants.'" He explained the evils of modern-day secularism and talked about the erosion of our cherished value systems. Most important, he understood the importance of our work and the importance of faith in the lives of Americans.

Near the end of the speech, Reagan addressed the evils of the Soviet Union and the "sad, bizarre chapter of human history" that was communism. He focused on our steadfast conviction that Bolshevism was the precursor to the Antichrist, who would lead us to the end of days. We understood the connection between leftist movements in the United States and international socialism as a grave danger fostered by progressives—cause enough to defeat their efforts. "We will never compromise our principles and standards. We will never give away our freedom. We will never abandon our belief in God. And we will never stop searching for a genuine peace," he continued, and then came the pivot. "But we can assure none of these things America stands for

---

* Lou Cannon, *President Reagan: The Role of a Lifetime* (New York: Simon & Schuster, 1991), 273.

through the so-called nuclear freeze solutions proposed by some." He urged us to use our pulpits to share with our communities the importance of defeating this terrible measure. Reagan's appeal left me and everyone in that room glowing with the rush of presidential affirmation. The speech went down in history as one of his greatest, and the nuclear freeze measure failed.

Almost a year to the day later, on March 6, 1984, I again attended the NAE convention, this time at the Hyatt Regency in Columbus, Ohio. Reagan was, for the second time, the keynote speaker, and it was not to be missed. The Gipper was his most engaging, charming, and riveting self. He began with a joke that brought the house down: "Talking to a church audience like this reminds me of a church in a little town in Illinois—Dixon, Illinois—that I used to attend as a boy. One sweltering Sunday morning in July, the minister told us he was going to preach the shortest sermon he had ever given. And then he said a single sentence. 'If you think it's hot today, just wait.'" We cheered and laughed and relaxed—we were in good hands.

Reagan peppered the speech with a laundry list of concerns that resonated, point by point, with every member of the audience: the search for religious freedom by the first American settlers; the Founders and their firm faith in God; his own identification with Abraham Lincoln's bended-knee prayers; and his recollection of a World War II war bond rally where he heard prizefighter turned Army private Joe Louis declare, "I know we'll win, because we're on God's side."

Reagan masterfully fused matters of church and state and, toggling between the sacred and the secular, the political and the spiritual: the problem of widespread access to pornography and the breakdown of the traditional family; teen pregnancies; big taxing and spending and a weakened military; a downturn in inflation and a cut in the prime rate; a long-awaited spiritual awakening with attendant increased sales in religious books and audiences for Christian broadcasters; and, of course, the intolerable number of abortions performed every day in our nation. The president ended his speech by appealing for the passage of a constitutional amendment permitting prayer in public schools: "I'm convinced that passage of this amendment would do more than any other action to reassert the faith and values that made America great. I urge you and all those listening on television and radio to support this amendment and to let your Senators and Members of Congress know where you stand. And together we can show the world that America is still one nation under God."

We leapt to our feet, applauding in a thunderous and sustained ovation. The ecstasy was similar to what I had experienced ten years earlier at the altar of that tiny Methodist church. When Reagan conflated biblical theology and Republican politics, the Bible and the GOP platform, my own world expanded immeasurably. All of my work had been geared to serving the Lord, but there was another force within me, a personal ambition, that had not yet found its full expression. I liked the idea of moving a large audience. The accolades, the occasional applause, the fund-raising results after a missionary appeal—all quantified my success. Reagan validated all these drives by showing they served a greater good for the nation. I had once wanted to be like Billy Graham, preaching Jesus to the multitudes and moving them to the altar rails for salvation. Now I wanted to be like both Graham and Reagan, moving those same people from the altar rails into the voting booths.

During Reagan's speech, something fundamental had shifted inside me. I experienced, as most born-again Christians do, a "turning." Turning is the start of everything: turning away from sin and toward God is how every Bible-believing convert begins his or her Christian life. As the president finished his speech, I felt as if Jesus himself had extended an invitation to me for another turning. This time it was to move beyond the familiarity of my missionary work and into the more expansive realm of political life. I felt liberated to proceed to a different level of engagement with my community and my country. The next steps weren't exactly apparent, but I was confident God would make my path clear.

8
FaithWalk

Politics were in the air in the summer of 1988 when I undertook a two-thousand-mile-long walk from Canada to Mexico to raise funds for the children in the garbage dumps.
Cheryl and I had planned this FaithWalk for over two years before we
set out in an RV, following a route along mostly low-traffic state high-
ways safe enough for me to walk along, from morning to night, five
days a week, stopping every Sunday to preach in churches on the way
and raise a penny for every mile my feet traversed. Cheryl and the kids
lived in the RV, where she homeschooled them. A support team took
care of everything else.

Over the course of the cross-country trek, my only connection to
the news was NPR, which I listened to every time I could get it on my
Sony Walkman. In one state after another, I passed miles and miles
of political posters—staked in lawns, taped in shop windows, and stapled to telephone poles—for George H. W. Bush, Bob Dole, and one
very familiar name: Pat Robertson. Just months before I started out
on the FaithWalk, Paul and I had hosted a fund-raising gala for Pat in
Buffalo. We had recruited a host of evangelical leaders from the region
to contribute money, manpower, and endorsements for the man one
pastor had called "the Moses of our times who will lead our people to
the Promised Land." I was excited to have an evangelical faith leader of
his stature among a credible lineup of candidates.

Even with the presidential election looming, I was more preoccupied with our missionary work, the church back home, and in the spiritual condition of the Christians I met every day in my life as a traveling preacher. So many seemed absorbed in their pursuit of a comfortable life. When I spoke in churches on weekends and described the suffering of the *pepenadores*, someone would often get up angrily and walk out. "I don't come to church to listen to people's misery," one woman complained. "I come to be uplifted. You ruined my morning."

From my earliest days of Christian life, I was trained to believe the gospel obligated us to take care of the poor. When I was a student at Elim, a faculty member admonished, "If God ever tells you to give something to someone in need, give them the best. If somebody needs a refrigerator, don't go out and buy a new one and give them the old one. Go out and buy a new one and give the new one to them! That's what God did. He gave us his best, his only begotten Son." It was taxing to think that I wasn't getting through to my charges, and at times I felt hopeless they weren't hearing me or understanding the call to sacrificial faith.

Often my thoughts would drift back to Buffalo and the ministry that Paul and I had built together. There were now four services each week at New Covenant, and our congregation continued to grow rapidly. We had a Sunday school, an overflowing nursery, midweek Bible study and home fellowship groups, leadership training classes, and schools: Covenant Academy K-6 and the slowly expanding Charles G. Finney High School, named for the famous nineteenth-century abolitionist revivalist.

My side of our operation was also increasing in scope. Besides my missionary fieldwork in some thirty countries, I oversaw Operation Serve in Mexico and Egypt and conducted what Paul and I dubbed "motivation and mobilization campaigns" in churches across the U.S., throughout Canada, in the U.K., and in Europe. The theme of these three-day seminars was "Out of the Pew and Into the Action." If our work could be distilled into one element, it would be the joyful knowledge of the love of God and the plan of salvation provided for in the death and resurrection of Jesus Christ. We knew if someone made their peace with God, their whole life would improve. The gospel message was clear: Love God; commit your life to Jesus; read the Bible and obey it; tell others about Christ and care for their spiritual and temporal needs. And so Paul and I would passionately make our case from pulpits, calling Christians "to walk your talk, turn your faith into works!" I would often direct our congregants' attention to a passage from the New Testament book of James that states starkly, "Faith by itself, if it does not have works, is dead." One of us would then "open the altar," urging people to come forward, kneel at the rails, and dedicate their lives to actively serving Christ. We would also send them off with a workbook that would guide them toward discovering their own gifts, talents, and resources to be put into service inside and outside the church, whether leading souls to Jesus, stocking shelves at a food pantry, or volunteering their professional skills on short-term mission teams to places such as the Mexican garbage dumps.

But outside of our work in the church, Paul's and my interest in politics was gaining traction, and we both spent time planning events and fund-raisers for evangelical candidates who could wield power in the public sphere. Before I left on my FaithWalk, Paul was organizing one of the biggest events of his career. If Pat Robertson and Pat Boone were crowned princes in the evangelical community, Billy Graham was the king. He was about to appear in our hometown and Paul would be one of his hosts. As the public face of the evangelical movement for decades, Graham was renowned for the crowds of hundreds of thousands attracted to his crusades. He was practically revered for having preached the gospel to more people than the apostle Paul. Powerful politicians, even presidents, sought his spiritual counsel, if not his political allegiance.

Long before I was introduced to Christianity, Billy Graham was a surprising regular feature in our Jewish home. We watched his televised events—especially his annual Christmas special—but with the same kind of appreciation for the spectacle that we had for the Ice Capades. Graham seemed to have everything: a gentle southern lilt; dashing looks; and easy engagement with every popular talk-show host, from mornings with Merv Griffin to late nights with Johnny Carson. When I entered the Christian world, my appreciation for Graham increased exponentially because I discovered how many people had "found the Lord" under his ministry. In Bible school, I studied Graham's unsurpassed pulpit method, his sermonic techniques, and his stagecraft, feeling that if I could master them, I'd surely succeed in my ministry. How was he able to command the attention of everyone in a packed arena or football stadium? What was it about one of his sweeping gestures that would move the throngs from their seats as if a single unit and flood into the field to receive Christ as Savior? Knowing the answers would be the key to moving the masses.

Finally, Billy Graham and his entourage were coming to our town for a visit that would affirm the importance of our community and, perforce, of us. Once a site was selected by the Graham organization, scores of highly trained professionals descended to inspect arenas, drive million-dollar fund-raising campaigns, and recruit, train, and mobilize hundreds of volunteers, dozens of churches, and appoint numerous committees to manage various aspects of the Crusade and its ancillary events. Part of this advance work involved contacting leading pastors to enlist their support. My brother received such a call from Graham himself, asking Paul to serve on the executive committee of "the Greater Buffalo–Niagara Billy Graham Crusade."

I missed all this excitement as I had left for my FaithWalk a month before the Graham event. When I was trudging along lonely and often abandoned country roads, Paul was in a whirlwind of activity. From small congregations to large ones, Paul reached out to fellow pastors and local civic and political leaders to organize their participation in Graham's visit. The layers of logistics involved—from selecting venues, to arranging mass transportation, to recruiting the choirs, to ensuring security, to enlisting volunteer support for the event itself—elevated Paul's prominence as a significant figure in the Buffalo religious community. Not that I was really aware of most of this, my long walk being the first time I had been almost completely out of touch with home base. In fact, it turned out I was out of touch in more ways than I could have imagined.

Somewhere south of Hamilton, Ohio, I stopped at a 7-Eleven for a drink and to glance at the news. I bought a copy of *USA Today* and was paging through it when I was startled to see a photo of Paul sitting in the back of a police prisoner transport van. I was so confused, I thought I had entered another dimension. What was my identical twin brother, the pastor of our home church, doing in a police van? The caption explained he had been arrested while praying with a group of pastors outside an abortion clinic in Atlanta after the Democratic National Convention. I immediately blamed it on his association with Randall Terry, whom he had known when they were both students at Elim. Randall had appeared at odd moments in our lives ever since, and I considered him at best eccentric, maybe even unstable. In an earlier phone call home, I had gotten sketchy information about Paul's possible protest at the convention in Atlanta, but because I knew he was tied up with the Graham visit, I didn't think it would happen. I was wrong. Looking at the photo embarrassed me, giving me the odd sense of looking in a distorted mirror when I saw Paul's familiar face and imagined it in a mug shot. What about our reputation? What about my brother's safety and well-being?

In those days before cell phones were popular, I had to locate a pay phone to get in touch, which also required a side trip to find plenty of change to feed it for a long-distance call. It took about fifteen very long minutes before I finally reached my sister Kathy. As soon as she heard my voice, she was concerned that something might have happened to me on the walk. I quickly reassured her and told her that Paul was the one I was worried about. She sounded relieved that I had checked in and then gave me some of the basic details. Paul had gone down to Atlanta to demonstrate with Randall and his anti-abortion group, known as Operation Rescue, at the Democratic National Convention. He initially went only to observe, but then had become much more involved by leading what they called a "pray-in" with pastors at an abortion clinic. Ministers and other believers would kneel at the entrance of the facility and pray for the babies who were about to be murdered. In the process, they also made it difficult for women to enter, so they were arrested for trespassing. Paul was taken into custody and with his trial and release date uncertain, he contacted our dad, who flew to Atlanta to bail him out. As I was talking to Kathy, Paul and Dad were in a rental car driving back to Buffalo.

My head was spinning.

I knew Randall had taken on his anti-abortion crusade as a singular mission. He was routinely arrested, and was wildly flamboyant in the way he communicated his message that abortion was equivalent to mass murder, genocide, ritual child sacrifice, and the Holocaust. That behavior was completely alien in the world Paul and I inhabited. After our stint as sidewalk evangelists during the coffeehouse days, and my bunking in with recovering addicts, we had opted for a more respectable brand of born-again faith. We dressed in suits with professionally pressed shirts, convened board meetings using *Robert's Rules of Order*, and employed the best and most professional manners when speaking in public. It was the kind of behavior that had won Paul an invitation to open Congress in prayer and for me to visit with top government officials in Mexico.

That was the world from which Paul had been summoned to take leadership in the prestigious Billy Graham Crusade. Nothing could have been more mainstream for us than that. And yet, here Paul was, arrested and changed into what I could only imagine was a crazy anti-abortion extremist. How could he be willing to sacrifice all that we had worked so hard to build for the sake of a fringe movement led by an unpredictable, marginal figure? As Paul looked ahead, would his future be filled with more arrests and court dates? Or with a growing congregation and influence in the evangelical world?

Of course, who was I to lecture him on being reasonable when I was walking to Mexico? Still, I saw my mission as a noble humanitarian one. I wasn't sure if that was true of Paul's new cause. When Kathy finished explaining what had happened, I sat down for a few moments to collect myself. Where would this activism lead Paul? This couldn't spell anything but disaster—for our reputation, for the church, for his family. I felt grateful I had a thousand more miles to walk: it would postpone our inevitable confrontation, in which I would be forced to ask him to choose between our work together and his work with Randall. There was a time when I was confident that, put this way, Paul would have sided with me. But the face that I saw in the paper, as familiar as it was, had on it the expression of a stranger. I didn't know what that would mean for either of us, and the prospect frightened me to my core. The earth was shifting beneath me and I knew all I had imagined would be familiar and stable when I returned was probably gone. I just didn't know what had taken its place.

Part II

My Second Conversion

"Christ as the center of history is the mediator between state and God in the form of the church."

—DIETRICH BONHOEFFER,
CHRIST THE CENTER

9
Joining the Movement

For six to eight hours a day, five days a week, for four months, I had been alone with my thoughts, with God, with my conscience, and yet I was distracted by my own anxieties. What was the meaning of the enormously consequential change under way at home? This was not just about Paul. I was worried that, during the four months I was gone in 1988, the community that had shaped me as a Christian and launched me as a minister was changing—and not for the better. It seemed to be morphing into something unrecognizable and malignant.

For years our church folks had listened almost exclusively to the local Christian radio station. The network's most popular on-air personality had been the kindly syndicated afternoon talk show host Rich Buhler—a Mister Rogers type of gentle soul who translated the best of pastoral care to the radio waves, offering warm, avuncular guidance about trauma, sex, broken marriages, alienated children, alcohol- and drug-addicted teens, and emotionally wounded friends. Whenever Rich appeared at Paul's church, the sanctuary was standing room only.

Now, instead of tuning in at noon to hear Rich, many of our constituents waited three hours for station manager Neil Boron's show, *Life-Line*, where hot political topics such as abortion and gay marriage were sprinkled into an otherwise anodyne lineup of spiritual exhortation, reports of answered prayers, and personal testimonies of salvation. But other folks had become hungrier for cultural combat and moved to the secular WBEN, where they were drenched by Rush Limbaugh's conservative fire hose. The migration from gentle Buhler, through the more topical Boron, to the inflammatory Limbaugh would portend an evolution in the church writ large.

After four months and two thousand miles, I finally crossed the last bridge and arrived in Mexico to an enthusiastic welcome with a mariachi band and a Girl Scout troop cheering me on. Thanks to the funds raised on the walk, Operation Serve was now poised to deploy even greater numbers of short-term relief workers to the most desperately poor people around the globe. I hadn't come close to raising the promised $1 million—a source of some tension with my Mexican partners—but we had recruited record numbers of doctors, dentists, and other health and hygiene workers, built two facilities, and deployed several mobile clinics.

When I got home, I had to piece together what had happened while I was away, particularly concerning Paul's involvement with Randall Terry. I thought back to 1987, when Paul and I joined thirty-five thousand other ordained and lay leaders at a church conference in the Superdome in New Orleans. In the exhibit hall, Cheryl and the kids manned a booth that showcased our work in Mexico, and our neighbor exhibitor was Randall Terry, whom I had first met at Paul's introduction back in our Bible school days. He was sitting cross-legged on the floor atop a Berber rug, handing out tiny plastic dolls made to resemble sixteen-week-old fetuses. Cheryl thought he was nuts, and that impression was reinforced throughout our stay. Randall berated us for ignoring the "abortion holocaust," and once followed my brother and me through the hallways demanding we "save these babies!"

We tried to avoid him, but when that didn't work, we agreed to watch an amateur video he had produced about abortion clinic blockades in the Hudson Valley of New York. The earnest blockaders reminded me of the antiwar protestors we knew in our youth. After we watched that video, Paul's opinion shifted—if not about Randall, certainly about the movement he was representing. When we got back to Buffalo, my brother spoke forcefully about abortion from the pulpit, even while many of his congregational leaders warned him about potential defections.

As Paul's anti-abortion sentiment was growing, I was preoccupied by the preparation and promotional work surrounding my walk to Mexico, and Paul was similarly consumed with preparing for the upcoming Billy Graham Crusade. I had already been gone a few weeks when Paul's office received a series of cryptic collect phone calls from Fulton County Jail in Atlanta. They were from someone who identified himself as "Baby Doe," the name Randall instructed all of his clinic blockaders to assume in order to slow down police processing and buy time to keep the clinics closed. What Paul initially thought were prank calls were coming from Randall. He was in Atlanta, where his newly christened "Operation Rescue" was sponsoring massive demonstrations outside the Democratic National Convention.

The name "Operation Rescue" came from a passage in the book of Proverbs: "Rescue those being led away to death; hold back those staggering toward slaughter." Evangelicals had historically interpreted this verse to mean anything from a command to evangelize the lost on their way to eternal damnation, to a believer's ethical duty to intervene when corrupt potentates mete out unjust sentences, such as capital punishment. But it never referred to the unborn—until Randall. Suddenly, the scripture had a novel and potent meaning. "Those being led away to death" were in the womb, the powerless and voiceless unborn.

Rescuers would assume the identities of "Baby Jane Doe" and "Baby John Doe" and sit at the clinic doors or lie down in clinic driveways, blocking entrance for abortion seekers, after which they were arrested. They then refused to provide names or identification, frustrating police procedure and consequently delaying the resumption of normal clinic operations. Randall Terry had called Paul from jail and urged him to come to Atlanta. Initially, Paul agreed to go only as an observer, but when he and a delegation of religious leaders flew down to meet Randall's ragtag crew of pro-life champions, my brother was impressed. Prayerful groups of pro-life activists sat and knelt in front of clinic doors singing, chanting, and putting their bodies between the perpetrators and the victims. They had been spit on, pummeled, and even manhandled by cops. After a few days Paul flew back to Buffalo, resolved to participate in demonstrations. He returned to Atlanta a week later with his family and was detailed to be the jailed Randall's surrogate, mostly recruiting regional pastors to the cause. Many pastors who would have avoided Randall as an embarrassing rabble-rouser now joined out of respect for my brother. As the days wore on, though, Paul felt he needed to practice what he was preaching, and so he participated in one of the demonstrations and got himself arrested.

The more I caught up with what had gone on in Buffalo in my absence, the more I worried about Paul's involvement with Operation Rescue and Randall. My skepticism had mostly to do with Randall's dubious reputation: he was something of a drifter, someone who never seemed to have a fixed address or a steady job. But there was also a theological dimension. I reminded Paul of Romans 13, in which Christians are instructed to be "subject to the governing authorities." Weren't Operation Rescue's tactics a violation of this New Testament tenet? Blockading was a form of trespass, and trespass was a violation of law. I worried about both the spiritual and the legal implications of all of this.

I became more and more anxious about my reunion with a brother who sounded very different from the one I had left in Buffalo in July. To say our encounter was tempestuous would be an understatement. I scolded him for his absurd embrace of Randall's extremism, rebuking him for violating Saint Paul's admonition to obey authority, and for compromising our stature by becoming a common criminal. He shot back that I was deceived by the murderous spirit of a pro-abortion culture and too cowardly to risk my comfort by challenging child killing. It was the nastiest exchange we had had since we punched each other out as kids.

Arrests had become routine for Paul, and each experience further galvanized his commitment to the anti-abortion cause. He had even established a new organization called the Western New York Clergy Council, a collection of ministers and priests who attended the sit-ins. Hundreds of people had been arrested in the "rescues" at "abortion mills" in and around Buffalo. Demonstrating at abortion clinics—or "businesses," as he referred to them—and "saving babies" by attempting to persuade pregnant women not to kill them had become part of his weekly work. The movement was primarily focused on doctors and the babies who must be saved.

A variety of tactics were employed with the intent of interrupting the ability of women to make appointments with abortion providers and of providers to carry out their work. Young women from our churches were recruited and coached in how to make appointments that would never be kept but would burden clinic calendars. Activists unwilling to risk arrest during blockades would be used to carry signs—often with gruesome photos of aborted fetuses reclaimed from medical refuse containers—outside the clinics, forming a sometimes impenetrable phalanx that would discourage timid patients. In rare situations, more experienced activists obtained jobs inside the clinics and surreptitiously destroyed equipment, shut off utilities, canceled supply contracts, and did anything else that would hamper smooth operations. The most effective technique, though, was to seal off the facility by placing large numbers of people against the doors, laying bodies across driveway entrances, and, on occasion, barging inside and chaining multiple activists to furniture, doorknobs, to whatever else was a well-anchored object. Later, women seeking abortions were targeted—as victims of a vast, profitable enterprise. To get an expectant mother to relent, rescuers only had to convince her she was about to murder an innocent child.

Paul had not only become more aggressive in his activism, willing to take risks that I considered unacceptable, he began focusing his energy on persuading me to participate in a rescue. I was ambivalent, to say the least, but all the ministers at our church and many members of clergy from other denominations joined the demonstrations. I couldn't bear to be excluded and finally capitulated: I would take in a rescue at some time, but not risk arrest. I would, as Paul once resolved, only "observe." I wasn't sure when, but I told Paul I'd let him know.

When I met Randall again, he seemed transformed by the experience of having created a movement that was taking hold across the country. His entire being seemed on fire with this cause. A year younger than Paul and me, Randall appeared to have been defined by the search for some crucible into which he could pour his energies. In saving unborn babies, he had found it. Randall had become a national figure, a movement leader, and the embodiment of an emerging element in American evangelicalism: someone who was not just rhetorically questioning popular culture but physically challenging it. He brought together Catholics and evangelicals, groups that had previously been highly suspicious of each other, on the same team. They were now literally linking arms as they steeled themselves against forced removal by police outside abortion clinics. But most notably, Randall had become a media phenom, ubiquitous on television, radio, and in print—and it wasn't accidental. His strategic operation included savvy young operatives influencing the shifting narrative around abortion for evangelicals.

In the early 1980s, many in the evangelical community felt as I did: abortion was not our key concern. Some denominations and national organizations even recognized a necessity for abortion access and supported the rationale of *Roe v. Wade*. I knew pastors who had recommended abortions to their congregants and, in some cases, had the church pay for the procedure. That was all changing as evangelicals—especially national leaders—were adopting a view of human life that placed its origin at the moment of conception, when sperm meets egg. Prior to the mid-1970s, the evangelical position on the beginning of life was murky. There were, to be sure, segments of the community that held conception as the beginning of life and therefore considered abortion immoral, but that was far from a widely held consensus. Once abortion became a principal concern, it was mostly because it was linked to promiscuity and feminism, not to morality or murder.

More than one evangelical leader made the case that the Nazis had proved a civilized society could sanction the heartless slaughter of the lame, the disabled, and the weak. Catholics had mobilized against abortion in the late sixties when states like California and New York first legalized abortions, but it was the high court's 1973 finding in *Roe v. Wade*—and in its lesser-known companion case, *Doe v. Bolton*, which permitted abortion at later stages—that ultimately swept evangelicals into the fray in large numbers.

Then came a series of films produced by evangelical theologian Francis Schaeffer with the future surgeon general Dr. C. Everett Koop. It connected biblical teachings about respect for human life with the scourge of abortion, euthanasia, and infanticide, because inevitably they led to the murder of "the least among us." Inexorably, something shifted. Schaeffer's books began flying off the shelves at Christian bookstores; they turned up in Sunday school classes and home Bible studies. Schaeffer himself was interviewed on numerous Christian radio and television shows, and even preached a sermon on Jerry Falwell's hugely popular *Old Time Gospel Hour* TV broadcast. His prestige as a certified intellectual, not to mention his exotic looks—a long white mane, goatee, and Swiss knickers—commanded attention and loaned gravitas to his views.

Paul made sure I got a steady flow of Schaeffer and other new theological publications making the case against abortion. I was at first reluctant to read them, thinking they were so much movement propaganda, but I soon did and found them quite persuasive. Paul collaborated with a pastor I admired, Richard Exley of Tulsa, Oklahoma, in producing a short book that borrowed one of Paul's pro-life sermon titles, "Pro-Life by Conviction, Pro-Choice by Default." It made the case that if we believe abortion was the deliberate ending of human life, we must act as though it is and do whatever possible to end such a flagrant violation of God's commandment "Thou shalt not kill." I read it in one sitting and was pretty much convinced Richard was right.

Reminding me of my pledge to participate in a rescue, Paul urged me to accompany him to one in early December 1988. It would take place outside the clinic that had first come to his attention when members of our congregation exhumed fetal remains from a Dumpster in its parking lot. I acquiesced to Paul's incessant pleading.

When the day of my initiation finally arrived, Cheryl was extremely unhappy about my taking this step, especially with the possibility that I might face criminal charges. I assured her my role would be on the sidelines, brokering possible problems with police but always obeying the law. I was not going to sully my record as a law-abiding, upstanding member of the community and responsible cleric. The sit-in was planned at the clinic at 666 Colvin Avenue in Tonawanda, a northern suburb of Buffalo with about sixty thousand inhabitants. The address was potent with meaning for Christians: the Book of Revelation described the three-digit sequence as the "number of a man"—a reference universally interpreted by evangelicals to refer to the Antichrist, the monstrous End Times character who would declare war against God.

My adrenaline started to flow when we arrived at the bland cinder-block office building. Well-trained "rescuers" emerged from every direction, some hopping out of cars, others approaching on foot. They sprinted to the doors, sat down, and slid backward until they created a sea of folded bodies, ten and twenty deep. Sometimes one of our side-walk counselors would approach a patient and ask if she would recon-sider her decision, tell her she was carrying a real baby and was about to kill her son or daughter. Then the prayers began. About an hour passed as demonstrators were methodically arrested. Women, feeling fright-ened, guilty, or uncomfortable, tried to enter the clinic with parents, partners, or friends, but couldn't. After about an hour of this, police cruisers whipped into the parking lot. Radios crackled and officers consulted one another on how to handle the situation. I was on the periphery, ready to do whatever Paul needed. An officer warned me to stay off the property or be arrested.

Police draped yellow crime scene tape across the parking lot entry-way. When Paul beckoned to me to come to him, I made my way across the lot and stood in front of a patrol car and was grabbed by a police officer who put my hands behind my back and handcuffed me. Another cop rifled through my pockets, pulled out my ID, read me my Miranda rights, and placed me in the backseat of his cruiser. I stared out the win-dow and watched the rest of the action, thinking of how disappointed Cheryl would be in me, but riveted, as if a film were unspooling in a pri-vate screening. The rescuers prayed and held signs—"Abortion Is Mur-der," "What About the Babies?"—and sang "We Shall Overcome" and other civil rights songs. I felt like I was really part of something, and the lingering guilt I felt about breaking my promise to Cheryl was eclipsed by exhilaration at having played a part in this experience. I began to see the pro-life movement as a battle for civil rights. Something deeply, morally wrong was taking place right in front of us, and we could not be among those "good people" who, my father had warned, "did nothing" when the Nazis were exterminating our people—the Jews.

Police custody was my initiation into the full extent of pro-life work. I now understood what had attracted Paul: the sense of purpose, the moral urgency, the community, the feeling of doing God's work to correct a catastrophic injustice. The sense of solidarity with all the others was reminiscent of the days back at Emmanuel, when we sat and sang intimately about "peace like a river" in our souls. We were united in a common cause that combined full engagement in real-life moral problems with our religious convictions. I felt the shock of a realization that what Paul and Randall and all the others in the movement were doing consolidated all our work thus far and moved us into a new and important realm. We were saving souls and saving lives. It was the missionary evangelism I had carried out in the Mexican garbage dumps, only now it was to save the babies that were being thrown into garbage bins in my own hometown. In fact, one of the Catholic groups we were now working with was called Missionaries to the Unborn. How could any missionary work be more important? This was God's work, this was God's call, this was God's heart for the most vulnerable children of all.

Paul wasn't arrested that day, but I was—and that arrest was sacramental in its importance. It was another baptism, and I was converted.

10

Spring of Life

From the moment I returned home after being held all day in a temporary police processing center, Cheryl noticed the change in me. It wasn't the energy I had from being with people engaged in high-risk behavior, or the solidarity that comes with being part of an anti-establishment cause, but rather the obvious disdain for human life that I thought I recognized in those coming to the clinic. In my mind, abortion was becoming a form of genocide. It had to be stopped. Interposition—the act of placing oneself between a victim and a perpetrator, in our case between a pregnant mother and the "abortionist"—seemed to me then the only effective and moral way to do it.

I had been marinating in the ideology, the facts, and the grotesque anecdotes for months. Paul shared the theological literature with me, along with Schaeffer's works and many photos of aborted fetuses floating in blood-red liquid. I was desperate to get up to speed on the issue—which should not have been presented as an issue at all but a moral catastrophe on a par with human slavery 120 years earlier. I came quickly to know that by ten or eleven weeks of gestation, all ten fingers and toes of a fetus were formed, and the face was clearly human. Sonograms were grainy and rough then, but there were plenty of photos, including in utero ones that showed childlike forms with cherubic faces and tufts of hair, some of them even sucking their thumbs. I also came to see that the Bible clearly condemned this, affirming the child in the womb as a full member of the human family. God told the prophet Jeremiah, "Before I formed you in the womb I knew you, and before you were born I consecrated you . . ." There was no nuance here, no relative meaning, no justification. Abortion was wrong in each and every instance.

If my newfound activism had created a widening rift with Cheryl, it was reestablishing my connection with Paul and making it stronger than ever. Becoming a part of Operation Rescue seamlessly integrated me back into the community at New Covenant, given how disoriented I was when I returned from my walk. I continued to travel as a missionary, but now—in addition to talking about our work in Mexico and among the homeless of Buffalo—I would call for an end to the scourge of abortion. When some people who knew me before I was part of the movement questioned my new cause, I reacted much as I had done with Cheryl: I tried to persuade them and moved on. I remained congenial but basically wrote off the disinterested or unconvinced as benighted souls, unable to see the terrible threat abortion was to humanity. I found my support elsewhere; evangelicals were rapidly embracing the pro-life movement.

Once I committed myself to working with Operation Rescue, I was part of an inner circle that included Paul; Randall; Reverend Patrick Mahoney, an energetic and often hilarious Presbyterian minister from Boca Raton; and Pastor Keith Tucci, who had recently been hired as the movement's director. FaithWalk had garnered some media attention in all the states through which I traveled, and I enjoyed modest fame that the Operation Rescue movement appreciated. We began orchestrating a massive nationwide movement to bring abortion into the consciousness of America. Randall was at the center of it all, barking orders, coming up with strategies, recruiting the soldiers in our pro-life army. He would pop up all over the country, getting arrested more times than I could count.

Yet, as prominent as abortion had become in our lives, at that point it was still not the sole focus of our activities. Paul and I had many other ministry outreach programs—for the homeless, ex-prisoners transitioning into freedom, and food and clothing pantries for Western New York's many underemployed and out-of-work families. Cheryl was extensively involved in these other aspects of my work and in Operation Serve, but she remained distant from the anti-abortion ministry. For me, though, as Operation Rescue grew, it became a near-singular passion. Cheryl and I never discussed the distance between us. The topic was so charged, and my own immersion in the cause left no room for questioning, much less her lack of unwavering support.

My hyperkinetic schedule took its toll emotionally. As is too often the case, the one safe place where I was free to be impatient, and often unkind, was with the people whom I loved most in the world. During a rare dull day full of errands, Cheryl and I were alone in our minivan when she mentioned a conversation she had had with her mother. The mere mention of Virginia, who once told me how embarrassed she was when a friend learned her son-in-law was "a fundamentalist minister," put me on high alert. I had also learned her mother was a new card-carrying member of the Pro-Choice Network of Western New York, the group that would later sue Paul and me for interfering with the constitutional right of women to seek abortion. Our family was a microcosm of the culture wars: progressive versus conservative, Unitarian Universalist versus born-again Christian, and, most important, the protective mother of a beloved daughter versus the guy who took her away. I was prepared for the worst when Cheryl told me she had spoken to my mother-in-law.

They had revisited an old conversation about Cheryl's need to finish her associate's degree so she could pursue her career in occupational therapy. Virginia was a formidable woman, and I had always known I would need to marshal all the emotional strength I possessed to withstand her pressure. As a teenager, I didn't appreciate how natural it was for Virginia not to want her daughter to make an irreversible mistake as a teenage bride. Cheryl knew she had disappointed and hurt her mother, so it was complicated for all of us.

But in the van that day, I was oblivious to the deeper dynamics. When I heard Cheryl say Virginia was coaxing her to go back to school, I felt existentially threatened by the modest proposal. My anger turned to rage and spiraled into an epic temper tantrum. How could she dare consider this? Did she have any idea what this could mean for me in our community? What about our children? I slammed on the brakes and pounded the steering wheel, frightening her. She looked stunned. I had never reacted this way before to what should have been an open and honest conversation.

The explosiveness of my anger was disconcerting even to me: it reminded me too much of my father's frightening and unpredictable rages. Seeing the shock on Cheryl's face in some way reflected my own shock at my similarity with my dad. I felt I was having an out-of-body experience, looking down from the van's ceiling, seeing myself menacing Cheryl—intimidating her, bullying her—caught between competing emotions of anger and shame. I took a deep breath to calm myself sufficiently to listen to Cheryl's reasonable plan. She simply wanted to go back to the community college and resume the work our marriage had interrupted twelve years before. My vision was still blurred by anger, but I could not ignore how meaningful this was to her. In my youth and my arrogance, I had been convinced I could be everything for Cheryl. But I would need to learn that no spouse can be responsible for fulfilling every need, and if anyone should know that, a minister who preaches about the universal human need for God should. But I didn't. Cheryl's academic ambitions threatened me. Agreeing meant she would outshine me on the educational front, but losing her over a diploma would be far worse. Reluctantly, and somewhat bitterly, I accepted it.

My male ego, far more fragile than I realized, had taken a serious hit. Even though I resigned myself to the new circumstances of our lives, my insecurities were reignited every time someone in my community looked askance at the fact I had "permitted" my wife to go to school. My defenses were triggered, frankly, with every grade of A that she brought home. These were two different forces at play: both potent, both playing beneath the surface to become a constant undercurrent in our marriage. The reasonable man I wanted to be, driven by a kind of gender-neutral egalitarianism, would time and again give way to the patriarchal fundamentalist forming in my psyche.

★★★

With its constantly escalating number of high-profile demonstrations, Operation Rescue had commanded increasing national attention since our first blockades in 1988. The staff already topped twenty-three, and we sent mail to over thirty-five thousand supporters, who rewarded us with donations that, as I remember it, reached something like a million dollars. Randall had become a real celebrity, and it was impossible to count how many supporters we actually had. Often the contributions were anonymous cash donations. The leadership had strategically chosen not to incorporate as a nonprofit organization, which meant normally careful record keeping wasn't required or desired. As for volunteers and boosters, we attracted hundreds, sometimes thousands, to our rescues, rallies, and other events. Paul and I worked nationally but also developed a highly visible local presence. We were intent on making Buffalo a linchpin in protecting the lives of soon-to-be-murdered babies. That first rescue in December was repeated over and over again at various clinics.

Paul's role during this period was primarily to recruit, orient, and showcase clergy dedicated to the cause. He and I were always ecumenically oriented, and that quality served the movement well. Paul brought ministers, priests, rabbis, and even an imam or two into our ever-expanding universe of sympathetic religious leaders. What had started as a small collection of mostly marginal, small-church charismatic Christian pastors soon ballooned into a network of major denominational representatives including Catholic, Evangelical, Orthodox, and Protestant.

My role was mostly as a rally speaker, a pro-life guest preacher for church pulpits, and media spokesman. I used the skills I had polished as an itinerant missionary evangelist to bring drama, humor, storytelling, and pathos to a subject that was too often presented in boring or pedantic ways. One of my particularly effective presentations was to tell the story of how a young girl, fourteen years old, had come to my office one day to ask for my help. She nervously explained to me that she was pregnant, and when she told her parents, her father exploded, demanding she get an abortion "or he'd do it with a kitchen knife on the dining room table." Then I would step to the edge of the stage, point my finger into the audience, and ask, "How much is that girl and her baby worth to you? A thousand dollars? Ten thousand dollars? Five hundred dollars? A hundred dollars? Are they worth as much as you pay for cable television? Your yearly vacation? A new large-screen TV? You decide which is worth more." Then I'd dramatically take out my checkbook and announce, "I know what it's worth to me—and it's not ten dollars or twenty dollars." Then I would take my position at the lectern, or podium, or whatever was on the stage, and slowly write out the check in front of the audience and call an usher forward so I could be the first to place it in a collection plate—or, if it was a rally, a clean Kentucky Fried Chicken bucket.

As time went on, I became more involved in the tactical planning for rescues. This included the who, what, where, when, and how of blockades. How many people did we need? Where would they be recruited?

Teams had to be selected to reconnoiter the targeted sites and choose which doors and driveways would be blocked, and by what means. Days and dates and even time periods were carefully selected to do as much damage as possible to the clinic's scheduled "killing." There were always highly experienced "captains" at the ready to keep the troops in line, especially if police would apply physical tactics to coerce compliance with their orders to disperse. Videographers and photographers were enlisted to document the entire experience, and pro bono lawyers were lined up to be available both on- and off-site to challenge court orders, police conduct, and arrests. I was often in those planning sessions, which were generally held surreptitiously in undisclosed locations known only to the participants.

In 1990 the Pro-Choice Network of Western New York—a group of abortion providers, lawyers, and advocates—found a pamphlet we had secretly distributed announcing our intent to shut down clinics with a blockade all over the western part of the state. Lucinda Finley, a law professor at the University of Buffalo, joined with ACLU lawyers and the National Organization for Women in a court complaint against Paul, charging that our plans threatened women's access to health care and deprived them of their constitutional rights.

In response, the court established the "fifteen-foot floating zone," a fluid boundary surrounding a clinic and those who entered it. Sometimes this distance would expand and other times it would contract, but demonstrators had to respect that sphere of privacy and stop talking to women or approaching them within those parameters. The day before the blockade was planned, federal district judge Richard Arcara issued a temporary restraining order prohibiting any activity that would impede clinic operations and women's easy access to facilities. Pro-life activist clergy were even ordered not use their pulpits to recruit participants for our rescues. Paul saw this as an attack on our First Amendment rights and was intent on challenging it.

We were determined to preach about it and distribute Bibles and tracts to women entering clinics and other passersby to get our day in court. The order came down and the pastors went to their pulpits and openly defied it. Paul was summoned to appear before Arcara. He went to his initial hearing without legal counsel. "I'm not a lawyer, but I have read the First Amendment," Paul told the judge, "and this fifteen-foot floating zone doesn't sound like the First Amendment to me." At the end of the hearing, Arcara upheld the floating buffer zone and included a new provision that created a fixed distance protecting the clinic entrances.

This judge's courtroom would become a familiar place for us, and a dozen other Western New York pro-life leaders, as we fought the restraining order, defended ourselves against more contempt charges, and filed our own complaints. For me, the courthouse became an extension of our mission field, a place to give witness to the truth, plead the cause of unborn children, and flex our constitutional muscle. Each appearance was an ordeal, but I began to enjoy them.

If we didn't block entrances, then we picketed. If we didn't picket, then we knelt and prayed silently as staff and patients came and went. If we were not praying, then we called a news conference, and if we were not in a news conference, then we handed out pro-life literature to anyone we encountered. We weren't restricted to the clinics; sometimes we demonstrated, prayed, and handed out literature in front of the homes of abortion providers. We even went after pro-choice churches, leafletting the cars in their parking lots. We were relentless.

In all of our communications, we avoided using the term "fetus," even if it seemed unnatural to do so. "'Fetus,'" I would announce to groups of activists in training, always carefully employing air quotes around the word to underscore my point, "is nothing but a pro-abortion propaganda term meant to dehumanize the unborn child." In my pro-life sermons, which Paul and I routinely delivered from the pulpit at New Covenant, and that I carried with me to my church visits around the country, I asked, "Have you ever seen a little child point to her pregnant mommy's belly and say, 'Mommy's going to have a fetus'? Why? Because even a little child knows what a baby is!" Who could disagree with that?

Our increased involvement meant more and more litigation against us, and we had to devise new tactics. Our opponents were videotaping the clinic blockades so they could use them to accuse us of violating the court orders restricting our activities. At one such blockade, Paul and I decided to make the videographer's job a little harder by ducking behind a building and switching our glasses and neckties. If we were misidentified in a contempt hearing, it would render the tape useless. It seemed ingenious at the time, but it backfired badly.

The inevitable contempt charges were filed, and as Paul was cross-examined, he was specifically asked if he and I had ever exchanged identities. It was a very important point in that particular proceeding, because Paul was being sued personally for having participated in the rescues. Flustered and taken by surprise by the question, Paul denied we had done such a thing. During a confidential lunchtime conversation with our lawyers, I brought up the discrepancy and suggested it would be prudent for Paul to correct the record, say he had merely been confused, and acknowledge that we had done the exchange. Paul agreed it would probably be a good idea, but a member of our legal team advised him not to, arguing it was "immaterial to the case." Paul was uncomfortable but went along with the advice. It proved disastrous.

In his decision to hold us both in contempt for violating his order, Arcara announced his additional finding that Paul had committed perjury by making false statements under oath regarding the neckties. He referred the matter to a federal prosecutor. This was a felony charge, and my twin brother potentially faced a year in a federal penitentiary and up to a $20,000 fine if convicted. But justice moves slowly, and other immediate demands confronted us. Nothing could stop the important work we had committed ourselves to. We organized smaller demonstrations and planned large ones, not only in Buffalo but also all over the country. I visited churches and preached about the sanctity of life and the evils of abortion. We were in a holy war, in which the forces of good would confront the forces of evil— and perhaps even triumph.

In July 1991, our most ambitious target was Wichita, Kansas, and we had our sights set on its three abortion facilities. We had become accustomed to traveling for our demonstrations, but this one was to be our biggest yet. Thousands of rescuers arrived from all over the country and were joined by an equal number of locals. No one was prepared for the scale of our presence. For forty-six days, thousands participated. We blocked cars, chained ourselves to clinic doors, printed and distributed "Wanted" posters of the doctors. We waved signs that read "Babies Killed Here" and passed out countless broadsides denouncing "baby killing" that included gruesome photos of aborted fetuses. I couldn't tell you how many women we approached, pleading with them not to abort—and offering to help them.

The city assigned nearly a quarter of its police force to handling us, and the rescue ended in nearly 2,500 arrests. At one point a judge ordered federal marshals to keep the clinics open. It didn't work. We managed to close all three facilities for a week. Our spokesman, Reverend Pat Mahoney, explained our strategy to the *New York Times*: "The abortion battle is not going to be decided in the trendy urban centers," he said. "It will be decided street by street, town by town, village by village. Wichita is the heartland of America. In capsule form, Wichita embodies what we will see in the next three to four years."

I arrived a couple of weeks into the campaign, after equestrian troops had been called in to scatter the blockaders. One morning I responded to a distress call from a site captain. A small band of nuns was occupying Women's Health Care Services, run by Dr. George Tiller, one of only a few providers in the country offering late-term abortion up to day of delivery. The facility was known to us as "Tiller the Killer's place," where, we were told, two thousand babies were aborted each year. Many in our movement compared his clinic to Auschwitz, complete with a fenced compound and a chimney. We were sure the smoke belching from the clinic's roof came from an incinerator and contained human ash—an argument that I can't say I truly believed at the time. I rationalized my discomfort by thinking that even if this was technically not the case, symbolically it illustrated the important connection between abortion and Nazi genocide. Who did not know about the smoke from the crematoriums in Auschwitz? The site captain called me, fearful the police horses would trample the nuns. He figured I might be able to reason with the police commander at the scene.

A horde of photographers captured the vivid and irresistible images: the sea of middle-class midwestern Americans, along with college and career kids who could have just emerged from Sunday school, young moms with Farrah Fawcett hairstyles, paunchy middle-aged men, elderly couples—all sitting, jammed against a wire gate in the fence surrounding Tiller's compound. On the sidewalk in front of them knelt nine nuns in bright yellow habits, praying with their rosaries. Wearing my clerical collar, I knelt with them. A few minutes later a phalanx of Kansas state troopers descended upon us and dragged us away one by one.

The horses came only after I was already in the back of a Ryder truck, heading to a local school where a cafeteria had become a processing center for arrestees. It was there I was told President Bush had sent someone to argue against the temporary restraining order that had been issued by a federal judge barring our activities. U.S. attorney John Roberts, future Chief Justice of the United States, was sent from Washington by President George H. W. Bush to argue the court order against us was unconstitutional. He prevailed and the court's action was struck down. We were victorious, and those at the highest levels of power were now advocating on our behalf.

If I had any doubts about what we were doing, our experience in Wichita assured me we were on the right side of morality and of history. I was convinced monsters like "Tiller the Killer" could not be allowed to continue. We were engaged in a resistance movement—daring, edgy, risky, even dangerous. We left the comfortable zone occupied by most others who called themselves Christians. We brought many with us to confront and defeat evil—or die trying. We could get away with a lot when the cause was just and noble. Randall, Paul, and I would often point to references in the Bible about spiritual warfare, as when the apostle Paul told his protégé Timothy, "I am giving you this instruction in keeping with the prophecies previously made about you, so that by them you may strongly engage in battle . . ." Despite our often extreme rhetoric, we adjudged the battle was never physically violent, which would have been to stoop to the level of the abortionist.

Paul and I returned to Buffalo from Wichita that summer convinced the time was right for us to stage a similar event in our hometown after such a successful showing in Kansas. We set the dates for April 20 to May 2. Randall mobilized his vast Operation Rescue network to help us. Our Catholic, pro-life mayor, Jimmy Griffin, welcomed our forces with open arms, saying, "I want to see them in this city. If they can shut down one abortion mill, they've done their job." We received letters of support from all over the country and even around the world. Mother Teresa, the famed Angel of Calcutta, wrote to say, "My prayer will be with you that you may allow God to use you more and more as instruments of his peace—the true peace that comes from loving and caring and respecting every person including the unborn child." Flyers were sent to pro-life groups and churches all over the Eastern Seaboard: "The Macedonian Cry Has Gone Out—'Come Over and Help

Us!' Please join us in Buffalo and Erie County for the Historic 'Spring of Life.' Let the church arise to move the gates of hell!"

We distributed a list of prayer needs for those who were unable to attend, urging them to ask the Lord to ensure the signs of division "in the pro-abort ranks ... would continue and that the Lord would send or release spirits of confusion, despair, fear and negligence among them." We implored heaven that "Buffalo's known abortionists . . . be led to publicly renounce the abortion profession and quit." We asked divine assistance for transportation that would be easily available for our pro-life demonstrators but delayed or prevented "to bring in out of town pro-aborts." We prayed that the Buffalo police would arrest "those pro-aborts who get out of hand."

After the success in Wichita, we needed a way to escalate the urgency of our hometown cause. An opportunity presented itself during a visit to a church in Tulsa, Oklahoma. After I preached at the service, my host pastor introduced me to a local pathologist, who explained he was responsible for conducting postmortem examinations on what he said were aborted fetuses. His responsibilities included issuing a death certificate for each one before destroying them. He wanted to show me what he had to face every day.

We arrived at the deserted pathology lab. Nothing prepared me for what I saw when he turned on the lights. Lining the walls were plastic buckets filled with fetal remains. The pathologist told me that before he destroyed them he would place a name on each one's death certificate, usually just "Baby Doe," but he wanted to do something more, wanted the babies to have proper Christian burials. I knew our network included plenty of people likely to have contacts with church cemeteries where these babies could be interred. Right there I pledged to do everything possible to get them into caring hands. The doctor said he would help me transport them wherever there were willing parties to bury them—in the process, confronting the public with the reality of death by abortion. We selected an initial four babies; he helped me to pack them safely with special solution in medical containers. The doctor then warned me it was illegal to transport them across state lines, so I stuffed them into the interior pockets of my overcoat to avoid detection at the airport.

Among our other objectives, Paul and I wanted to use the Buffalo demonstrations to show the public what an aborted baby looked like. During an afternoon press conference, we decided to display the largest baby I had brought from Tulsa: a perfectly preserved, fully formed African-American girl who was at approximately six months gestation. Gently cradling her in his hands, Paul laid the baby out on a table. Pastor Johnny Hunter, the single African-American rescue leader among us, had christened her "Tia." Cameras crowded around us, with reporters shouting questions: "That's not real, is it?" "Are you kidding me?" "Where did you get this?" "Is that legal?" "Goddamn—that's fucking real!"

The next day hundreds of protestors assembled in front of 50 High Street, a medium-rise medical building that housed an abortion clinic on its fourth floor. Paul faced the "pro-deathers," deliberately goading them into a confrontation by speaking softly and announcing he loved them in the name of Christ. They shoved him, and I boiled with rage. Ducking around a corner, I called a staff member and asked him to quickly bring me the remains of Baby Tia.

Within minutes I had a small tub in front of me. I exhumed the pinkish form from the liquid preservative and took her to the front lines, parading her in my hands along the yellow police tape. Pro-choice counterdemonstrators surrounded me.

"Is this what you are advocating for?" I asked repeatedly, passing the form beneath their chins. "A dead baby? Is that what you want?"

Many screamed and expressed their disgust at me, and when someone lunged and attempted to grab Tia, I lost my grip on her and she fell to the ground. I was appalled by the further abuse this innocent baby had to endure, but the spectacle served well in illustrating to the world how callous the pro-deathers were toward the unborn. I reclaimed the remains and held her now torn flesh high in the air. The whole thing was working perfectly, and I accused the mob of desecrating a child as police swooped in and arrested me. At first I held on to the baby, which was easy, because the officers didn't want to touch her. Finally a lab worker in a white coat and gloves appeared and forcibly took the remains from my hand. Paul and I were charged with disorderly conduct, the police citing a law that prohibited "creating a physically offensive condition."

After a night in jail, Paul and I appeared on *Nightline* with Ted Koppel, who devoted his entire show, "True Believers: Abortion Clash in Buffalo," to the events leading to our arrests. When he introduced the segment, Koppel said, "The people you will see tonight on both sides of this issue are, as best we can determine, genuinely committed to their points of view. Nevertheless, the confrontation currently playing out in Buffalo has been staged with a certain degree of cynicism on both sides to be acted out as a contemporary morality play on television. When all is said and done, as you will see tonight, everything that happens is done with one eye on the camera."

I would never have admitted it then, but he was right. Media exposure was enormously important to us. Our immediate goal was to close the clinics, as we had done in Wichita, but we also knew a key anti-abortion case, *Planned Parenthood of Southeastern Pennsylvania v. Casey*, was being argued before the Supreme Court. After *Roe v. Wade* established abortion rights, this was the case that had the potential to roll them back by creating a new legal standard giving states greater leeway to regulate the procedure. Even if it were impossible to destroy *Roe v. Wade* completely, it could be undermined incrementally. A Pennsylvania law, signed in 1989 by Democratic governor Robert

Casey Sr., had made abortion much more difficult to obtain: a twenty-four-hour waiting period, informed consent rules for women seeking abortions, parental consent rules for minors, and the requirement that married women notify their husbands before terminating a pregnancy. Planned Parenthood sued to overturn the law, but so far the courts had ruled in our favor.

Months earlier, the liberal Supreme Court justice Thurgood Marshall had resigned, and the epic confirmation fight for Clarence Thomas got under way. The effectiveness of our anti-abortion work depended on justices like Thomas on the high court. The pro-abortion side decided to put the *Planned Parenthood v. Casey* appeal on the fast track, so it would be decided during the 1992 presidential campaign. Even though justices were ostensibly above political or public pressure, we knew they were aware of what was happening in Buffalo.

Paul and I now played leading roles on the national stage. The price was high: we were in deep legal trouble, spending enormous sums we didn't have. The emotional toll on our families was also enormous, and there were days I wondered if it was all worth it. Still, we soldiered on. We were getting attention for a noble cause. I could announce a news conference, often with only hours' notice, and see twelve trucks with satellite dishes roll into the church parking lot. But I was blind to the human implications; I ignored the anguished expressions on women's faces as they tried to enter the clinic for this procedure and had to face our censure. I ignored how much I was losing my perspective on what was truly important.

Buffalo would prove to be only the dress rehearsal for a much bigger drama in New York City during the upcoming Democratic National Convention.

11

Conventions and Courtrooms

I t would have been difficult to find a presidential hopeful whose values were more contrary to ours than William Jefferson Clinton. He tried to convince voters he was a Christian and a moderate Democrat. To us he was a traitor. In 1986, when Arkansas was struggling with the issue of state funding for abortions and Bill Clinton was governor, he was completely evasive on the subject, which many of us took as evidence of his pro-life convictions.* We were aware that, at some point in the late eighties, he had signaled he believed abortion was morally wrong, but he changed his tune completely when he became a national candidate in 1992. We assumed he realized, or had been schooled by party leadership, that no Democrat could secure the nomination by being anti-abortion. That year he told the National Abortion Rights Action League, "The government simply has no right to interfere with decisions that must be made by women of America to make the right choice." It looked to us that Clinton embodied the party he wanted to lead: unrepentant in legitimizing the murder of babies, unsupportive of any pro-life politician in his midst, and ready to experiment with God's design for human sexuality.

If Reagan's presidency set us on the path of combining our faith with political action, 1992 was the culmination of our dominance within

---

* Rickie Solinger, ed., *Abortion Wars: A Half Century of Struggle, 1950–2000* (University of California Press, 2001), 114.

the Republican Party. Reporters routinely called Paul and me to comment, politicians from many states courted us for help in fund-raising efforts, and Rush Limbaugh extolled us to the masses. We received invitations from all over the country to preach at rallies, in large and small auditoriums, and in medium- to mega-sized churches. We often took our cues from Ralph Reed, the executive director of Pat Robertson's political creation, the Christian Coalition.

Pat Robertson was determined to inject our values into the political conversation, too. He and Ralph Reed helped draft the Republican platform for the 1992 convention in Houston, ensuring the culture wars would be front and center. They condemned the liberal commitment to abortion, contraception, homosexuality, and obscene art and music. For the embodiment of our principles, we turned not to President Bush, who was a liberal Episcopalian and therefore suspect on abortion, but to his conservative Presbyterian running mate Dan Quayle and his wife, Marilyn.

Meantime, we were orchestrating a demonstration that would publicize our convictions when the Democrats gathered for their convention in New York City. The same pathologist who had given me Baby Tia for our demonstrations in Buffalo was willing to provide babies for this demonstration as well. We arranged to get several and intended to find an opportune time to present an aborted baby to Clinton and his running mate, Al Gore, and capture the moment on film for an ad we would call "The True Face of Pro-Choice America." A courier from Tulsa delivered several fetuses in bags by strapping them to his body. We arranged to meet him aboard a train between Newark and Manhattan to reduce the chances of being spotted by pro-death monitors at our hotel. But New York had a large and important Catholic community that was extremely sensitive about the proper burial of fetal remains. We didn't want to do anything to alienate them, so we checked with John Cardinal O'Connor, the prelate of the New York archdiocese, who approved the plan, provided that the remains were treated with respect. That's all Randall needed to hear. Against my advice, he and Pat Mahoney impulsively called a news conference to announce our intentions to present the candidates with the unborn babies. We only had to look for the right opportunity, which we thought might be in or around Madison Square Garden, where the convention was being held.

New York attorney general Robert Abrams immediately asked the court to block our actions, and U.S. District Court judge Robert Ward issued an injunction prohibiting anyone from "presenting or confronting either Governor Bill Clinton or Senator Albert Gore with any fetus or fetuses or fetal remains." The injunction also established a speech-free zone around clinic doors, barred intimidating doctors at their homes, and prohibited any kind of blockade at a convention gathering. We were even required to inform our adversaries of any protests we might otherwise plan twenty-four hours before they were scheduled.

What was meant to discourage only emboldened us. We felt then that our civil disobedience would be in the grand tradition of historical acts of conscience, from the Boston Tea Party to the civil rights movement. Enlisting the help of the sympathetic Tulsa pathologist, not to mention all the other surreptitious moving parts in our effort, was the stuff of grand conspiracy, played out on a national stage. Any apprehension I might have felt about going too far—or disappointing Cheryl even more—was pushed away by the comradeship and energy of the movement. Becoming a Christian had brought me a new and loving group of friends. Becoming a pro-life activist had brought me into an intense, competitive, high-minded group of men—a kind of fraternity. It might not have been comforting, but it was thrilling.

When we reached our New York hotel, I opened the box the courier had placed the babies in after he landed at the airport. One of them was a perfect little boy, whom Paul named Nathan after the prophet who confronted King David with his sins of murder and adultery. I met up with Randall, who was adamant about carrying out our protest plans even though they violated the court order. In another news conference he announced: "We are coming to be a witness against the Democratic Party's brazen embrace of child killing *and* homosexuality." For some time Randall and a few other movement leaders had begun stringing together abortion and homosexuality as tandem sins. I didn't see it that way and even felt it diminished the life issue, which I considered paramount. It was indicative of Randall's religious populism, which I found distasteful. He knew the crowds at our rallies would be riled up by the fact that gay activist groups were joining forces with the pro-choice protestors and he fully exploited all that emotional volatility. As cameras rolled, Randall tore up Judge Ward's order prohibiting our convention protests—a dramatic gesture that would cost us all dearly.

The day before the convention began, we moved from our hotel to the InterContinental—Clinton's headquarters. We wanted every possible opportunity to gain access to him so we could spring the babies on him, his wife, Hillary, or Al Gore. As we were checking out, I asked my group where Nathan and the other babies were.

I had forgotten them in our room.

We raced back upstairs to a chaotic scene with a sobbing maid, some New York cops, and a few hotel security guards. While cleaning, the maid opened the box to see what had been left behind. She was traumatized. When we arrived to claim the box, the police returned it to us, unaware of what we had planned to do. That evening at the Intercontinental, with two other Operation Rescue insiders, Joe Forman and Harley Belew, I prepared a small jewelry case, lined with a tufted paper towel so it looked like a tiny casket, into which we placed Baby Nathan's little form.

The next morning I awoke to the sound of Harley banging on the door. He was beside himself with excitement and urged me to turn on the television, because he had managed to present the baby to Governor Clinton and CNN was there to catch the encounter. We were shocked to see it playing out on the screen: Clinton in his jogging outfit, Harley standing awkwardly behind police tape, holding a bulky copy of the *New York Times*. He had taken it upon himself to go downstairs early, knowing Clinton would go out for his morning run.

Harley filled us in on the details: He had positioned himself at the entrance of the hotel behind the rope line. When Clinton emerged, he asked for the governor's autograph but was initially ignored. The governor then turned back toward him and Harley offered him a pen to sign the *Times*. As Clinton leaned forward, Harley revealed the fetus.

"What about the babies, Governor?" Harley demanded.

Clinton threw the newspaper at his feet in disgust, then followed Secret Service agents to his limo, speeding away without comment.

After we made ourselves presentable, we raced into the hotel's press area to announce a news conference. Reporters jostled each other, pushing and shoving as we all crammed into a hallway where I explained the rationale behind what had just taken place. Soon the Secret Service showed up and escorted us to our room, where they interrogated us for almost an hour. When they left, the NYPD arrived and took their turn. We were charged with violating the city health code governing "Improper Disposal of a Fetus, Transportation of a Fetus into the City, and Removal of Human Remains from the Place of Death." I was enjoying the adrenaline high all this drama provided—and I felt satisfied we were dealing a blow to pro-abortion culture in our country. Still, anxiety was beginning to creep in. I knew we were in real legal trouble. What would happen if I ended up in a federal prison? What would become of Cheryl and the kids? Never mind—there was no time to indulge such self-pity. We had to win this war.

The three of us were given summonses to appear in court and told to promptly get out of the hotel. As much as I was in denial about the legal dangers looming for me, I couldn't really contain the anxiety that increasingly became part of my experiences. I worried about managing the media or figuring out the downstream consequences when we celebrated what seemed like a victory. As frequent as my interactions with the court system had become, I could never celebrate them the way some in our group did. Cheryl acted as my link to another kind of reality: her disapproval was rarely articulated but always close to the surface. With the other guys at Operation Rescue, each summons was a new medal of honor. At home, it was a source of tension and shame.

We were told Judge Ward had ordered each of us to surrender to federal authorities. I quickly realized I needed to get out of town before I was forced to either surrender or face a warrant for my arrest, so I grabbed the first train back to Buffalo. When I arrived home, I was exhausted but had no time to enjoy reuniting with the kids and Cheryl.

All I wanted to do was take a shower, get into some clean clothes, and spend time with my family, who were clearly showing signs of strain. But a warrant had indeed been issued—while I was in transit—and I had to return to New York, so I could surrender to Ward in the morning. He had been contemplating criminal charges against Randall and civil contempt charges against Harley, Joe, and me. I tried to maintain a calm exterior, but inside I was sick with the thought of prison and bankrupting judgments. I struggled with other biblical mandates, like properly caring for one's family and living at peace with all people. Was I, in fact, in conflict with my own faith? What about Cheryl? I could see the sadness and fear all this caused her: she wore it in her eyes, in her more frequent frowns, and, worse than anything else, in her tearful retreats to our bedroom. In New York, Judge Ward reserved his ire for Randall and scheduled an October hearing for me. I returned to Buffalo, relieved by what felt like a stay of execution.

★★★

In the beginning of August, just a few weeks before the Republican National Convention in Houston, I had another court date. Two months earlier, I had been arrested along with twenty-nine others during our Spring of Life demonstrations in Buffalo. Finally, my trial was going to take place—bookended between the two political conventions. Paul and I felt blessed with a remarkable attorney, the retired New York State Supreme Court judge William J. Ostrowski, whom we called "Judge O." A tall, bearded, and elegant man, a reader in his Catholic parish, and an amateur Shakespearean actor, he was an ardent opponent of abortion and admired our pro-life work. When he heard about our arrests that April, he reached out and offered to defend us pro bono—a gift from God. He walked us through the complications that we might face in every step of our legal journey, but his patrician manner and long history serving on a prestigious bench reassured us we were receiving the best possible representation.

On August 6, Paul, another rescuer, Gary Oyer, and I—along with about thirty others charged with trespass, resisting arrest, and disorderly conduct—arrived early for the evening court session. We knelt outside the doors, heads bowed in prayer, and were immediately stopped by the bailiff, who warned us we were engaging in an unlawful demonstration. When we were finally called into the courtroom, Judge Sherwood Bestry didn't pause to deal with any of the specifics of our case. He ordered our attorneys and the prosecutors into his chambers, where he harrumphed about sending anyone to jail who dared disrupt his courtroom while our attorneys argued he had no legal authority to do so. He said he could do whatever he damned well pleased in his own court, including sending our attorneys to jail for contempt, whereupon Judge O. told him that that, too, would be illegal.

When Judge Bestry reconvened the court, he swore in the jury and then, as is commonly done in a part-time night court, dismissed them for the evening, as it had already been a restless wait for them. Once out of their presence, the judge turned to us and sternly warned he would not permit singing, religious ceremonies, praying, or any demonstrations at all. He was asserting his control over his courtroom and was determined to keep religion out of it. He assured us that if he heard this occurring, we would be in contempt of court—having disrupted proceedings and violated courtroom decorum—and he would send us to the Erie County Correctional Facility for thirty days. I thought of what the apostles Peter and John had done after they were arrested and were warned never again to "speak or teach in the name of Jesus." They admonished the civil magistrates, "Judge for yourselves whether it is right in God's sight to obey you rather than God. For we cannot help speaking about what we have seen and heard." I also thought that this just might prove to be a thrilling opportunity for a case about religious freedom and the First Amendment. At the time, I couldn't stop working all the angles that might have been available to bring attention to our cause and, perforce, to us.

In court the next evening, our group once again dropped to our knees and prayed. The bailiff impatiently herded us into the courtroom. Judge Bestry again ordered our lawyers into chambers and, in their absence, several of us again knelt—this time at our seats, as if in a pew—and prayed quietly while the jury and spectators talked, laughed, even occasionally cursed. It's hard to describe how righteous I felt in that moment. We were obeying God while they were deriding him. When the judge and the attorneys reentered the courtroom, Bestry immediately announced that Gary and I were in contempt of court, summarily sentencing us to thirty days in jail. I was delighted: this was both a form of suffering for Jesus and another chance at being a principal in a classic First Amendment case.

The officers pushed Gary and me down a hall, stripped us of our belts and shoelaces, and held us in two cells in the back of the courthouse. My door was solid metal except for a narrow window of very thick glass. I could see everyone on the other side talking furiously but could not hear a word. I was so eager to always be involved, to know what was going on and participate in the process, that to watch the pantomime was frustrating for me. It didn't take long before I deduced what had happened, as Paul was escorted through the same hall, also in handcuffs. I figured he had likely done the same thing Gary and I had. Later on I would learn he had done so in grand style, walking right up to the front and opening his Bible, reading Psalm 94 to the defendants:

> The Lord is a God who avenges.
> O God who avenges, shine forth.
> Rise up, Judge of the earth;
> pay back to the proud what they deserve.
> How long, Lord, will the wicked,
> how long will the wicked be jubilant?

The judge asked him to close the Bible and stop praying. Undeterred, Paul dropped to his knees and offered the Bible up to the bench, and swiftly received the same sentence as I had. Was Paul provocative as a witness to God? Or was he being provocative because he, too, wanted to clock some time in jail during this high-profile case? We never discussed it.

Late that night, we were all transferred to the Erie County Holding Center in downtown Buffalo and placed in isolation cells. On the same block as the psychiatric inmates, I could hear various anguished voices in the halls. As I sat in my cell, I took stock of where I was. The walls were smeared with dried excrement and the lone toilet was jammed with wads of soiled paper and feces. I tried to mitigate my nausea by reminding myself that Jesus had suffered far greater indignities. But it was an enormous relief when we were moved to a large, secured room with sixteen other prisoners.

Meanwhile our lawyers were working through the night, preparing an appeal based on the fact that by jailing us when we prayed, Judge Bestry had violated our First Amendment rights of both religion and freedom of speech. There is a thin line between acts of demonstration, which are universally banned in courtrooms on every level of government to protect the integrity of justice from the intimidation of the mob, and the free exercise of religion guaranteed in the Constitution. The fact that we were reading from the Bible and praying—quintessentially religious activities—forced the court to either permit it or risk doing the very thing the First Amendment prohibits the government from doing: establishing a religion by redefining these activities as acts of protest, not religious ritual.

Just after midnight, Erie County judge Joseph McCarthy granted our release pending a future hearing. He eventually dismissed the charges of contempt against me, but, for reasons I can't recall, Paul and Gary remained as defendants and would be sentenced to time served. When I returned home, Cheryl was exhausted from worry. She had been getting periodic and often breathless phone calls from acquaintances who were attending the trial, and with each installment of news she would fret more about my safety and our family's security. I emphasized that what we were doing was necessary and important work. She found my political activism at times deeply distressing, but she wanted to be supportive. Still, she couldn't understand why a social cause was more important than our family's well-being. I never had a good answer for that.

Because of my detention, I had missed my next court appearance and so my charges were separated from the others, and my next hearing was scheduled for the following February. To be prosecuted alone was not an advantage. I would be the subject of Bestry's undivided attention, and the focus of his anger over the contempt dismissal. But the delay allowed me to temporarily resume life as usual, which included a trip to Houston for the Republican National Convention. Paul and I wanted to use the RNC as a platform to keep child-killing at the forefront of the Republican consciousness and exploit the media exposure guaranteed to be available to us there.

Friends of our movement who were high-end donors to Republican causes helped us get the equivalent of all-access passes. We mingled on the convention floor with the delegates. I received backslaps of approval as I stood holding a sign, "Exorcise the *Demon*-crats!" On the night the president and vice president were to speak, the mood on the convention floor was optimistic, even euphoric. We were never convinced George H. W. Bush was sincerely engaged with the issues most important to us. We all knew his family had supported Planned Parenthood and that was enough to make us suspicious. On a broader level, the party was already divided between the old-line conservative Republicans—the Nelson Rockefeller types—and the religious right, with Pat Robertson and Pat Buchanan. Bush was from the earlier generation, which we considered namby-pamby on abortion, the gay agenda, and secularist encroachment on religious freedom; but we were reassured by the presence on the ticket of Dan Quayle, whom we knew and trusted.

The festivities began with Pastor Ed Young of Houston's enormous Second Baptist Church leading us in prayer, followed by a gospel choir. All around the arena, my fellow Republicans bowed their heads. It could have been a revival meeting. After President George Bush accepted his party's nomination, he delivered a strong, optimistic speech extolling free markets, tax relief, small-business opportunities, and new schools ready for the twenty-first century. But it was his penultimate words that night that calmed our fears about whether he could be trusted to follow through with his promises to us: "I happen to believe very deeply in the worth of each individual human being, born or unborn. I believe in teaching our kids the difference between what's wrong and what's right, teaching them respect for hard work and to love their neighbors. I believe that America will always have a special place in God's heart, as long as He has a special place in ours."

12

"A Mighty Threshing Instrument"

I n the weeks following the convention, I preached plenty of anti-Clinton sermons, referring to his unequivocal embrace of abortion and suggesting he needed it to be legal so he could get out of the trouble his lascivious lifestyle brought to him. In private conversations and at clergy gatherings, I also did my best to convince pastors they should steer their people toward the Republican and therefore pro-life ticket.

We had all hoped the election of 1992 would be about values, but those concerns were hijacked by "the economy, stupid," which was what most worried Americans, as Clinton's brilliant campaign strategist James Carville put it. That segment of the electorate included plenty of blue-collar people in the congregations I routinely visited. Of course, the economy was important, but millions were equally worried about America's collapse of moral values and its marginalization of religious faith. I worked hard to coax them over to the Republican side. The Clinton administration was determined to undo any progress we made under Reagan and Bush, but we were equally determined to keep that from happening. We planned to show Congress and the American people that Clinton's victory did not guarantee enacting a corrupt and dangerous agenda.

For my part, I wanted to continue to fight for the causes that were consistent with our Christian values: stopping abortion, putting a halt to the advancement of the homosexual agenda, and bringing back prayer in schools and public life. So I accepted an invitation from ministers in Fort Walton Beach, Florida, to address a pro-life rally on January 16, 1993—four days before Bill Clinton was inaugurated as the forty-second president of the United States. I encouraged the rally participants to continue the great work they were doing and the significant contributions they were making to the most important cause of our lifetimes. I spoke about the sanctity and inherent value of every human life, including the most fragile and vulnerable of God's creatures in the womb. I compared our times to biblical days when Molech was the false idol to which humans were sacrificed. "We, too, worship false gods," I said, "the false gods of selfishness, of financial security, of a better life, and we are offering our children as human sacrifices on that idol's altar. *That* is an abomination in the eyes of God."

As I bowed my head in a closing prayer, I heard "Amen!" and a smattering of applause. I loved preaching to these communities across the country. The energy of believers in small-town America provided emotional and spiritual nourishment and the reassurance that, however dire the political culture seemed, there was resilience and deep goodness that would sustain us—not to mention the adulation from the crowds.

But I was tired. Preaching is a demanding experience. As a minister, it was often difficult to truly enjoy worship unless I was on vacation with my family. To be a guest preacher is tantamount to being a minor celebrity. There is a constant stream of people who want to talk before and after the service—and sometimes even during it. As energized as I was by the rally and the warmth of the reception and the weather, on this Saturday night I looked forward to some solitude in my hotel room. I had a lot to think about.

The months preceding my visit south were filled with enormous stress for both Paul's family and mine. The lawsuits against us had become a constant burden, weighing us down with the possibility of financial ruin and even long-term incarceration. By now our risky and consuming work fighting the scourge of abortion had expanded far beyond Buffalo. Paul had built an important church over the last dozen years, with nearly two thousand attendees and influence beyond our locale. I had established three external organizations that were active around the world. But our increasing notoriety and the looming Democratic administration, which we dreaded, indicated we needed to redirect our energies away from demonstrations, blockades, and civil disobedience and toward advocacy that would lead to systemic change. We just weren't entirely sure how, especially since our resources were concentrated on our pending court cases. An evening alone to reflect in peace and quiet felt necessary.

My hosts had other ideas. They wanted to share worship with me, and when the last of the participants had left our big rally, they took me to the Abundant Life Church. I had heard about the pastor, Dr. L. M. Thorne, from Tommy Reid. Thorne had been a global missionary in Belgium, China, South Africa, and Korea before arriving in Fort Walton Beach in 1976 to create his independent charismatic congregation.

With a few thousand members, Abundant Life was an "apostolic prophetic church," where preachers and attendees speak in tongues, offer prayers for healing, and engage in demonstrative worship. I was escorted to a seat in one of the middle rows. An organ played quietly in the background, its music confirming we had entered a sacred space. This kind of southern Pentecostal culture is in many ways informed by black church tradition. Southern preachers work with their organist as if playing a duet; the organ propels the service emotionally and spiritually while the pastor provides its theological content. Abundant Life was a predominantly white congregation, but—as often happens in the South—the minister employed a more dynamic and engaged black preaching style, including a technique known as call and response, in which congregants verbally react to the message of the preacher, calling out "Amen, Brother!" "Come on!" "Keep preachin' it!" "That's right!" Dr. Thorne entered the sanctuary platform accompanied by a rumbling bass.

"We have a guest minister with us tonight," he announced. "Reverend Rob Schenck, please stand." I slowly rose to my feet, expecting a brief introduction to the congregation and a few words about Operation Rescue. But I was wrong. In my archives, I still have a cassette recording of what transpired that night.

"I have a word from the Lord for you," he said.

I instantly felt awkward and embarrassed. As a charismatic Christian, I accepted the reality of what is called in some circles "personal prophecy"—a specific divine revelation to an individual delivered through a third party. Still, even from the very beginning of my Christian life, I maintained a quiet skepticism about the public airing of what was purportedly a direct message from heaven. Most of the time it had nothing to do with me and seemed harmless enough, but here I was in the spotlight. I kept my face impassive, my mind racing as I tried to imagine Dr. Thorne's possible motivations for singling me out. I was regularly in the news, making headlines. Maybe he wanted to showcase a visiting notable, or even put me in my place. Notoriety is a blessing and a curse in Charismatic-Pentecostal culture, a source of both celebration and criticism. Our worshippers like it when their preachers get attention from the outside world but worry that too much attention can swell a minister's head. "Pride goeth before destruction," the King James Version of the Bible warns in Proverbs, "and an haughty spirit before a fall." The atmosphere in the church became more charged and the music more intense as Dr. Thorne continued.

"I believe that God said to me to say to you that He's been setting you up. All this notoriety you've been getting—He's been *setting you up* because He knows He can trust you to do what He said 'Do.'"

Maybe this was the point: an elder saying to his junior, *I know you're a famous guy, but I'm going to tell you what God is really doing in your life. You may think that you've arrived but you haven't.* Maybe God was using Reverend Thorne, in his three-piece suit and aviator glasses, to rein me in a little bit and hold me accountable. I probably needed a dose of humility. Was this southern preacher channeling God's plan for me? In my heart of hearts, I doubted it.

"God's gonna use you, my brother," Dr. Thorne continued, his voice and the organ both swelling with emotion. "But God's raised *you* up and He's set you up. I saw you like on a launching pad, getting ready to be launched. You will be used like a mighty threshing instrument to the glory of God."

The pronouncement simultaneously appealed to my ego and embarrassed me. Standing there uncomfortably, I hoped he would soon end.

"You will see the hand of God working, and God is going to use you, Brother, in a mighty way in this country. Brother, you are going to stand before the leaders of our nation and you're going to declare the Word. It will be for His honor and praise but also for His church. It will also be in more ways than the abortion issue." The organ grew louder, as did his words. "Brother, you will be launched now. Praise God! Amen!"

The organ burst forth and the congregation joined him in the amen chorus. "I welcome you! Praise God!" Reverend Thorne finally paused as the music retreated into meditative strains. He then emerged, as if from a trance, saying, "I think that the Lord deserves a clap of the hand." And I stood nodding, sweating, and smiling uneasily as the congregation applauded.

After it was over, my hosts introduced me to the pastor. In his mid-fifties but youthful, he was warm, slightly formal, but friendly, like a boss who had just informed an employee about a big promotion that would also involve a total disruption of his and his family's serene life. *"Brother, you are going to stand before the leaders of our nation and you're going to declare the Word."* What could that possibly mean? It excited me to think I might stand like one of the prophets of old in the chambers of America's potentates—in the halls of Congress, in the Oval Office, maybe even in the Supreme Court—reading authoritatively from my Bible, preaching to them about repentance from sin and obedience to God. That night in my hotel room I imagined myself as another Billy Graham speaking into the ears of presidents, taking their hands in prayer, and giving them guidance on how to serve a holy God as the chief executive of the United States.

When I returned to Buffalo, though, the thrill was already wearing off and the pastor's message receded in my memory. There were so many pressing demands, I had little time to ponder whatever future greatness God had in mind for me. President Clinton wasted little time in enacting policies that aligned with his party's views on gay rights and abortion. He immediately lobbied Congress for the "Don't Ask, Don't Tell" legislation prohibiting discrimination against homosexuals in the military. It was a policy that, for our movement, signaled an unleashing of sodomy and perversion in the unlikeliest of places, the armed services. For me, the gay issue was more complex. I knew a gay classmate in high school and had contact with gay people throughout my Christian life. I held to a quiet, internal conviction that God loved all people—all sinners—and I was one as much as anyone else. How could one category of sinner be any worse than another? But that notion wouldn't fly in the climate in which I now ministered, so I capitulated to the zeitgeist and railed against Clinton for both his horrifying attack on the unborn and pro-lifers and his infatuation with all things homosexual.

Clinton also dismantled a series of Reagan and Bush administration abortion restrictions, ending a ban on fetal tissue research, a move that, to us, signaled treatment of the remains of babies like little more than specimens in petri dishes. He limited restrictions on abortion counseling at federally funded family planning clinics, and permitted importing the French "morning after" pill, RU-486—what we saw as making abortion just another form of birth control. He permitted abortions in U.S. military hospitals overseas, and he overturned one of our earliest victories under Reagan, the prohibiting of foreign aid to organizations that provided abortions.

Long before I was involved in the anti-abortion movement—but every year since January 22, 1974, which was the second anniversary of the *Roe v. Wade* decision—people opposed to abortion would gather in Washington, D.C., usually in punishing weather, to demonstrate in what became known as the March for Life. It was the largest pro-life manifestation in the United States, founded by a nun. Paul and I always participated, but with Randall and others in Operation Rescue we were considered the more radical wing of the pro-life movement, so we did not command a place on the dais or as speakers. Nonetheless, we were enthusiastic participants, and the march that year was the largest ever, with over seventy-five thousand people showing the new president our force and fury. Morale in our movement was high. One of our fund-raisers quipped, "Who would think Bill Clinton would be our best friend?"

Meanwhile, Paul and I were still simultaneously fighting several lawsuits. We were in court for displaying the fetus, for "provocative" demonstrations, and for defying an explicit court order. At the end of January, I returned to Judge Bestry's courtroom for my arrest eight months earlier at our Spring of Life protest. The trial lasted two weeks. The jury convicted me of resisting arrest and disorderly conduct. There was a grim expression of satisfaction on Bestry's face when he heard the verdict and scheduled sentencing for April 19. Hundreds of people wrote letters to him vouching for my integrity, character, and sincerity. I was hopeful they would make a difference when it came to my sentence, but I was still apprehensive about ending up in jail for months and months. I tried to remain optimistic, especially for Cheryl and the kids, but my bravado might not have camouflaged my deep worry over what lay ahead.

Then, on Wednesday, March 10, 1993, an abortion doctor was murdered.

Paul and I had repeatedly reassured ourselves the movement was entirely nonviolent. We trained our people to endure abuse without fighting back. By then I had seen many of our numbers, of all ages and in all states of physical condition, prayerful and motionless as cops wrenched, dragged, and hurled them from the front of clinics. We were the model of peaceful social change—or so I thought.

Then came the news from Pensacola. Dr. David Gunn had been shot in the back three times. We had staged numerous demonstrations at his Pensacola Women's Medical Services. Randall had once created a wanted poster for Gunn that he distributed at a rally in Montgomery, Alabama, where the OB-GYN also provided his services. The doctor's face, phone number, and other identifying information were clearly displayed. We all instructed our people to restrain their language and actions when confronting abortion providers, and rescuers were required to sign a statement that read, in part, "I commit to be peaceful, prayerful, and nonviolent in word and deed."

I didn't appreciate, or allow myself to see, the contradiction between the pledge and our increasingly inflammatory rhetoric. We would use stark language—"baby killers," "mass murderers," "pro-aborts"—and outline battle plans in which we referred to abortion providers as "the enemy," and asserted that sometimes people may break lesser laws to avoid committing the greater evil of murdering innocent children. This was in keeping with long-held Christian moral theology. But none of us considered the vulnerability of those who, for one reason or another, could not discriminate between literal and figurative concepts. There were also people bent on doing harm, and all they needed was religious permission to do so. And one such person had just committed murder in the name of our movement.

When Paul summoned me to his office and told me Gunn had been shot, we called our contacts in Florida. Before Michael Griffin unloaded three rounds from his .38 caliber revolver into Gunn's back, the killer had been a sometimes marginal rescue activist with fundamentalist church ties. As he gunned down the doctor, he yelled to his victim, "Don't kill any more babies." Rescue America, another pro-life organization that competed with us for funds and followers, was picketing Gunn's clinic that day. We considered the group's swaggering leader, Don Treshman, an embarrassment to the pro-life movement. A Texan who wore a ten-gallon Stetson and oversized metal belt buckles, Treshman fancied himself a pro-life purist compared to the Northeast-establishment Randall Terry. Treshman was bombastic, indiscreet, and unpredictable—especially when it came to peaceful, nonviolent action. His Pensacola operative, a lay preacher and former Marine named John Burt, was worse. It was Burt who oversaw the protest the day of the shooting. To outsiders, there may have seemed little difference between us, but we saw the difference as fundamental. "Abortion Kills Children" and "Stop Abortion" typified signs at our events. "Execute Baby Killers" typified theirs. On the day of Gunn's murder, Treshman told the New York Times, "While Gunn's death is unfortunate, it's also true that quite a number of babies' lives will be saved."

We issued a news release: "Our commitment to the dignity of life stands for the born as well as the unborn." Reverend Joe Foreman, who had worked with Randall since the beginning of Operation Rescue, told the press that we had "been saying for years that if the government insists on suppressing normal and time-honored dissent through injunctions, it turns the field over to the rock-throwers, the bombers and the assassins." At the time, we all believed that the more the government attempted to control what we considered to be peaceful acts of civil disobedience, the more room they gave to extremists who felt they had no other recourse than to bomb, burn, and shoot in order to be heard.

The story of Gunn's murder was still in the news when I returned to Judge Bestry's courtroom for my sentencing hearing in April. I knew that didn't bode well for me. I had written to my supporters about my impending sentencing date, and they crowded the courtroom.

Judge Bestry called the court to order.

He ignored the thick file of letters pleading mercy on my behalf. I had asked for permission to make a statement before he pronounced his sentence, and he granted it. I was as careful about composing it as I had been for any sermon I had ever preached. I asserted that I was a pastor of souls, resolved to right whatever wrongs God enabled me to rectify, and explained my action as simply an expression of the principles by which I lived. I tried to impress on the judge that I was a good and generous man, and described my work in the Mexican dumps and how I created the Hearts for the Homeless shelter program in Buffalo. I closed with a prayer that the judge would grant mercy for me, my co-defendants, and for his own soul "from the God who is Himself merciful." I was intoxicated by my eloquence and considered that speech the most important one I had ever delivered: I was Moses before Pharaoh, the prophet Elijah before King Ahab, Saint Paul before the procurator.

Our family and hundreds of my supporters waited, tense and prayerful. After I finished, Judge Bestry sat pensively for a few seconds. Then he let me have it. He told me how reckless my actions had been a year before, during the Spring of Life demonstrations, when I could have incited a riot. He called me "a publicity hound" and said my punishment had nothing to do with abortion but with my lawless actions.

He sentenced me to nine months at Alden, a medium-security state penitentiary. I could hear gasps of shock behind me.

The bailiff handcuffed me and whisked me away without even a chance to kiss Cheryl or hug the kids. I'll never forget their faces, frozen in horror. I was cuffed to a line of several prisoners who had been sentenced for other crimes that same night. We were pushed into a transport van. As we drove, I felt as if I had joined the long list of Christian martyrs who had sacrificed their lives for their own true faith. I wondered what kind of torture by hardened criminals I might expect in jail, and if I would have the courage and the faith to withstand whatever was in my future. And yet, shamefully, none of these lofty thoughts included how all this would affect Cheryl. She had to return home with Anna and Matthew, comfort them, and try to explain what they had just seen. Only years later did I learn just how traumatic this was for them, particularly for Matthew, who was then twelve years old. I had been my boy's hero, and now he heard the parents of other kids ridicule me and got into a fight on the school bus defending my honor.

Meanwhile, I was thinking only of myself and how I was going to survive the indignities of jail. After trading my clothes for a jumpsuit, I was escorted into my cell, a tiny, austere cement cube with a bench on one wall covered by a thin foam mattress for a bed. The first night I tried to rest, but it was nearly impossible; above my door was a brilliant lamp that was never turned off, and every few hours throughout the night, guards would noisily make the rounds.

The next day a prisoner threw a copy of the *Buffalo News* at me. It was opened to a headline that read "Minister Gets Jail in Protest Case." The editorial page opined "A Just Sentence for Schenck: He'll Pay for What He Did, Not His Beliefs."

I spent that first day coming to terms with what would be the parameters of my life for the next nine months. There were two televisions on my cellblock and plenty of board games to pass the time.

Cheryl had left a Bible at a designated drop-off window in the visitor center. There were a couple of angry inmates who seemed bothered by my presence, and I did my best to befriend them. To many of the other inmates, I personified the enemy: white, middle class, educated. I had never felt so paranoid, constantly looking over my shoulder, afraid to use the shower because it made me feel too vulnerable, and wondering when someone was going to challenge me to a fight. I was enormously relieved when they moved me to a different cell in a mostly empty gallery. Grateful for the solitude and quiet, I looked around and figured this would be my home for close to a year. I imagined where I would place my books, and other personal items, perhaps a computer, if I was allowed to have one.

When Cheryl visited, we were separated by a thick glass pane and talked through a telephone handset. She looked drawn and broken-hearted, and rightly so. She was nervous about my safety, anxious about the kids, and worried about the reaction to all this at her school, where she was taking final exams. I was still getting a paycheck from our ministry organization, but I couldn't be sure how long that would last, given I had to go out and raise the money that paid me. She put her hand on the window and cried. I wanted to as well, but all I could manage were some empty pastoral words of reassurance. The fact was, deep inside, I thought the mission of changing the culture even eclipsed the needs of my family. I was losing sight of the message I had once preached from the New Testament, warning that a man who didn't care for his family was worse than an infidel.

When I returned to my cell, a guard met me and abruptly ordered me to collect my things, as I was being moved to yet another cellblock, without further explanation. The day passed slowly, but that evening after dinner the heavy cell door buzzed and opened. No guard was present. I hesitated, thinking something might have malfunctioned or maybe some prison ambush awaited me. I sat up with all my senses highly attenuated but relaxed instantly when I heard a familiar booming voice from below the second-tier walkway outside: "Revvv—vehr—runnnd Schenck!" This exaggerated diction could only be Judge O.'s.

There he stood, with his shock of white hair, neatly trimmed goatee, and pressed pocket handkerchief. He looked up, raised his arm, and told me to collect my things, because I was getting out of there.

I didn't ask for details but grabbed my few belongings and met the guard, who escorted me out. Judge O. informed me he had filed an emergency appeal on my behalf. A county judge vacated my sentence and released me pending a full appeal. Judge Bestry had overplayed his hand, Judge O. said, by demonstrating bias against me. We were going to get his draconian sentence reversed.

Throughout the days leading up to this, I maintained strict control over my emotions. I couldn't permit myself to recognize, much less feel, the enormity of what was happening to me and my family. I bottled up any honest feelings until I arrived back home and sat on our couch with my arms around Anna and Matthew. I wept with relief and regret for all I had put them through.

Bestry's nine-month sentence for resisting arrest and inciting a riot was vacated, but my conviction for disorderly conduct remained. For that I was sentenced to fifteen days. I had already served that much time, but technically I needed to "process out," so I returned to prison before being immediately transferred to a "halfway house," which was really just an older wing of the facility. I had steeled myself to spend fifteen days in this unpleasant environment, but it ended up being only one day, because of the arcane formula they use to calculate time served. As the guards processed my paperwork on the way out, I looked around with relief but also guilt. I was starting to see a criminal justice system where someone with white skin, privilege, and an impressive legal team was released in record time. The other men were stuck, represented by overworked, underpaid, and unappreciated public defenders. Who knew how long they would remain there, much less what would happen when they finally went to trial? The problem nagged me, but I had to get back to my family, to the babies—and to the movement.

My return home was less dramatic this time, and we all settled back into our routines. But the aftershocks were evident on Cheryl's countenance, Matthew's constant anxiety about where I was, and Anna's near-forensic questioning about my schedule. I tried to reassure everyone by diving back into work, acting as if not much had happened, and pretending everything was normal. It wasn't.

13

A Reprieve and a Draconian Sentence

While I was in the middle of lawsuits, arrests, prosecutions, and jail time, Cheryl was juggling her own demands. I did what I could to help maintain a home and parent two young kids, but my presence was sporadic and unpredictable. Cheryl was now virtually a single parent and also attending the University of Buffalo full-time, having transferred from her community college program into a bachelor of science track for occupational therapy. Over the years, I came to accept Cheryl's academic interests—even embraced and celebrated them—but I also constantly had to defend them to many in my community.

In the churches where I preached and in the pro-life universe where I was a leader, being a full-time wife and stay-at-home mom was thought to be a woman's greatest source of fulfillment and happiness. There were, of course, exceptions. Dual-income couples were not excluded from our churches, but they were anomalies. Among pro-lifers, women were to be mothers, first and foremost, with *lots of* children—eight, or ten, or even fifteen. Not only did I now have to hide Cheryl's professional status by evading questions that had to do with her college life, I also had to excuse myself for *only* having two kids. (Paul, in contrast, had six.) Fewer than four children suggested the couple might be "contraceptors," artificially interfering with God's intended abundance from the womb. We did, in fact, use contraception but never would have acknowledged it. Disclosing that could have taken me out of the pro-life leadership. Cheryl's bout with cancer—though totally unrelated to reproduction—became my convenient excuse for having only two children.

It was more difficult to keep her education secret. The University of Buffalo was viewed by pro-lifers as the dark citadel of the cursed law professor Lucinda Finley, lead counsel for the Pro-Choice Network of Western New York. But Finley was only part of the broader problem; the campus paper considered us enemies, and student groups would often counterdemonstrate when we showed up at clinics. For many in my world, UB was a damnable place.

Not for Cheryl, though. She loved being a student there. She had a group of friends and favorite professors—and graduating from UB would be her gateway to the profession of her dreams. In my world, I didn't dare say a word about my own wife's association with such an alien institution. Compounding the problem, though, was my real, unspoken concern that Cheryl would be receiving a prestigious degree before I did. Still, she was my center of gravity. No matter how many demands pulled at us, the love that had brought us together as kids deepened and became more complex over the years. We may have been growing and changing, but I knew we could rely on this constant. I put my concerns aside and tried my best—which didn't amount to much—to celebrate her academic accomplishments.

During these years I found myself having to navigate between several different worlds and formidable personalities. There were the pastors who thought my arrests for anti-abortion activism bordered on anarchy, because I was distracted from my true ministerial obligations. Then there were the hard-core Operation Rescue types who thought I should do more jail time, not less, to symbolize the sacrifice our work demanded. My supporters were a heterogeneous group: some lavishly rewarded me for my moral courage, and others withheld their support until I stopped saving babies and returned to saving souls, as the Bible commanded me to do. I wanted to do everything at once—save souls and save babies—and not disappoint anyone.

The vision that first drew me to ministry, of the parson, the shepherd caring for his lost sheep—Fred Dixon, Peter Bolt, Tommy Reid— was getting lost in the oversized, frantic, belligerent warrior priest, the model of a pro-life activist clergyman that I had become. Some days, in my fantasies, I would leave the culture wars behind and retreat to a little clapboard country church where common folk came to find spiritual solace, newborns were dedicated to the Lord, and the elderly were visited at home before I buried them in the churchyard. In those daydreams, people would call me "Pastor Rob," not "Reverend Schenck." Some nights I would lull myself to sleep thinking what a beautiful life that would be for Cheryl, Matthew, and Anna. But I knew that when morning came I'd eagerly dive back into the fray.

In October 1993, hundreds of friends and supporters joined us to celebrate the tenth anniversary of our ministry. As Cheryl and I looked around, seeing our children and all our friends, we felt blessed by the world that had opened to us since we moved back to Buffalo. But the revelry was a rare moment of ease that fall. We otherwise seemed to be constantly preparing for, appearing in, and recovering from a date in court. The lawsuits from our demonstrations during the Democratic National Convention continued to haunt us. I was facing a $25,000 penalty for displaying Baby Nathan, and nearly $100,000 in claims against me by abortion providers for damages to their businesses and monetary penalties for violating court orders. Later that month I was set to appear again with Harley Belew and Joe Forman before Judge Ward in New York.

After a colorful trial during which pro-choice spies who had infiltrated our secret planning meetings testified, videos of half-naked, lesbian protestors were shown, and Harley Belew detailed how he had presented Bill Clinton with a dead baby, Judge Ward offered us a deal. He would hold collection of a twenty-five-thousand-dollar judgment if we would agree not to engage in such public displays of activism for a year in his district, which included Manhattan, parts of the Bronx, and Brooklyn. His offer meant incredible burdens would be removed from my family and me. I accepted on the spot. Besides, our anti-abortion efforts had already moved into a new phase. We would continue more modest demonstrations at clinics, but we were planning more strategic action in the form of federal and state legislation. For me, Ward's deal was tantamount to a slap on the wrist.

The year before, Paul was not so lucky. His denial that we switched identities sometimes to fool the surveillance cameras had come back to haunt him. His false statements under oath became the centerpiece of the case against him. A grand jury had been impaneled by a federal prosecutor. On November 4, 1993, he was charged with perjury, and his lawyers prepared for a trial. Paul was mortified. While he would be the first to acknowledge his many faults, dishonesty was not one of them. That single injudicious remark had mushroomed beyond all reasonable proportion, threatening his and his family's future.

The burden of the criminal case seemed to act as a kind of catalyst for Paul to change his ministry. I wondered if he might not have felt ashamed in his own congregation about the charge of perjury and needed to flee from what he thought was their disapproval. I had always been the itinerant preacher, and Paul had been the homebody. But increasingly he began traveling more frequently and spoke about expanding our ministry to Washington, where the real decision makers lived. Our old Operation Rescue comrade Pat Mahoney was now living in D.C., and he told Paul about his vision for a church on Capitol Hill that would actively engage the culture of Washington: the bureaucrats, the staff and members of Congress, and the federal judiciary.

Paul had been down in Washington several times and he and Pat had already assembled a core group of activists who had pledged time and money to a new church start-up. As we slowly distanced ourselves from Randall, and as Operation Rescue itself began to lose its momentum, replaced by more mainstream advocacy organizations, we, too, wanted to be viewed less as the bomb throwers and more as the judicious figures in the movement. We had a national reputation, and it seemed only fitting that we would work in the seat of power in the nation's capital.

Paul not only supported the effort, he wanted to move from Buffalo to Washington and build the new church. For the founding pastor of a large and successful congregation to leave and undertake a new start-up was highly unusual. But Paul believed those who lived and worked in Washington might not be literal enemies—despite the presence of the Clinton administration—but instead were most in need of being reminded of the importance of Christ's moral and spiritual instruction. The new congregation would be under the aegis of the Assemblies of God, which did not have a congregation on Capitol Hill. Paul would be the first to bring the values from Main Street, from the small churches all over the country, into the metropolis of Washington. This was the job of lawmakers. Why couldn't it also be the job of ministers? "The kingdom is to be in the midst of your enemies," said Martin Luther, the catalyst for the Protestant Reformation, whom we claimed as one of the founders of evangelicalism.

Our plans were still inchoate, but a few important people had caught wind of them, including Hans Helmerich, the CEO of an oil and gas drilling company out of Tulsa. He was a significant financial supporter of our Operation Serve program in Mexico, and even though he was often critical of our pro-life activism, he had bailed 150 people out of jail during the Spring of Life demonstration. When Hans heard about the Washington possibility, he wanted to introduce me to his friend

Senator Don Nickles, an outspoken Christian and pro-life advocate, and arranged for us to lunch with him in the Capitol Building. In late autumn of 1993, Hans picked me up in his corporate jet and we flew to Washington.

This was my first time inside the U.S. Capitol, and I tried not to look like an overwhelmed tourist as we entered the private Senate Dining Room for lunch. I took note of the well-known lawmakers sitting at tables around us—Bob Dole, Alan Cranston, John McCain, Chuck Grassley, and Ted Kennedy. I was in awe, and yet felt an odd sense of belonging.

The conversation immediately turned to our common concerns about the spiritual state of the nation under the Clinton administration. Senator Nickles, who was in his third term and was the youngest senator to be elected from Oklahoma, called himself an "evangelical Catholic." He had a long record of appearing at Southern Baptist and charismatic churches, so we shared the same language of faith. We discussed how the erosion of traditional values in our country could be traced to the widening distance between the decisions our representatives made and the Christian faith espoused by most of the American Founders. An essential ingredient of campaigns was the appearance of candidates at local churches, but any sympathy with faith often disappeared once they were in office. And yet, there were so many people of deep religious faith—like Senator Nickles, who longed for a kind of local infrastructure to support that faith in his work as a lawmaker.

Yes, there were chaplains in the Congress, but this work was internal, politically neutral, and largely ceremonial. What was needed would be a kind of missionary to Capitol Hill. Someone who was tethered not to a particular state but to a state of grace—and a rack of principles. He would be able to evangelize lawmakers, advance Christian morality, and communicate what was really going on in Washington to people in the pews of America's churches. He suggested I bring my ministry to Washington. He assured me he would introduce me to the power brokers and open doors for me throughout Capitol Hill. He said our national lawmakers needed to hear the Word of God, learn to pray, and get some common sense told to them about right and wrong. He gave me a brief tutorial on how such a minister would make his way around Capitol Hill, where the minefields were, and how to navigate the complex relationship between church and state.

The conversation with Senator Nickles marked the final link in a chain of events from Pastor Thorne's word to me from God to the discussions with Paul about relocating to D.C. and planting a new church. As we spoke, a vision of what was possible took shape in my mind. I was not entirely certain of the details, but I could see the unique role Paul and I could play in these halls of power. I took it as confirmation that it was God's will for me to expand my ministry to the most powerful city on earth. Suddenly I felt liberated not only from the strictures of blue-collar, working-class, Democrat-dominated Buffalo but also from the social marginalization of Bible-believing Christians that Paul and I endlessly carped about in sermons, interviews, and even in a book Paul had published entitled *The Extermination of Christianity: A Tyranny of Consensus.* In it, he argued that an unwitting conspiracy between modern education, the media, left-wing politics, and popular culture was bent on wiping out all vestiges of traditional Christian beliefs, practices, and adherents from the American landscape. A formal invitation from a United States senator to bring our work inside the U.S. Capitol, arguably the seat of power in our system of government, seemed the cure for our social and political ostracization.

When I got back home to Buffalo, I walked into the kitchen, where Cheryl was washing the dishes and cautiously but with resolve asked how she felt about moving our family to D.C. before the next school year began. We had been talking about the possibility since Paul started his exploration there, so she wasn't unprepared for the question, but until that moment it had only been theoretical. She paused for a minute, asked about a variety of details, then said, "It feels right. I think we need to go." I was the one surprised by her easy agreement, which I took as an answer to my prayers. Over the next few months we gently explained our plans to the kids and listed our house for sale. After Cheryl graduated summa cum laude from the University of Buffalo as a fully trained occupational therapist in June of 1994, she began applying for jobs in the metro Washington, D.C., area.

Cheryl's graduation spurred me on to fill out my own academic credentials. In early 1994, I found Faith Evangelical Seminary, a small school in Tacoma, Washington. "Faith" had been established in 1969 as an independent Lutheran seminary to combat the creeping liberalism in that denomination. It had since expanded its constituency considerably, enrolling more Baptists than Lutherans. I flew to Washington State for an interview with Dr. Michael Adams, who was then the dean. He was aware of my work through the national media, and complimented me, saying having an alumnus with national name recognition would benefit the school. Given that, he was willing to ease some of the requirements to accommodate me. He allowed me to enroll in a combined bachelor's and master's program. In the end, I would obtain a BA in religion and an MA in Christian ministry. I was able to complete the program by way of intensive short-term classes and long-term research projects, which culminated in 1998 when I received the degrees. No big ceremony for me, however—I was too busy. And still dreaming that one day, I might be able to complete a doctorate.

The summer of '94 was unimaginably frenetic. My longtime friend Charles Nestor, pastor of a large congregation in Manassas, Virginia, thirty-five miles west of D.C., and his wife, Belinda, offered to be our area guides. We were stunned by the prices of everything, but especially homes. In Buffalo you could get a nice house for $75,000; that wasn't even a down payment anywhere near Washington. When I asked pastors in the D.C. area what they paid their office workers, it was as much as a well-tenured senior pastor made back in our hometown.

I looked for creative ways to get things done at the lowest possible cost and tapped every major donor I knew for substantial gifts. We decided to move to Manassas because, even with the seventy-mile round-trip commute, it would be significantly cheaper to live there. And we would be close to the Nestors, the only friends we had in the area, in a community we thought more closely resembled what we had left behind in Buffalo. I would work out of a small shared office space on Pennsylvania Avenue, midway between the White House and the Capitol. It wasn't ideal for church work, but it was the best I could do on a missionary's start-up budget. When Cheryl landed a job with the local school district as a therapist, it was a big relief. We rented a small house and, with the help of one of our ministry supporters, eventually built a lovely home with four bedrooms. Still, the challenge to remain financially viable became my biggest exercise in faith.

Before Paul could join us, he had to face a potentially merciless sentence in the federal court, one that would be unbearable for Becky and the kids, and so he decided to accept a plea agreement. As they had for me in Bestry's court, hundreds of people—including our Democratic congressman John LaFalce—wrote Paul's sentencing judge, asking for leniency. On August 12, 1994, we stormed heaven with prayers for mercy. The sentencing guidelines for perjury recommended a year in prison and a fine of up to $20,000. Instead, the judge remanded Paul to thirty days in the Federal Correctional Institution, McKean in Lewis Run, Pennsylvania, followed by five months of house arrest. He also fined him $500. "Mr. Schenck, you are not known to be a deceitful man," the judge said, adding that "lying in court is an inexcusable crime that attacks the foundations of the American justice system."

Paul and his family were in the final stages of making their move to Washington, and suddenly nothing was easy. Shortly before he was scheduled to report to prison, the American Center for Law and Justice, his representation in the case, urged him to join its team as vice president in charge of operations. A public-interest religious-liberty law firm, the ACLJ was established in 1990 by Pat Robertson as an answer to liberal juggernaut ACLU. In its short history, the organization had already scored a big Supreme Court victory guaranteeing the freedom of Bible and prayer clubs to meet on public school property. The successes kept mounting and the organization developed a reputation within the evangelical world for legal rigor that was often missing in our fight for religious liberty. Teams of lawyers with Ivy League educational credentials—Harvard, Stanford, Yale—were working cases that would advance Christian freedom in all sectors of public life. The new offices were at Regent University, a graduate institution also founded by Robertson and situated at the Christian Broadcasting Network's sprawling headquarters complex in Virginia Beach, Virginia. This job would be a wonderful opportunity for Paul and his family, but he was conflicted. We had already obtained the necessary permission from the Potomac regional office of the Assemblies of God to form what we had named the "National Community Church on Capitol Hill." Paul felt as if he would be letting me down if he went to Virginia Beach, but I urged him to go, promising I would take the reins of our work in Washington.

Before Paul could move anywhere, however, he had to serve his time at McKean. His incarceration was the darkest period of his life. Prisoners were there for every imaginable crime, and many were violent offenders. During my phone calls with him, he expressed greater fear than I had ever heard in him before. Inmates routinely threatened each other, and sometimes followed through. We both knew the Protestant chaplain there very well, and I figured Paul was in good hands. But I was wrong. He was lonely and terrified.

My brother was now a convicted felon. Once released, he would be required to check in regularly with a parole officer and wear an ankle bracelet for five months to ensure he only traveled to and from his new office. Worst of all, he was banned for life from voting in federal elections. It proved a terrible time to up and move. Both Paul and Becky were attached to their extended families, and the sudden separation from siblings, parents, cousins, and lifelong friends was traumatic for all of them. For the first time in his life, my brother sank into a paralyzing depression.

There had never been such an extreme disparity between our states of mind; I was at a loss to know how to offer comfort or reestablish our brotherly bond. So as I did so often when confronted with complicated emotional demands, I plunged into work. And there was so much work to be done. Not just the logistics of organizing our move, but the more important ones of informing my supporters of this change. I had developed an extensive mailing list over time, and needed those people to be more generous than ever in their support. When I visited the small churches that had been so much a part of my life over the years, I described my plans for working in Washington, assured them that I would be their voice in that political wilderness, told them I would keep them informed, not just of our work, but of other issues and activities they could never learn about from watching the daily news or reading their papers. The abundance of their response was proof that I was on the right track.

At the turn of the year, I wrote a New Year's letter to my friends and supporters outlining my new plans.

DURING THE LAST TWELVE MONTHS WE HAVE WATCHED OUR GOVERNMENT DECLARE OPEN SEASON ON UNBORN CHILDREN, AUTHORIZE THE USE OF THEIR BODIES FOR GRUESOME EXPERIMENTATION, PROMOTE HOMOSEXUAL-

ITY AS A LEGITIMATE AND EVEN PREFERABLE LIFESTYLE, ATTEMPT TO PERSECUTE CONSCIENTIOUS CHRISTIANS THROUGH DRACONIAN LAWS, AND DISMISS ADULTERY BY DESCRIBING IT AS "NOTHING WRONG." ISN'T IT TIME WE DO SOMETHING ABOUT IT?

The answer was clearly yes, and I asked my supporters to become members of what I described as "Gideon's Army," an allusion to the biblical story when a ragtag militia of three hundred Jews defeated a heathen horde of tens of thousands. We would preach in our new mission field made up of elected and appointed officials and those who worked for them. I was very clear about the long-term objective: "All of this will be done with a view toward 1996 when spiritual, moral and religious issues will be very prominent in the debates surrounding the next presidential election. We want to be in Washington when all this happens so that God can use our voices if He so desires." I dubbed the new effort "Operation Save Our Nation."

14

Planting and Replanting a Church

My original plan was to divide our ministry between Sunday worship with the attendant congregational programs—nursery, children's church, youth group, Sunday school classes—and public policy and pro-life advocacy. Our focus was on young adults; I imagined mobilizing thousands of twenty- and thirty-something White House, congressional, and Supreme Court staffers, not to mention those who worked at federal agencies, to channel political influence with a strong moral and religious focus.

We would engage these young professionals and they would, in turn, invite their closest friends to "Andrew Parties," named after the disciple who brought his brother to Jesus, where they would hear the Gospel preached. Thereby a community of conscientious Christians who learned what it meant to be disciples of Jesus would be created. They would return to work and live out their witness to him by bringing Christian moral teaching to bear in their work in government, even speaking to their colleagues about the transformational experience of having Christ in their lives. Our model was a kind of utopian "trickle-up" theory: having gained a critical number of these members, our influence would move higher and higher up within the government, until we got to the top, my ultimate target—members of Congress, U.S. senators, cabinet secretaries, Supreme Court justices—even presidents.

I thought that if I evangelized the ungodly men and women whose decisions and actions so negatively impacted American life and culture, the proponents of abortion and the gay agenda would reject those pursuits and embrace values that would restore the moral core to our American civilization. I believed if we changed their hearts, we could change their minds and eventually their policies. I envisioned leading these reprobates to Christ in droves and seeing individual spiritual changes reflected in the way they thought, behaved, and, ultimately, governed. To get all this done, I wanted to put together a missionary body, poised to take on the big issues of the day while aggressively advancing a Christian witness to top government policy makers.

But the reality was I had no idea what Washington was like. I was shocked to discover that it was not, in fact, a godforsaken place. White evangelicals attended the Capitol Hill Baptist Church, a longstanding, theologically sound congregation. I missed it in my surveys of the Washington religious landscape, because Baptists existed in a different sphere than the Pentecostal-charismatics I kept company with in those days. Baptists don't practice speaking in tongues or believe in modern-day prophecy or miracles, and as was the case with this congregation, they often do not engage in the political debate. There were also vibrant African-American churches of every size and denomination, with rich histories, some dating back to the 1700s, and they were ubiquitous throughout the city. Of course, they were virtually all Democratic leaning in their political orientation, which made them, lamentably in my view, allies with our enemies. There were also myriad Catholic and Protestant congregations to choose from, all with committed parishioners, and they were a mix of conservative and liberal, but mostly the latter. So, realizing we had these faith communities to compete with, I thought of forming instead a residential community of Christian workers—something like a Protestant version of a monastery or convent. Eventually I realized the notion of taking the city by religious storm by creating a Christian community—and other fanciful ideas as well—all were technically impossible, and I became resigned to simply being a parson for a little while.

Every day, I returned home and complained to Cheryl about how difficult this was proving to be and wondering if I had made a mistake. My best option, I thought, would be to pursue the conventional model for "doing church." I searched for an existing congregation that would rent us their sanctuary for Sunday-afternoon services and found one at Capitol Hill United Methodist. By now we were a wide-ranging and diverse team made up of a public school teacher, a devoted homeschool mom, a law school student, the director for a U.S. Marine training program, a lawyer working for a U.S. senator, an inspector for the Environmental Protection Agency, and a forensic accountant for the FBI. Together we implemented a nursery, a children's church, a Sunday school, and even a youth department. On the outside, National Community Church was in every way a "normal" church, but inside we were defined by certain core convictions that set us apart from other congregations. The sanctity of life was our nonnegotiable guiding principle.

At this stage of my ministry I still harbored an inner conflict. The pastoral side of me just wanted to care for souls, but my political ambitions were quickly gaining control over my way of seeing the world. The measurement of a Christian, in my mind, was no longer Jesus and his timeless Sermon on the Mount, but fealty to a party, its platform, and its personalities. More than proclaiming the gospel, I wanted to keep our pro-life, pro-family message on the front pages.

In two short years, President Clinton had accomplished a great deal in attacking our pro-life movement, culminating in the Freedom of Access to Clinic Entrances (FACE) Act, which he signed in May 1994. The law was designed to make it impossible for us to exercise the time-honored and constitutionally protected right of protest by strictly limiting our access to clinics. This law eliminated any gray zone that might have existed and effectively criminalized what we had been doing for years. And it worked. Over time, FACE would all but put Operation Rescue out of business. It still existed—Randall was still demonstrating—but the wind had gone out of its sails, its previous adherents had found more mainstream ways to advocate for life, and donations had dried up. There was a shell of an organization, however, one that never fully disappeared.

We were all forced to devise new tactics in our pro-life advocacy, and I, for one, found that to be a relief. I had matured and looked back on all the arrests and the court confrontations with some pride—we had succeeded in bringing the subject of abortion into the mainstream conversation—but I harbored some regret for the toll that it had taken on Cheryl and our family. We were beginning a new life, and with it came the need to come up with new approaches to address this existential crisis in our country.

Increasingly, I thought about the families of aborted children, often seen as only bit players in a much bigger drama. There was at least a father to every mother, and sometimes siblings to the unborn children. On January 22, 1995, the twenty-second anniversary of *Roe v. Wade*, my new church held the first National Memorial for the Preborn and Their Mothers and Fathers. We invited guests to acknowledge the value and dignity of every human life, and to grieve if they had been touched by the loss of abortion. To attract the media, we included a tiny casket containing the remains of an aborted child. We also invited members of Congress. We knew most would not appear, but all we needed was one or two. We thought that by putting the casket in the same room with sitting members of Congress we would be guaranteed coverage in the major papers. And we were right: radio, TV, and print media swarmed our event. We deemed it a great success, but on Monday morning I received a call from Dick Stetler, the pastor of the church we were renting space from. His voice was strained. His church leadership demanded we restrain our pro-life activities and keep a very low profile. I said no. A few days later we were told we could no longer use the facilities.

I had to find a new home for our fledgling congregation. We soon settled in a decrepit elementary school right on the border of a dangerous neighborhood in Southeast Washington, D.C. It was a neglected and desolate place, but at the front of each classroom, near the chalkboards, were prominent white-and-blue signs that read "Thou Shalt Not Kill." To see the Sixth Commandment, the most succinct summation of the reasons for our Operation Rescue work, in every class of a public elementary school in a sketchy part of the city was a sign to me that this was God's place for us.

As National Community Church settled into its new space, something was stirring inside of me. I looked back with longing to the halcyon days of Operation Rescue, when we demonstrated and faced arrest, to my long walk to Mexico and the deep satisfaction I received from my mission work in the putrid dumps. I had felt this before, way back in Webster, when the staid and worthy demands of parish life left me restless. This time, though, there was another mission field much closer that beckoned. Needy souls were gathered inside the Capitol Building, where the power to change our country resided. If ever we were going to stem the tide of abortion blood, if we were ever going to hold back the runaway train of immorality in the culture—if we were ever going to acknowledge God as we should, and needed to—it was going to be because those who operated the levers of power acted to do it. My little flock was precious but powerless. I would exchange it for members of Congress.

15

Faith and Action

In the winter of 1995, not long after we had moved the National Community Church into the Giddings Elementary School, I was at a meeting in the Capitol with Ralph Reed, the head of Pat Robertson's political action group, the Christian Coalition. To most of us in the pro-life movement, Bill Clinton was a disaster, but for Ralph and the coalition, he was the gift that kept on giving. In just a short time, the coalition's membership had soared from 250,000 to over 1.6 million with 1,600 chapter affiliates spread across the country. With all those members came Pat Robertson's unmatched fund-raising prowess, and the organization's budget grew to almost $25 million. I had spoken at many coalition events over the years, but this was one of my first high-level meetings with them in Washington. The room was filled with friends and allies. It was a propitious time after the GOP triumph over Democrats in November. With his perfectly coiffed dome of hair, starched shirts, and tasseled loafers, Ralph was visibly basking in success. I liked Ralph and he was always congenial, even deferential, with me, but there was a lingering sense that he had really arrived in D.C., while I remained on the margins. I needed only to look at the prominent people he had assembled in this room for proof.

The purpose of the meeting was to lay out the strategy for consolidating the victories from the midterm elections. Many of us there were members of the clergy, and Ralph was careful not to begin electioneering, but there were strong hints on how congregations, pastors, and high-profile ministry personalities should be mobilized. After discussing demographics, election trends, and hot-button issues, I remember Ralph leaning forward, looking around the table, and announcing, "We don't just want a *place* at the table," he said, pausing for dramatic effect. "We want to *replace* the table with our own."

His brazen ambition and the way that others reveled in our collective destiny left me feeling momentarily uncomfortable. But perhaps this was the way one needed to play the game in this city. Everyone was confident that with Ralph we could realize our goal. I put away my doubts and, like a sponge, absorbed everything about the way Washington worked. If I felt any pangs of conscience, I soon dismissed them as simply part of the learning curve. I was using muscles I had never flexed before—of course they would twinge—so I took my cues from the experienced insiders.

The effects of the Republican Revolution would soon be felt. Those fifty-four new seats in the House and an additional eight in the Senate had given Republicans control of Congress for the first time in four decades and delivered many friendly new lawmakers to Capitol Hill. Odds were in our favor for the passage of legislation that rolled back some of the measures of the Clinton administration, or might at least stall further advancement of what I, at the time, considered a wicked agenda.

I naïvely attempted to make appointments with senators, representatives, and even federal judges, and was repeatedly though very politely brushed off. I needed to get closer to power, but I was having a hard time gaining access. I had to get creative. What would happen, I wondered, if I simply rode the elevators in their office buildings during the early-morning hours or late at night? Perhaps members would be more accessible when they were not on the floor, or in committee, or obligated to constituents and lobbyists, when the halls were not crawling with tourists.

As I prepared for my first elevator ministry, I put on my time-honored sartorial uniform first suggested by Pastor Fred Dixon: a sober suit, white shirt, and understated tie. But with one special difference. Someone I knew with experience on the Hill explained that a lapel pin was essential to signal my stature and experience. It would demonstrate to all who knew the code that I was a member of a special organization and, as such, I was worthy of their attention. Luckily, I had a pin from the National Clergy Council, or NCC, which Paul and I had founded back in the early nineties, while we were still in Buffalo. It was a network of pastors and ministry leaders we would call together on an as-needed basis—for a pro-life demonstration, say, or a news conference. My title was originally secretary-general, but when several of our members suggested it sounded too "communist," it was changed to "president." Being "president of the National Clergy Council" was proof of my national bona fides—and my new handsome lapel pin proved it.

One early morning in March 1995, I appeared for my first day working the elevators, wearing my pin, with my National Clergy Council business cards tucked in my pocket. As I approached the security detail, I remembered my father's admonition that the only thing separating success from failure is confidence. I crossed the Capitol Rotunda, heading for the proprietary subway that connects to the Hart Senate Office Building. A police officer raised his hand to stop me and said he didn't recognize my pin. I looked as surprised as if he had not recognized the American flag, even though I knew our council was not on any clearance list. With exaggerated patience, I pointed to the pin and informed him that it was the National Clergy Council logo. Looking embarrassed, he encouraged me to proceed.

I walked confidently to the railcar and hopped onboard. From there I got in the elevator and my vertical chapel was officially open for business. Senator John Kerry of Massachusetts was a visitor; I had not thought that I would have such a famous lawmaker, and prominent representative of our enemy, as my first visitor. He entered and I greeted him and introduced myself, explaining that I was the president of the National Clergy Council and eager to meet members of Congress. He gave me a polite response, went to his floor, exited, and someone else came in and hit the down button. And so it went, floor after floor, often with staffers and occasionally a bold-faced name: Tom Daschle, Arlen Specter, Ted Kennedy.

Some took my business card and gave the impression they would use it, and they did, calling me later—sometimes to ask for spiritual counseling, sometimes to ask if I might be interested in running a small Bible study group in their offices. But most simply reaching out to explore what political networking opportunities might come with a clergyman like me.

Slowly I discovered portals into the world of the political elite, learning to navigate the corridors of power. Senator Nickles was a constant help to me, but the congressional class of 1994 for the first time ever included lawmakers from my own denomination, the Assemblies of God. The transformation of the Senate and Congress during the middle of Clinton's first term in office created a congenial landscape, and I made some good friends. One of them was Ed Buckham, the new chief of staff for Texas congressman Tom DeLay, the majority whip in the House of Representatives. Ed was well-connected on the Hill. He had been head of the Republican Study Committee, a caucus of the most conservative members of the Republican Party in the House of Representatives. A lay evangelical minister—and a charismatic—he would often walk the grounds of the Capitol, praying in tongues. We understood each other entirely and he tutored me in the ways of the House. He explained which members were likely to be open to my elevator approach and those not worth my effort. He prayed with me, made sure I was on the guest list for various events, and warned me about political charlatans and enemies.

There was so much to absorb and so many moving parts. The demand fragmented my life. I spent my days trying to establish myself in Washington while my family was making the same effort in Manassas, thirty-five miles away, in a completely different community and disparate culture. Companies in Washington gave their employees incentive gifts of tickets to the opera; in Manassas they gave out tickets to the stock car races at the county fairgrounds. Cheryl and the kids were living in a whole other world, and the vast gulf between our experiences often made it hard to relate to each other after long days.

In addition to the toll that it took on my family life, the inroads I was making into Capitol Hill increasingly took time away from my congregation and my work as a pastor. But I felt a strong gravitational pull toward the Hill, the personalities, and the possibilities. I turned my eyes away from my humble little flock and toward the potentates, who I believed could literally change the course of the nation.

When I told my denominational supervisor I wanted to give up the church, he was relieved, but reluctant to grant permission unless I could suggest a suitable successor. Mark Batterson was an impressive young minister teaching at Washington's Urban Bible Training Center, an educational program for inner-city pastors. Over lunch, when Mark and I discussed how he would lead such a church, it was clear he would do something special. I asked if he would assume the pulpit if I were to resign. Without hesitation, he said he would. Cheryl and I were done. National Community Church was now in the hands of a new leader, who remained and went on to build it into one of the largest and most effective evangelical congregations in the metro Washington, D.C., area.

Finally, I was positioned to fully commit to the work that had drawn me to Washington in the first place. Jerry Falwell, Pat Robertson, James Dobson, Chuck Colson, and D. James Kennedy had preceded me in working the levers of power on a policy level, but I wanted to do something more immediately accessible. I wanted to become the first missionary to Capitol Hill. It would be an opportunity to bring biblical truth to bear on not only elected officials but those appointed and confirmed by them. My mission field would now be not only Congress and the White House but also the federal judiciary, including the Supreme Court justices—and I would do it up close and very personal.

With limited resources to pull it off, I had to take on just about every job to pay the bills. The American Center for Law and Justice and a few other sympathetic groups hired me as a consultant. Meanwhile, I worked every church connection I had, spending pretty much every weekend on the road preaching in pulpits all over the country, raising support wherever I went. I quickly built a small team of full-time employees and lay and clergy volunteers. Our work was to challenge the political leaders in Washington by exposing their machinations, rebuking their moral turpitude, reminding them they were all accountable to a higher authority than themselves, and reporting it all back to our supporters across the country.

In the end, this translated into support of Republicans and criticism of Democrats. I would look at their speeches on the floor, their legislation, sometimes the groups with whom they met, and talk to their staff members, sometimes to the members themselves. I wrote a monthly newsletter that I would send to the now several thousand people on our mailing list—folks who lived in small communities in Oklahoma, say, or Kansas, or Alabama, or rural Washington State—and I would zero in on the issues most important to us, such as abortion, and report on the nefarious doings of the Democrats and the rectitude of many Republicans. Then I would return to Capitol Hill and meet with like-minded officials in a prayerful way, to engage them in thinking about their work with an eye to the Lord.

We renamed ourselves Faith and Action in the Nation's Capital and devised a simple mission statement: "To challenge Capitol Hill with

Biblical truth and to change the nation, one policy maker at a time." I wanted to lead every needy soul to the Savior so they could find forgiveness of sins and, consequently, change their thinking and actions when it came to public policy. "The solution to the mess in our country," I said in many a Sunday sermon, "is the gospel. When a heart is changed, a head is changed. When a head is changed, a policy is changed. When a policy is changed, a nation is changed. That's how it works, folks, plain and simple."

This change, I thought, would get done through individual witness, which meant sitting and talking with members of Congress and their staff in offices, in those elevators, across lunch tables, in group Bible studies, and in special events. I was exhilarated and engaged. I was on a first-name basis with some important people, funders came on board, and I even made some friends in the Clinton White House. Every day offered a new opportunity to evangelize, to connect with power brokers, to do an interview with national media, to explore new territory. I was in my glory. I could feel the working of the Holy Spirit in everything I was doing. From the small events where a few staff members from Congress appeared for Bible study, to the day a Supreme Court justice reached out to ask for my counsel in a family crisis. This was heady stuff. Sometimes, I would remember Pastor L. M. Thorne's words at the Abundant Life Church, "God's gonna use you, my brother, in a mighty way in this country and it's going to be for his glory, honor and praise."

I was beginning to believe it.

16

Rev. Schenck v. Pro-Choice Network of Western N.Y.

When I arrived in Washington in 1994, the tensions around questions of American morality that had begun in the 1970s had reached their zenith—or nadir, depending on your point of view. Shortly after I stepped away from the National Community Church, I was up on the Hill, talking to a senior congressional staff member about my concern over the deteriorating spiritual condition of our country. Our conversation became more and more frustrating. The more I talked about what I considered the most pressing problems, the more impassive his expression became, as if he could neither hear nor understand what I was saying. This was obviously not the first time I had spoken to someone who was secular, but it did make me realize just how entrenched this nonreligious worldview was in official Washington, D.C., and I wanted to do something about it. It also impressed on me how our divide was not just religious but, in a sense, linguistic: he spoke the language of secularism, and I spoke the idiom of deism, and from that difference all else followed—a cascade of misunderstanding and miscommunication—which I felt was deleterious to the moral fabric of our country.

I returned to my office to pray over and ponder what I had just experienced. Even though the congressional aide and I were roughly the same age, came from the same part of the country, and shared an

intense interest in politics, the gap between us seemed virtually un-
bridgeable. Could there possibly be a common point of reference? Was
there any place to begin a conversation?

Impatient for answers and looking for a sign, I pulled a magazine
out from under a stack of papers, the *Biblical Archaeological Review*, a
journal on modern-day discoveries of artifacts supporting the Bible
story. As I scanned the pages, my eyes caught a small ad for imitation
marble carvings of the Ten Commandments with a painfully amateur-
ish photo. And yet, even as I flipped the pages forward, I kept going
back. The ad was for Covenant Marble and Granite Works, located in
Roaring River, North Carolina. Suddenly I felt the surge of adrenaline.
I thought, *Maybe this is where to start the conversation, at the very beginning, with the Ten Commandments.*

The purpose of the Ten Commandments is to offer instruction on
sin and righteousness, to lay out starkly the difference between right
and wrong, to hold us accountable and force us to face ourselves in
the mirror. The "Great Words of Sinai," as I had called them in many
a sermon, can also be a locus of tension between my evangelical community and the outside secular-dominated world. But I also thought
most people probably had a memory of the Commandments from their
younger days in either Sunday school or catechism—or they at least
had a rudimentary knowledge of them passed down from parents or
grandparents—and that familiarity would facilitate conversation. The
Commandments also had a kind of universal status, recognized not
just by Christians and Jews but by Muslims and many other religions.
I figured it would be pretty hard for politicians to turn away from such
a widely recognized moral code.

I called the 800 number and spoke to a young woman who sounded
as if she were in her kitchen. Her husband made the die-cast plates of
the Ten Commandments, which came in small, medium, and large
sizes and could be mounted in frames. As she carefully explained stone

polymer construction, felt backings, color variations, and volume discounts, a vision played in my head: these tablets hanging in offices all around Capitol Hill, testifying to God's basic moral requirements for humankind, and sparking just the right kind of conversation about good and evil, right and wrong, sin and salvation. She would send me some samples.

Using the Ten Commandments to introduce the concept of transcendent moral truths—a universal standard to which every human being and institution is held accountable—would make it possible to return the Word of God to the halls of government and to the national conversation. Like Johnny Appleseed, I would distribute the plaques as seeds of righteousness to elected and appointed officials in Washington. I did know that ethics rules would make it difficult to give works of art, no matter how low-grade, to congresspeople. I would need to get around that problem and it didn't take me long to come up with a solution. While gifts to congressional members and other officials were prohibited, because they could be construed as bribes, awards were not. I would mount the tablets on wood frames and apply an inscribed plate announcing it as the "Ten Commandments Leadership Award."

Before talking to my ministry team about this new tack, I did a little research on how the Ten Commandments were positioned in society. Did people indeed identify with them in any way? Were they being referenced anywhere outside the religious world? That's when I discovered Roy Moore, a county judge in Alabama who was making national news after he hung a small, hand-carved plaque of the Commandments on his courtroom wall. The ACLU had sued for its removal, but the judge prevailed when the state supreme court ruled the plaintiffs had no legal standing. I invited the "Ten Commandments Judge," as he was being called by his supporters, to Washington for his first national news conference, during which we officially launched the "Ten Commandments Project."

Republicans in both houses had just passed a resolution applauding Moore for his stand and calling for the public display of the Commandments, something I helped to bring across the finish line by recruiting last-minute votes. I would go on to forge a tight relationship with Moore, staying as a guest in his home, traveling the country with him speaking to enthusiastic audiences, and, eventually, campaigning for him when he ran for chief justice of the supreme court of Alabama. I was with him when he installed a highly controversial monument of the Commandments in the Alabama Judicial Building, where the Alabama Supreme Court convenes, and I went to jail in support of his action after federal marshals were ordered to remove it. He was ultimately removed from the bench for his defiance of a federal court order, but ten years later would reclaim that post in a landslide election. I stuck with him through it all. The notoriety helped us not only to launch the effort but also to raise substantial amounts of money to keep it going.

Back in Washington, I always expected the plaques would be well received, especially if offered through the National Clergy Council and presented by a delegation of ministers and other religious officials who would provide the gravitas cherished by the denizens of Capitol Hill. Plus politicians know the value of a good photo op, and we would offer it. In return, our delegation would demonstrate that we wielded enough influence to bring important people together. It would be a winning strategy to announce to a member of Congress, a cabinet secretary, a judge, or even a president that a delegation of religious leaders wanted to present an award. My hunch proved right. Prospects, all of them Republicans, almost always said yes.

The Ten Commandments became a kind of calling card for me. The project expanded my identity on the Hill. I was not just the "pro-life reverend" anymore. What I missed at that early stage was the divisiveness of even this nearly universal symbol. While a wide spectrum of religious believers revered the Commandments, it was also true that they divided believers from nonbelievers, moral traditionalists from social progressives, and westerners from easterners. It didn't take long for me to jettison my intentions of bringing people together and instead to use this universal symbol of moral behavior to leverage the divisions. In retrospect the painful irony is obvious; at the time it wasn't. Implicit in my message when awarding one lawmaker the Ten Commandments was that there were others who did not deserve them. Emphasizing the point, sometimes I would ask for suggestions for nominees for those who *broke* the most commandments. That line was not only an easy laugh, it also created a conspiratorial bond between us that further solidified our connection.

As I took up the Ten Commandments crusade, my anti-abortion efforts aligned perfectly with the new message. In fact, when discussing abortion with reporters, I was always careful to point out that the commandment "Thou shalt not kill" is displayed in an image of Moses bearing the tablets that was situated just over the heads of the Supreme Court justices as they sit on their lofty bench. I suggested it was a perennial reminder to them that *Roe v. Wade* and every other abortion decision was an affront to the universal moral code, and the justices would eventually need to grapple with that fact.

That moment came for us on March 19, 1996, when we learned the high court agreed to hear Paul's case from back in 1990, when he and I handed out literature in front of the Buffalo clinic and were accused of breaching the fifteen-foot zone. Of some seven thousand cases to choose from during each year, the Supreme Court accepts only seventy to eighty, and ours would be one of them; we were, in the language of the court, granted *cert.* It was a very big deal for us and for the pro-life movement. The basic question boiled down to whether judges can establish so-called buffer zones to prevent demonstrators from obstructing clinics. At issue was the fifteen-foot no-protest zones and whether they unnecessarily burdened free speech.

On October 16, 1996, Paul and Becky and their two oldest kids, Leah and Ari; Cheryl and I, and Anna and Matthew; and my father, Hank, stood outside the marbled Temple of Justice, with its august columns and grand staircase. Although I had been to the court a number of times, to be a litigant was an otherworldly experience for me. We arrived at the crack of dawn, because, unlike lower appellate courts, where parties to the case have special standing and are virtually guaranteed entrance, this does not happen for petitioners before the highest court in the land. Our legal team was so large, it filled every reserved seat in the court available to our side. Paul and I and our family members could only hope to be among the first fifty public observers allowed in for the entire argument.

We achieved our objective and were ushered into church-like pews in the front of the ornate courtroom. Everyone stood as the justices filed in. With a single rap of the gavel, Chief Justice William Rehnquist announced: "We'll hear argument first this morning in Number 95–1065, *Reverend Paul Schenck and Dwight Saunders versus Pro-Choice Network of Western New York.*" Paul and I winked at each other, knowing we had made history with that "Reverend" in his name. It had been a minor victory when we persuaded the court that "Rev." should remain before Paul's name, even though we had been told repeatedly that legal briefs never included such titles. Paul knew that even if the justices didn't see it that way, our supporters and opponents needed to. "Reverend Paul Schenck" ensured we could cast the conflict as a religious liberty case and not one about blockading clinics.

Sitting in front of Paul and Becky were Pat Robertson with Ralph Reed. Beverly LaHaye, the founder of the largest conservative Christian women's organization, Concerned Women for America, sat behind me. Our most vicious opponents were also there: Eleanor Smeal of the National Organization for Women, Kate Michelman of the National Abortion Rights Action League, and Gloria Feldt of Planned

Parenthood. More than six years of searing conflict would culminate here, in a civilized argument before the justices.

When our legal team leader, chief counsel Jay Sekulow, was invited to the podium, he sprang up and began so loudly that the Chief Justice chastised him and told him to tone it down. It was a rough start to what was otherwise a masterful presentation. No successful advocate before the most demanding tribunal in the country does it without exhaustive preparation, and Jay was no exception. He and his team had spent months combing through documents, interviewing principals, consulting with top legal experts, drafting briefs, and staging moot courts, in which law professors and retired judges playing the justices peppered Jay with endless questions.

One hour was allotted for the argument with each side given thirty minutes to make their case. Jay argued for us. On the other side was our old enemy, the abortion rights activist law professor from the University of Buffalo, Lucinda Finley. Any sitting president may ask special permission of the court for the solicitor general, the country's top civil attorney, to take a short amount of time to present the government's point of view in the controversy. Clinton had sent Walter Dellinger III to present the administration's opinion that the fifteen-foot no-speech zone was consistent with the First Amendment.

The arguments progressed in rapid fire, with justices interrupting attorneys, sometimes before they could finish a sentence. Toward the end, when the solicitor general discussed Judge Arcara's finding that Paul and I had physically obstructed women entering the clinic, he asked rhetorically, "What's a trial judge supposed to do in the face of that kind of finding?" Justice Anthony Kennedy leaned forward and retorted, "Well, one of the things he's supposed to do is read the First Amendment." Paul turned and whispered to me, "We just won the case."

As I reflected on what my brother had just said, my eyes wandered around the magnificent chamber, with its towering, gilded ceiling; dappled marble walls; impressive columns; and famous friezes on the four walls, with a pylon symbolizing the Bill of Rights on the frieze above the justices' bench. One of the figures on the frieze on the south wall especially distracted me: that image of Moses holding the tablets of the Ten Commandments written in Hebrew. The folds of his robe obscured most of the words, but the only ones clearly legible were *Lo Tirtzach*—*No taking of innocent life.* I thought of how many times I had referenced it in news conferences, but I was seeing the real thing for the first time. At that moment, it left me thinking we had been right all along.

After what seemed like sixty of the longest minutes of my life, the Chief Justice struck the gavel and ended the session. We all paraded outside to watch Jay as he addressed reporters gathered on the plaza. Standing there, looking at the gaggle of lawyers, I thought of how much hung on the outcome of this case: the rights of pro-lifers all over the country, the future of the rescue movement and its nonviolent direct action, the parameters of free speech, and religious expression—not to mention the Schenck name—and, of course, the lives of innocent unborn children. It didn't occur to me at the time that I had prioritized those concerns in precisely the wrong order.

There is no rule when it comes to how or when the Supreme Court must render its final opinion in a case. It could take days, weeks, months, or even years. Advance notice of a decision is never given. The parties learn their fate only after the case is suddenly and unexpectedly read from the bench by the author of the majority opinion. The long and agonizing wait began. Six months would pass before we would hear anything.

17

Christmas with the Clintons

The potential of my mission in D.C. was dazzling: 435 members of Congress, one hundred senators, and more than two thousand staffers; tens of thousands more working in the other branches of government; the Supreme Court justices and their clerks and assistants; the president and vice president as well as their closest advisors; plus other cabinet agencies including Justice, State, Defense, and on and on. If I included the military, there would be hundreds if not thousands more executive-level officials.

I knew I couldn't reach everyone, but that wasn't the point. I wanted to be present and available to whomever God placed in my path. But in D.C., there was a certain balancing act I needed to sustain: visible enough to be taken seriously by powerful people, but careful not to fall under somebody's disapproving gaze. I had seen how the slightest departure from lockstep conformity to partisan messaging, or a breach of protocol or even decorum, could lead to being blacklisted and therefore banned from critical access points. It had nearly happened to me when I managed to get onto a special invitation list to a closed-door hearing, then went and bragged to the media about it. I got an angry call from a committee staffer who barked, "Don't you know that I can block you from ever getting into any meeting here?" I apologized profusely and had my office send her a large basket of fruit and nuts with a formal letter admitting my faux pas. If my ministry was going to be successful, I would need to reign in my natural embrace and be discreet.

My main vehicle for visibility on the Hill was the Ten Commandments Project. It seemed to have answered a need among many Christian lawmakers for public recognition of their faith they hadn't previously found. It also signaled their sympathies on a whole range of issues: abortion, the gay agenda, religious freedom. In offices and ceremonial meeting rooms, I presented oversized wood mountings of the tablets, took a few photos, and then published the recipients' names among a list of men and women who reached a certain standard of courage in their public professions of faith. Most of our honorees were Republicans who shared our moral mission at the time. One then-little-known congressman, Mike Pence of Indiana, accepted the plaque and quickly displayed it in his office. He especially liked my line "When you find yourself in trouble, take two tablets and call Him in the morning." (He asked if he could steal it—missing the irony entirely.)

Security guards and other personnel now greeted me with warm and familiar smiles when I arrived. I walked through the halls with confidence, and was often stopped for brief conversations or button-holed into quick meetings with lawmakers or members of their staffs. Each interaction became a moment of pastoral care, an opportunity to inject an instant of biblical truth or Christian sensibility into the political conversation, and to forge an alliance. It paid off.

In the spring of 1996, several lawmakers asked for my help supporting the Defense of Marriage Act, or DOMA—a measure denying federal recognition of same-sex marriages—introduced by my friend Senator Nickles of Oklahoma. It explicitly defined a "spouse" as one half of a heterosexual couple in a legal marriage, which aligned with everything preached and taught in our churches. He and I spoke about the important role of marriage in the Bible and its theological underpinnings. I explained to him how the term "abomination" in our lexicon was reserved for only a few things, among them the future false prophet associated with the Antichrist—and sexual intercourse between persons of the same sex. Our community was unwavering on this point: homosexuals were driven by the supremely immoral impulses of lust, perversion, self-absorption, and rebellion against both God and society.

For us, holy matrimony was only one thing: a union between one man and one woman in lifelong monogamy. At one time this meant divorced and remarried people were relegated to second-class status in most evangelical churches and unwelcome in others, but we had resolved that problem. Social trends demanded pastors find a way not to demote divorced members or turn new people away. God's grace was emphasized in place of the previously legalistic interpretations of certain Bible passages, and soon marital status became pretty much a nonissue. By the time I entered ministry, there were growing numbers of newly single and remarried couples in our pews and even in some pulpits—something that would have been terribly scandalous a decade earlier.

There were no such attempts to accommodate gay couples. In May, the Defense of Marriage Act sailed through Congress with large, veto-proof majorities, which meant already committed gay couples were barred from receiving any kind of federal benefits—taxes, insurance, Social Security survivor benefits. Back then, the real human consequences of this policy were of only minor interest to me. I would revisit that evolutionary trajectory years later as I looked critically at my own attitudes on the way our churches treat LGBTQ people.

My side had long objectified homosexual persons to make them easy to depersonalize, and to diminish their humanity in order to reduce a vast, diverse group of men and women to their sexual preference. The next logical step was to demonize them and rob them of any recognition of our common humanity. Looking back, I am shocked at how easy this completely un-Christian behavior was, but I couldn't see it then. My organization routinely exploited garish public displays of sexual license at gay pride parades in cities like New York, San Francisco, and even Washington, using the images to induce the kind of revulsion and rage that generates interest and big fund-raising dollars from our evangelical Christian supporters all over the country. Small donors would send checks for ten dollars after one of our campaigns, while we could expect thousands from others.

A lot of moral and religious issues surfaced during the presidential campaign of 1996. Paul and I again attended the presidential nominating conventions and were disconcerted by slippage we saw in the commitment of the Republican Party to the pro-life cause. Since 1976 the party had championed a constitutional amendment banning abortion, but Republicans in several important states expressed discomfort with an outright ban. The nominee, Bob Dole, was a hardheaded pragmatist who had been shaped politically in the sixties and seventies, before religious conservatives dominated the party. His was the Republican Party of Gerald Ford, not Ronald Reagan. While he gave lip service to our issues, he demonstrated no passion for them. Our inner circle was determined to remind Dole and the party of our importance. Ralph Reed spoke for all of us when he told the *New York Times,* "For the evangelical and Roman Catholic voters who have poured into the Republican Party in recent years, this is an issue on which a signal of compromise or accommodation would lose their enthusiasm and probably their votes."

For our part, Paul and I went to the convention in San Diego and organized a memorial service for aborted children, which we held outside the convention hall. We challenged the so-called moderates who were urging the party to abandon the pro-life plank of its platform, reminding them that the Republican Party was founded during another time of moral crisis in America, when it had stood up against the abomination of slavery, and we needed to stand up for American values yet again. In the end, our hard work succeeded: the party platform reaffirmed the "fundamental individual right to life" for an unborn child and supported a human life amendment to the Constitution.

Turnout for the election was historically low, with only 49 percent of the country showing up to the polls to reelect Bill Clinton. We were discouraged by the outcome but managed to hold on to our congressional majority. Another four years of Clinton stretched before us like a vast, dismal desert, but there was something of an oasis on the horizon: my fund-raisers were now reporting record returns on our direct mail, thanking Clinton for the bump. And I was engaged in blood sport, eager to win, succeed, and do my part to damage the other side. I suppose I was a quick study: the new arrival in Washington who felt uncomfortable with the hubris of Ralph Reed's declaration about "replacing the table" now felt the same way.

In early December, Cheryl and I received a prized invitation to join other conservative leaders in attending the annual Christmas Eve service at the famed Washington National Cathedral. Its soaring Gothic spires, intricate stained-glass windows, and beautiful gardens made it one the city's notable landmarks. The cathedral was envisioned in its 1895 congressional charter as a "House of Prayer for All People," and it had hosted countless national events, including memorial services for thirteen presidents. My family arrived an hour early and the massive sanctuary was already a hive of activity, with a forest of poinsettias on the altar. The small brass orchestra was tuning up, the choir donned their robes, and the extraordinary combination of dignitaries and regular folk began to fill the rows.

Rumor had it Vice President Al Gore would be attending, which explained the presence of Secret Service and the long lines for security clearance. The cathedral always delayed announcing the presence of a president or vice president, both for their safety and to avoid distracting attention from the sacred nature of the gathering. It wasn't until the service began that I realized it wasn't Gore in the front row but President Clinton and his family.

My intention that night had been to simply participate in a meaningful observance of Christmas, but as soon as I learned the president was there, my activist ambitions crowded out all other thoughts, most of all the beauty of the momentous celebration of Jesus' birth. Clinton had recently vetoed the Partial-Birth Abortion Ban Act, and I couldn't miss this opportunity to confront him about it. I had advised members of Congress who had crafted that legislation, and here was the man who had undone all that noble work. He needed to be called to account, and the celebration of Christ's nativity made the setting symbolically profound to me. I found further justification in Galatians 6:1: "Brothers, if anyone is caught in any transgression, you who are spiritual should restore him in a spirit of gentleness." My spirit of gentleness was raring to go.

Mentally, I put together a plan of action, impatient for the moment while sleepwalking through the service. My opportunity was nearing and my heart rate was increasing as I prepared to go forward to the altar area and receive Holy Communion. As the ushers organized congregants, I deliberately chose the line that would pass by the president's seat. When I arrived there, I leaned toward him and said in a measured but quite audible voice, "God will call you to account, Mr. President."

Clinton's face flushed red but he stared straight ahead. I proceeded to the altar rail, knelt, and received Communion, then returned to my seat. That's when I heard the familiar crackle of law enforcement radios nearby. Three Secret Service agents were positioned near our row, blocking any path I might take once the congregation was dismissed. I knew I was in trouble. As my family and I prepared to leave, one of the agents said we needed to talk. I could see the dread and fear on the faces of my family: they had been victims of so many of my encounters with law enforcement, and this would be another one—and on Christmas Eve.

A younger man flashed his badge and became aggressive, telling me I could be sentenced to twenty-five years for threatening the president of the United States. When I heard the words "warrant" and "arrest," I realized this could be more serious than I had anticipated. I needed to call my lawyer—at 1:30 on Christmas morning. So I took out my cell phone and searched for his number, explaining that I needed to talk to my legal counsel. What I didn't know at this point was that in all the jostling of my phone, I had somehow hit a speed-dial number that called our home. The automated system tied to my computer answered. As I held the phone at my side, the voice mail recorded the encounter.

Cheryl and the kids stood a few feet away, waiting for me; she was humiliated and smoldering, and Anna and Matthew were clearly distressed. The crowds in the cathedral had dispersed—headed home, perhaps, for a cup of celebratory eggnog before going to bed. But my family was wide-awake, despite the late hour, coping with memories of my previous incarcerations. I paid no attention to how tired and stricken they were. In my activist mind-set, there was just one thing that had to be done that evening: confront the president on his murderous embrace of partial-birth abortion.

The younger agent searched through my wallet, handed it back to me, and let us go. The crisis, it seemed, had passed. It was a somber drive home. My mind was feverishly going through every detail of the encounter while Cheryl sat grim-faced beside me. The kids stared out the windows. Finally, Cheryl broke the silence and asked if I really needed to do this on Christmas—a rare display of criticism in such a highly charged moment. I didn't answer. I could have ruined the whole holiday, she protested, both angry and sad. She even sounded afraid. I kept my eyes on the road, torn within a swirl of my own emotions: my anger at her criticism, my silent acknowledgment that she may have had a point, my relief that I wasn't spending Christmas Eve in a D.C. jail. Thirty minutes of silence later, as we walked into our home, Cheryl saw the red indicator light on our computer. She played the recording and announced that the whole episode was on the answering device. Whatever misgivings I may have had disappeared. I was jubilant that there was some record of the incident and suspected, correctly, I hadn't heard the last of it. Cheryl did not share my euphoria, and after sending the kids to bed she somberly started putting presents out for Christmas morning. She only wanted to salvage the holiday.

The next day, when news started circulating that a clergyman had been detained by presidential security at the Christmas Eve service, a Secret Service spokesman told Reuters that no such thing had occurred. When other journalists came calling, I simply played the recording and took the opportunity to reemphasize my message to the president— and embarrass the Secret Service. A twofer. I had substituted Christmas festivities with a stream of reporters with their microphones, cameras, and steno pads. Our family Christmas was a fiasco, and I was the center of attention; my drama dominated our holiday.

Did I convince the president of the evils of partial-birth abortion? Of course not. It would be another ten years and a different administration before a bill restricting the procedure would be signed into law. But at the time it didn't matter. I congratulated myself on having provided a prophetic witness. I likened myself to the prophet Amos, who confronted the corrupt political leaders of the day, or to John the Baptist, who was witness to King Herod's evil behavior. To be a prophet is always to be ready to call out sin, especially when perpetrated by the powerful on the innocent. How could anyone possibly take issue with that?

Although I would later come to regret it, back then I was thrilled that I had confronted the president—and now had a priceless anecdote to share with others who called and congratulated me on my courage. But inside our home unexpressed questions hung in the air. Did I need to do this on Christmas Eve? Why did I put my family through the embarrassment and discomfort? Was there any reason why Christmas that year needed to be overshadowed by my political gamesmanship? What about the sanctity of the cathedral that Christmas Eve? What about my wife and children?

18
Family Matters

One of my favorite photographs from my walk to Mexico is of me and seven-year-old Matthew. We are walking hand in hand, sporting identical Nike gear—T-shirts, shorts, socks, shoes, and baseball caps—and matching packs. I loved showing off that photo and pointing to my boy, literally walking in my footsteps. But that scene was from what felt to be a lost, idyllic time. In the fall of 1997, nine years after my walk, Anna had gone off to college and Matthew had started to change. He became inordinately withdrawn and moody.

Adolescence is never an easy time, and Anna and Matthew confronted Cheryl and me with all the usual conflicts: Matthew wanted to stay out late with friends and girls; Anna wanted to go off for a weekend with classmates without adult supervision. However, all the normal tensions were amplified by the special anxiety I brought to my parenting—anxiety that had nothing to do with concern about the welfare of my kids. I was haunted by the fear that any of their transgressions would be seized upon by my enemies as an example of the contradiction between my public rectitude and private vulnerability. I tightened the standards of what was acceptable, constantly worrying that a normal family conflict would be revealed as a pastor's private life out of control.

Mine was not an idle worry: many ministerial careers had been ruined by less. Dysfunction among rebellious preachers' kids was well known in my community. The pressure to appear "perfect," to live up to unrealistic expectations, can lead families to act one way in private and the other in public, making kids feel as if they are surrounded by hypocrisy. My own insecurities about who I was—too young, under-educated, a Pentecostal minister—combined with my increasing visibility as someone members of Congress and their staff would turn to for spiritual help, made me even more demanding that my family *always* did the right thing. Matthew and Anna each felt the pressure in different ways.

Anna never went in for wild music or daring fashion and was always serious about her worship, her youth group, and her Bible reading. Matthew never fit that mold. He was culturally adventurous—into heavy metal bands, albeit the Christian version, with names like Stryper, Whitecross, and Leviticus. By his sixteenth birthday, he had ventured into secular genres, including, egregiously, the Rolling Stones. When he stapled a photo of the flagrantly immoral Keith Richards—the embodiment of everything I then condemned—to his bedroom wall, I imagined photographers ambushing the room to capture the image of what Reverend Rob Schenck—president of the National Clergy Council, head of Faith and Action—permitted his son to do. In my world, the behavior of a minister's children determined whether he was legitimate and worthy of financial backing. Faith and Action was now a growing organization with an increasing number of donors who appreciated the importance of having my evangelical presence among lawmakers. Not only did I have my family to support, but a dozen people now worked for me and depended on my success in fund-raising for their financial security. I constantly worried that my supporters would discover something wrong with my kids and judge me as deficient, and our income would plummet. This preoccupation affected my relationship with my children in very negative ways.

Conflicts between fathers and sons are part of the natural order of things, but I saw Matthew's behavior not as adolescent individuation but as an act of betrayal—against God, our family's mores, and, most important, against me personally. It wasn't just that he was drawn to pagan music, ear piercings, and even nose studs—clearly, he didn't want to follow in my footsteps anymore. Now, when I looked at our FaithWalk photograph, it seemed to reproach me. How could he have gotten so out of sync with me?

The crisis in our relationship came to a head after Anna had gone off to Grove City College, a prestigious Christian school north of Pittsburgh. One day Matthew's girlfriend's mother called Cheryl to tell her she had found a used condom in her daughter's room after Matthew had left. At that time, one of our cardinal beliefs was that sex between teenagers constituted a serious sin. Numerous Bible verses unequivocally ban sex outside of marriage. Every message we conveyed to our kids about sex was consistent with these biblical passages and was reinforced in their Christian schools, their Sunday school classes, their Bible studies, and the teachings of their youth pastors. Cheryl and I spoke frankly about the serious nature of sexual relationships and the grave consequences of promiscuity. Both our kids knew full well that sex was reserved *only* for marriage.

I was incredulous, and I was furious. I worried what this could mean for Matthew—a pregnancy, an STD, eviction from the church's youth group. And what did this mean for us as a family? How could I parent a child who wasn't a virgin and who had crossed the line of adult intimacy? And what about God? What did this imply about Matthew's relationship with Christ, with Christianity, with other Christians? By the time I confronted my son, I had amassed an overwhelming case against him. I returned to the danger of pregnancy, his inability to pay for a baby. I went on and on, doing everything possible to convince him he had made the worst mistake, taken the greatest risks, and inflicted the most grievous injury to our relationship, to another member of our church, and to God. If he wasn't sufficiently guilty already, I hoped he was now. For me, this was a crisis of monumental proportion, demanding that every weapon in my arsenal be deployed.

Cheryl watched this unfold and realized in ways I couldn't that this was a family problem that required professional help. We went to see our friend and pastor Charles Nestor in hopes he could refer us to a good Christian counselor. I dreaded how exposed I would be, how I would be judged an utter failure as a father, a minister, a faith leader, a Christian man. I had always been haunted by the verse from the apostle Paul's letter to the young first-century pastor Timothy: "If someone does not know how to manage his own household, how will he care for God's church?" Many of my efforts in resolving Matthew's misdeed were designed to circumvent public criticisms of me that could damage my credibility in the churches and on Capitol Hill. This wasn't only about Matthew and the family; it was fundamentally about me and my ministry. These worries occupied my entire field of vision.

As I sat in Charles's office shamefully recounting what had happened, I was surprised that he wasn't more concerned or more censorious. In fact, he was reassuring. He acknowledged the seriousness of what had occurred but did not turn it into a wholesale indictment of Matthew, our family, or me. I almost longed to be criticized, but instead Charles referred me to a Christian psychologist, Dr. William Bixler, who was trained at evangelical institutions and had a degree in theology. Going to see a shrink was enormously controversial for evangelicals. Psychologists were often vilified as the high priests of a new, pagan, anti-Christian religion—*anti*-theists who attempted to use worldly philosophy to replace God's wisdom.

I had never imagined that I would find myself in a therapist's office. Paying someone to listen to one's troubles seemed a waste to me. Then there was how my religious community viewed the practice: when we were troubled, the cause was not psychological and the solution was not secular. All human problems could be addressed through our relationship with God. And then, if I dared to admit it, I couldn't bear the thought of being judged by a stranger as I shared my shortcomings and vulnerabilities. Now I found that I had to face not just the world but myself in ways I had never even considered.

Notwithstanding all my objections, I took small, hesitant, and not fully engaged steps in this new process, but even then it did give me some insights. I saw early on that I lacked internal awareness of what constituted appropriate boundaries—in relation to my family, my staff, my donors, the churches, the media, the outside world. So much of my thinking, my motivation, my decisions, my actions, and my relationships were predicated on how others felt about me; what others would do with me, to me, and for me; and how my actions affected them. Dr. Bixler gave me my first glimpse into the possibility that my self-perception as a paragon of virtue or Christian perfection might not be particularly healthy. In fact, I was one big porous mess, and it eroded my relationship with Cheryl—and had for a long time—and it was central in the dysfunction in my relationship with my son. I could not metabolize the advice Dr. Bixler gave me that day and wouldn't for years. But he had planted a tiny mustard seed in my psyche.

While my participation in therapy was fleeting, Cheryl and Matthew kept going individually. It became a profound source of help for her, and for Matthew as well. We seemed to be back on an even keel. Still, there was trouble beneath the surface. Cheryl hinted she was not content with the state of our marriage, and that bothered me. I didn't ask what she meant, and she did not go further. Our focus was on Matthew, so I didn't think to look at how our marriage might have been a part of Matthew's problems.

I was far more worried about what had happened in the youth group, and whether it would get into the broader church community. They never condemned me for the sins of my son, but I continued to be ashamed over what I saw as being my failure to properly parent him. I didn't pay attention to the more forgiving gospel message of the Prodigal Son. In my family, God had become the harsh judge, not the merciful father. For so many reasons I grew increasingly uncomfortable at Manassas Assembly of God, and I started thinking about moving the family to a different church. Matthew felt ostracized by the church's young people, and Cheryl was longing for a different kind of Christian community to nurture her soul—one that did not impose exacting demands, strict conformity, and unrealistic perfection. She craved meaningful relationships, friends who not only accepted her with all her imperfections but affirmed her in them as she longed to do for others.

She found such a church meeting at the elementary school where she spent most of her working hours, where the incipient congregation of Christ the Redeemer Episcopal Church, or CTR, was renting space. In our circles, the Episcopal Church was considered irredeemably liberal and, therefore, unfaithful to the gospel. The Episcopal Church in the United States of America may have been the oldest continuous line of churches in the country—George Washington and Thomas Jefferson were both members—but since the 1970s it had taken on a distinctly progressive or what we considered apostate stance. It was one of the first Christian church institutions to sanction birth control and applaud *Roe v. Wade*. In the past, I had repeatedly thundered against one of its most famous bishops for denying the core doctrines of the Christian faith, including belief in the literal resurrection of Christ, for evangelicals the sine qua non of being a Christian.

I was shocked when Cheryl wanted to attend a congregation associated with all these profanations. Her decision left me in turmoil. On one hand, much of our early formation as Christians was in ecumenical circles that included Episcopal and other liberal church bodies. In theory, I liked the idea of being in a church that welcomed a variety of opinions on what I felt were not cardinal doctrines of the faith: whether speaking in tongues was a legitimate supernatural gift, what version of the Bible was the truly inspired one, or when and how Jesus might return to claim his people. The formalities at CTR were familiar—the structure of their services, the vested clergy, the weekly observance of Holy Communion. And as it turned out, CTR was thoroughly evangelical in its orientation and, as such, an outlier in the Episcopal world. It eventually passed my theological and social litmus test, but it would be impossible to justify our membership in an Episcopal church to my supporting evangelical pastors and top-level donors. I worried if I acceded to Cheryl's selection, the ecclesiastical grapevine would soon be filled with rumors of my unreliability. But my wife had found a Christian family where she felt at home and unconditionally accepted, and one that she believed would be healthy for our family. After Cheryl and the kids visited the church together on a weekend when I was away preaching, they were convinced: CTR was going to be their new church home.

It didn't take long before some of our donors caught wind of a change and raised concerns. Not that I had become a full-fledged Episcopalian—far from it—but that I had left the Assemblies of God entirely. Separating from Manassas Assembly of God over Matthew's crisis had induced me to look more critically at my overall church affiliation. It had become impossible for me to continue espousing the denomination's idiosyncratic doctrines, especially the necessity of speaking in tongues. Every year that I was a member of the Assemblies of God, I had to sign a form indicating I did not differ with *any* area of the doctrinal statement, and specifically on "speaking in tongues as the initial evidence of the baptism in the Holy Spirit." I just couldn't accept such an assertion, because it didn't comport with reality. Plenty of good Christian people I knew—including icons like Billy Graham—had never spoken in tongues, but they were clearly filled with God's Holy Spirit. I could no longer in good conscience sign the agreement. I needed to move to a different credentialing body.

While Cheryl's search for a specific congregation led her to the new Episcopal parish, my search for a new denominational affiliation led me to the Evangelical Church Alliance, or the ECA. One of America's oldest ecclesiastical networks for independent evangelical ministers, missionaries, and military chaplains, its tenets of faith weren't as narrow as the "Fundamental Truths" of the Assemblies of God. I was especially attracted to one of its bylaws, "In things essential, unity; in things non-essential, liberty; and in all things, charity," which would allow me to relate to a much broader field of churches.

My transfer to the ECA, while hardly controversial, was noticed, and two reliable Faith and Action donors peppered me with questions about why I had left my former church and demanded to know what church I now attended. One longtime and very generous supporter cried when she learned I was keeping company with Episcopalians. She and other benefactors began hinting at withdrawing their financial support from my nascent organization if I couldn't assure them I still believed and preached the truth. Repeatedly, I answered their interrogations and reassured them that I had not drifted left, and that I still believed the Bible to be the inerrant Word of God in its entirety. I needed to reinforce that my organization had become an important point of reference on Capitol Hill, and that there were still many battles left to fight during Clinton's second term. My defense seemed to assuage most of the complainers, at least in the short term.

All our big denominational changes coincided with Matthew's last two years of high school. His grades were good and he stayed out of trouble, even volunteering for a pro-life youth organization, but my relationship with him continued to be stormy. He always seemed to be testing my authority, and I often took the bait. I hate to admit that I was relieved when it came time for him to go to college. We had steered him to Valley Forge Christian College, a small school in Pennsylvania. It was affordable, and I knew some of the administration and faculty personally. With our kids in two fine Christian academies, Cheryl apparently doing well, and my ministry booming on Capitol Hill, I thought that 1999 was turning out to be a wonderful year.

In December, my ministry achieved a new level of belonging in Washington by purchasing a row house for Faith and Action right behind the Supreme Court. Putting down permanent roots at the center of Washington power—across the street from the Supreme Court, a block from the Capitol, and ten minutes from the White House—was a real boost to our credibility. Even though all finally seemed to be right in my world—better than just right—Cheryl kept asking me for a deeper emotional connection. I had no idea what she was talking about, and besides, I was too preoccupied with pressing national matters. As far as I was concerned, we had fixed what needed fixing and we could all move forward.

19

Murder and Impeachment

On Friday night, October 23, 1998, in the Buffalo suburb of Amherst, abortion doctor Barnett Slepian—whose clinic we had demonstrated against for years—and his wife returned home from annual memorial prayers for his father at their synagogue. He stood in the kitchen heating some soup for his dinner while talking to one of his four sons when a single sniper's bullet pierced a window, severed his spine and aorta, and narrowly missed his son's head. Two hours later he was dead. New York governor George Pataki described the shooting as an "act of terrorism," and Attorney General Janet Reno said the Justice Department would begin "actively investigating the possibility that Dr. Slepian was murdered because of his work providing abortion services" and that "the federal government would continue its vigilant defense of constitutionally protected rights to provide and to obtain reproductive health services."

Immediately a tsunami of blame began to swirl around Operation Rescue and especially the Schenck brothers because of our work blockading his clinic during the Spring of Life. In one instance Dr. Slepian had begged me to back off, but Paul tried to block his car as he denounced him for being a "pig" who spilled innocent blood. Slepian emerged enraged. I can remember his face and voice. This was not someone who was just another name. I knew Barnett Slepian.

When I heard the news, I was in New York City for a speaking engagement. I wish I could say my immediate reaction was pastoral compassion for the doctor and his family. Unfortunately, by then, my pastoral sensibility had been dulled by my concern about the pro-life movement and my reputation. I didn't ask what this would mean for his wife and now-fatherless children. A torrent of emails and phone calls from movement leaders convinced me that I needed to go to Buffalo to make some statement distancing us from this act. They urged me to do something publicly healing and do it fast.

I flew directly to Buffalo and twenty thousand feet above the usual distractions and demands, I started asking myself the hard questions: Who in our world would ever perpetrate such a horrible act? Was it possible someone under my spiritual care was an assassin? Our people put themselves in harm's way to prevent murder; how could one of them commit one? Had I ever said or done anything that contributed to this terrible event? Could I have prevented it? For Paul and me and so many of the activists around us, "abortionists" were not real people but had become symbols of the worst of liberal and secularist ideals, manifestations of a selfish and materialistic culture. But as I looked back on how my life had intersected with Dr. Slepian's, remembering our encounters and even our exchanges, I had a sense of understanding him. He was not just the embodiment of work I found abhorrent but, indeed, was a real human being who had been murdered by someone who claimed to be one of us. The implications were too terrible for me to fully absorb.

As the plane made its familiar descent into Buffalo, my more meaningful reflections were cut short when my old defensive reflexes sprang into action. I had a job to do and that was to control the narrative somehow, so that our anti-abortion work—and the Schenck brothers in particular—would not be connected to this vile act. By the time we landed, I decided to make a symbolic pilgrimage to the slain doctor's office, where an improvised memorial had already been created.

As I emerged into the airport terminal, reporters ambushed me:

Was I acquainted with the man who murdered Dr. Slepian? Was he part of your organization? Did I feel any personal responsibility for the shooting? The pro-choicers had pointed to our work in their attempts to assign blame. I emphasized that the murder was wrong, sinful, and cowardly, and that the Sixth Commandment was clear in its prohibition of the wanton taking of human life. I felt desperate to convince everyone that shootings or arson had no place in the fight against abortion. I wanted to be sure that none of Dr. Slepian's blood stained my hands.

On my way to the memorial site, I picked up flowers and contacted other Western New York pro-life leaders to join me in a delegation there. When we gathered in front of the modest storefront clinic, I remembered all the rescues, the calling out to pregnant women who still had a chance to save their babies during our numerous large-scale blockades. I recalled denouncing Slepian for the killing of unborn children and accusing him of murder. I watched him go from his car to his office door, climbing over rescuers deliberately inserting themselves in his path. I remembered his rage when we showed up outside his home—that same house where he would bleed out on his kitchen floor—and how he swung a baseball bat, smashing the back window of a minivan carrying our protestors.

Clearly what had happened violated the basic tenet we all held dear: respect for life was at the core of everything we did. But much as I condemned his actions, I could not condemn the man, who was a loving husband and father—just as I was. And a sinful human being—just as I knew I was. I knelt on the lawn and laid my bouquet amidst others. I thought of the prayerful crowds who had once assembled there and winced at some of our tactics. I would not accept any responsibility for the violent act of one madman, but I regretted, painfully at that moment, the incendiary language we used to get our point across and acknowledged the harm it may have caused.

The place where I was kneeling was not just an abortion clinic but now a makeshift shrine of mourning and loss. Flowers were piled atop the steps, and the door we had so often blockaded was covered with loving messages of sympathy and sadness. I bowed my head, confused and ambivalent, praying for an end to all violence, inside and outside abortion businesses. While the prayers I was saying in the aftermath were important, I remember thinking more about the optics. This was just what was needed to correct the perception that our movement endorsed this kind of violence. At the same time, I felt an unfamiliar but profound sense of moral culpability and grief.

Then I stood up and stepped back. I explained to a reporter that each flower in the bouquet I laid there was symbolic: a red one commemorated his death and that of all the babies who had died in his clinic, a pink rose was for his widow, four yellow roses were for each of his sons, and a single white rose represented the hope that someday God would end all violence. I had envisioned this modest ceremony as proof that, in the end, pro-lifers were reasonable and considerate. We cared—even about our vilest opponents.

It was as if I had pulled a pin from a hand grenade.

One columnist called me a "hypocrite and a charlatan." Lynn Slepian, the doctor's widow, later collected my bouquet, smashed it, and sent it back to me with an angry note. She blamed me for the violence against her family, citing the inflammatory language my cohorts and I routinely used about her husband, charging it had provoked her husband's murderer.

The more the accusations piled up, the more my need to assert our innocence grew. Nobody I knew would ever condone cold-blooded murder. We may have been a bit intemperate during the Spring of Life, but an unstable person could be set off for many reasons. Who could ever know what the murderer's motivation truly was? It seemed to us that the name calling, blame shifting, scapegoating, and false accusations against highly visible Christian leaders was part of a much broader pattern. We were under siege by the media establishment and others.

★★★

In October, the House of Representatives impeached President Clinton following perjury charges against him after he lied about an affair with a White House intern named Monica Lewinsky. Owing to the president's misstep, the folks in my circles could not imagine the midterm elections of 1998 would be anything but a wholesale repudiation of Clinton and his administration—a replay of what had happened in 1994. We miscalculated. The Senate voted not to remove the president from office, Republicans lost five seats in the House, and Newt Gingrich was forced to resign as speaker.

The official explanation for Gingrich's abrupt departure was that he bore the blame for the loss of Republican seats in the 1998 elections. But nothing is quite so simple. A year after Gingrich had lost his speakership, he divorced his second wife and married a former staff member with whom he was rumored to have had an extramarital affair. But it didn't stop with him. One after another, prominent members of our trusted Republican leadership demonstrated they had a great deal in common with the president they vilified when it came to infidelity.

It's a peculiar experience to be a clergyman when the misbehavior of people in the public eye is revealed. We're charged with being the moral center of gravity, an earthly authority on rectitude because we have devoted our lives to the Lord and, in doing so, are supposed to be above it all. Every day back then, it seemed, I was asked questions like "What do you think of this, Reverend?" and "Did you expect this?" I tried to be measured, talking about compassion, the importance of marital vows, how God's laws transcend partisan divides, but it was difficult to sustain the moral high ground of the Christian right and the Republican Party in the face of the revelations that many of our political allies were acting immorally. Whatever partisan triumphalism I might have experienced with Clinton's serial humiliations quickly faded with the barrage of embarrassing news that followed concerning the secret behavior of some of our luminaries. And yet, even as it was causing no small measure of pain and many accusations of double standards and outright hypocrisy, I was almost grateful for the period of reckoning that transpired during those months. It seemed a moment when our system might be purged of such sinful behavior and perhaps we could start again.

There is much to be said for public penance and atonement. I knew Clinton's excesses had become a part of his character, but similar ruptures of marriage vows and violations of basic decency existed on both sides of the aisle. I tried to maintain the façade of objectivity, pointing to questions of law, accountability, checks and balances. Inside, though, I felt differently. I thought of the families, the Clintons and the Lewinskys. I even thought of Clinton himself. I tried not to allow any empathy to enter too far into my consciousness, because the stakes were too high, but sometimes I thought that I had to acknowledge he was human like me. Who among us would have wanted our private, most embarrassing sins litigated by federal prosecutors, the United States Congress, producers, directors, and journalists? This all started to feel more like political retribution than anything else. And in private times of reflection, I was ashamed.

As members of the Christian right, we had dominated Republican politics throughout the decade, but we realized after Clinton was acquitted that our power and our values did not seem to be a part of any broad consensus. It seemed inevitable after the Lewinsky scandal surfaced that Clinton would be defeated, and yet he was more popular than ever, abortion was still generally accepted, and gays had made great strides into the mainstream. What had we done wrong? What did we not understand? "What has alarmed me throughout this episode," James Dobson wrote to his supporters, "has been the willingness of my fellow citizens to rationalize the President's behavior, even as they suspected, and later knew, that he was lying. I am left to conclude that our greatest problem is not in the Oval Office. It's with the people of this land."

Our mandate was to reverse what one of our revered philosophers, Robert Bork, referred to as our nation "slouching towards Gomorrah." We needed to redouble our efforts, work harder to mobilize fellow Christians, and make a difference in the next election. I relished being an underdog. The experience of being underestimated had served me well over the years. For members of the religious right, the Clinton presidency and impeachment catalyzed a period of taking stock; we had to come to terms with how we communicated our values and failed to engage the American people. For me it confirmed that I had made the right decision in coming to Washington. My mission seemed to be even more urgent.

As Faith and Action became more successful, and I took my place among influential figures in the Republican Party and among the religious right, my unguarded midnight thoughts became more uncomfortable. I struggled with how oversimplifications of difficult and complex human problems and actions were a convenient shortcut for me. If I could make them into binary equations—the right-thing-versus-the-wrong-thing, full stop—people and problems became easy to handle. But was that truly the way people lived? By morning I would tuck those pangs of conscience into the deep basement spaces reserved for ideas unserviceable to The Cause. Nuance, ambiguity, conundrums, even the once-hallowed concept of spiritual mystery neither motivated people nor raised the money necessary to accomplish our goals. No appeal letter that included lofty concepts about human frailty and tough choices would succeed. Decades later, that cheapening of the human experience would haunt me. But not yet.

20

The Providential Election

Given all our hard work in the Christian Right to establish ourselves within the Republican Party, many of us could no longer mask our disenchantment with those who appeared so impotent in Washington. Jim Dobson, for one, had even threatened to leave the party if the leaders weren't more responsive to religious conservatives and things didn't change. And yet, for me, perhaps because of all the turmoil, I came into my own during the nineties; my ministry expanded, my roots deepened, and my work became a point of reference for those on the right.

In only five years, our little group had gone from just an idea to an established organization with almost unrestricted access to the most important decision makers. I routinely attended social functions at the Supreme Court, and our monthly events in the Capitol were packed. When I sent out a news release, the media often quoted me verbatim. With only an hour's notice, we turned out record numbers of reporters and cameras in front of the Supreme Court Building, on the steps of the Capitol, or at the White House gates. Despite clear challenges, evangelicals—and, more broadly, all brands of conservative Christians—were firmly cemented into the Republican Party platform and strategy. When top-level operatives of the RNC met, they included me. At the Conservative Political Action Conference—the major yearly gathering of conservatives hosted by the American Conservative Union—I led a panel discussion. I was writing a book on the public display of the Ten Commandments, and many others cited me in their books.

I felt consummately able to handle any controversy, and I was rewarded for engaging in the fray. It was there I received the praise and unconditional admiration that fed me. When I entered my ministry world up on the Hill, with the people in power, my confidence knew no bounds. Especially during an election year. Especially when I had become so important.

My opinion of myself was reinforced when I was invited to fill a seat on the board of governors for the Council on National Policy, the most influential group of conservative thought leaders in the country. The CNP had been formed in 1981 by one of my heroes, Baptist celebrity pastor, writer, and speaker Dr. Tim LaHaye, who, with his wife, Beverly, had made such an impact on my early marriage with their Christian manual on sex. He was the author of the blockbuster *The Battle for the Mind*, an exposé of secular humanism that forcefully positioned evangelicals against what we viewed as the dominant culture. Having stepped down from his church to focus on political activism, Dr. LaHaye enlisted the help of Nelson Bunker Hunt, the Texas billionaire oil tycoon, and together they recruited the CNP's four hundred members who were the cream of the crop among conservative leaders.

Ministers, moguls, corporate executives, politicians, think tank scholars, and intellectuals joined. It was a veritable who's who of powerful conservatives whom I had come to respect and from whom I longed for approval. Richard Viguerie, the all-time greatest direct mail fund-raising genius; Paul Weyrich, the brilliant strategist behind the Heritage Foundation and Jerry Falwell's Moral Majority; and even Oliver North, Reagan's clandestine military operative, were all members. Add to these boldface names nearly two hundred wealthy CEOs, Fortune 500 chairs, and entrepreneurs, and the Council for National Policy was ground zero for the conservative elite. For a membership fee of $5,000 a year, which I eagerly paid, I was included in the three annual, private, off-the-record meetings, in which we discussed everything from the Defense of Marriage Act and anti-abortion strategies to military defense and a return to the gold standard.

It was at a CNP board meeting where I first heard about the possible presidential candidacy of George W. Bush, the scion of George H. W. Bush and the colorful governor of Texas. Bush was often complimented for getting Democrats to go along with his policy initiatives and soon began to win large numbers of mainstream conservatives and evangelicals to his side. The younger Bush wasn't the fervent pro-life candidate I'd hoped for, but begrudgingly I conceded he was our only hope for a morally responsible standard-bearer. Any hesitation I may have harbored was immediately dispelled during a primary debate when Bush was asked, "Who is your favorite philosopher?"

"Christ," he responded. "Because he changed my heart."

That cinched it. By now, not only did we have a true conservative, but we had a born-again believer with a clear testimony of personal salvation.

My publications in those days identified the sanctity of human life, marriage, the family, and religious freedom as important to God, to our Founders, and to us. I told provocative stories about life under Bill Clinton and the Democrats—how he aggressively persecuted pro-lifers and dragged them in front of a secret grand jury. How he instituted a "Gay, Lesbian, Bisexual Day" for federal employees. How he embraced liberal religious leaders over bedrock Christian traditionalists. I would contrast this iniquity by describing our Republican "brothers and sisters" who had weathered those storms. Steve Largent, a popular, good-looking, pro-football Hall of Famer representing Oklahoma; Helen Chenoweth-Hage, a tongues-speaking, miracle-believing charismatic who was the only Republican woman to ever represent Idaho; Mark Souder, the rock-solid Hoosier and quiet-as-a-church-mouse elder;

Tom Coburn, the pro-life Oklahoma country doc. They exemplified the qualities and convictions we held dear, and when I mentioned them, I could see the nods of agreement in the congregations where I preached. My approach was successful. Standing in the lobby after my sermon, shaking hands with parishioners and chatting, many would say something like, "You helped me make my decision about the upcoming election. It's clear Bush is God's man." I smiled with silent agreement, never having mentioned the nominee.

Of course, I knew if we had to, we'd get through another Democratic administration just as we'd managed Clinton's eight years, but we needed to bring in fund-raising dollars. By now I had engaged marketing and fund-raising companies that used the technique they called "Fear and Anger." One of our consultants explained that if we told people about our programs, we would likely get a little money. But if we instilled fear and anger, if we made our readers very afraid and very mad, they wouldn't send just a little money, they would send a lot of money. And he was right.

As Election Day approached, Faith and Action employees and volunteers planned for our "A game" should Bush win, which would entail a formal event at our new building, followed by various inaugural galas. If Gore won, we would implement our "B game," in which our deep bench of experienced pastors and street-level activists would be deployed throughout key areas in Washington to loudly and visibly denounce what we then considered to be the ungodly, militantly secularist, morally compromised future of the presidency, the executive branch, and the Democratic Party. It would not only get attention, it might provide some catharsis for our disappointed supporters.

Tuesday, November 7, began with a morning prayer service at our ministry center. Contrary to Jesus' admonition "When you pray, go into your room and shut the door and pray to your Father who is in secret," I put out a press release announcing our gathering. As television lights glowed and video cameras and tape recorders whirled, Paul, Pat Mahoney, and I convened a small circle of pro-life leaders, many in clerical collars. The room was filled with media, some supporters, volunteers, and other clergy. "Lord, let righteousness roll down today and deliver our nation by giving her your servant in the White House," I implored. There were many audible amens. Another beseeched, "Oh God, we pray for victory for George Bush, a man who loves and serves you. Use him as the chief executive of this country and commander in chief of our armed forces."

That night, pivoting back and forth between victory and defeat for our candidate, our prayers alternated between praise and lamentation, between A game and B game. For two weeks the election hung in the balance, mostly because of the way punch-hole ballots in Florida were counted—and for which candidate. House Majority Whip Tom DeLay, with whom I had developed a close relationship, tipped me off with details gathered by staffers he had dispatched to observe vote counting procedures in the Sunshine State. As the outcome came down to just a few hundred votes, lawsuits were filed by both sides. I knew the case was likely headed for the high court, and on Saturday, November 25, the clerk's office announced oral arguments would be heard that Friday, December 1.

I was determined to attend and thought that I might have a tempting barter deal for the chief of the court's police department. I told him that our office would provide facilities for the hundreds of people who were bound to be in line for the arguments if he would reserve two seats in my name. He agreed. By Wednesday morning there were pup tents, clusters of golf umbrellas, and beach chairs near the court building. The line would grow to over four hundred. I recruited two dozen volunteers to work three daily shifts, and my three paid staff members worked round the clock.

Early in the morning on December 1, Paul and I went across the street and took our reserved places in line. Groups of ten at a time were escorted into the courtroom. There had already been several court decisions regarding what was going to happen, but the one at issue that day was from the Florida Supreme Court, which had ordered a statewide manual recount. We listened to the arguments and prayed silently for Bush's success, sometimes holding hands. It was like staring at a coin on its edge: one side meant the grim continuation of the pro-abortion, pro-homosexual, liberal policies of the Clinton administration; the other meant a new beginning with a conservative, born-again Republican. The stakes could not have been higher for the country—or for us. That next Monday morning, when the justices filed their unanimous order vacating the Florida Supreme Court's decision, I wasn't sure whether God had granted our entreaties or not. The election outcome remained in question.

A week later the drama continued when the case came roaring back from Florida. This time I watched it unfold at the Supreme Court inside the office of the marshal of the court because the courtroom was filled. As I listened to an audio feed of the arguments, I saw Senator John Ashcroft just outside in the reception area. He was a superstar in my world. His father, Dr. J. Robert Ashcroft, was a revered academic who had developed several Assemblies of God colleges into credible institutions of higher education. I had spent time with then senator Ashcroft in his cramped Capitol Hill apartment while he played his favorite hymns on a battery-operated keyboard. But the election of 2000 handed him a defeat, and he looked forlorn when I came up to him and assured him that God had much bigger plans for him.

The next day, satellite trucks lined the entire city block, reporters did stand-ups in front of cameras, and police officers struggled to separate crowds of protestors on either side of the political divide. Evening had fallen and it was dark as I stood on the court's front steps. A news producer finally scrambled from the clerk's office and down front to his waiting correspondent. The reporter flipped through the pages as others tried to read the text over his shoulders. "Bush wins," he said. "Bush is the president-elect." The emotional rush put beads of sweat on my forehead.

All my hard work behind the scenes paid off with fifty tickets to the official swearing-in ceremony at the U.S. Capitol in January 2001. We invited many of our most generous donors and, under cloudy skies, listened to Bush's thoughtful, values-filled speech that spoke to what we agreed was most important in America: "That edifice of character is built in families, supported by communities with standards, and sustained in our national life by the truths of Sinai, the Sermon on the Mount, the words of the Koran, and the varied faiths of our people," he said. We applauded, some of us with tears in our eyes. At last we had an administration that would protect the unborn, strengthen traditional marriage and morality, and support religious freedom, especially our rights as Bible-believing Christians. That he watered down that declaration with politically correct jargon about the other religions didn't matter. We knew he meant the best parts. And, most important of all, we had a chance to get solid socially conservative justices on the Supreme Court. What a glorious contrast to the previous eight years!

Thus began the halcyon days for my brother and me, our ministry team, and our constellation of churches, volunteers, donors, and political allies. Evangelical and Catholic conservatives pretty much had the run of the Bush White House. Pentecostal John Ashcroft was picked for attorney general, and Bible study leader Don Evans became secretary of commerce. Tim Geoglein, a Missouri Synod Lutheran—the closest thing to a fundamentalist in the German Reformed Church—worked in the White House's Office of Public Liaison, which assured an open door to conservative Christians of every stripe. People like Jerry Falwell, James Dobson, Lou Sheldon of Traditional Values Coalition, Jay Sekulow, and Chuck Colson were regular visitors there. The new arrangement assured me of plenty of access to the administration. I led Bible studies and prayer meetings, delivered invocations and benedictions, and said grace at all kinds of functions at the various departments, State, Commerce, Labor, Health and Human Services, Justice, and the Pentagon. With Republican majorities in the Congress, the door to the legislative branch was also wide open, which meant that when lawmakers wanted to determine the moral underpinnings of a piece of legislation—like the Defense of Marriage Act, for example—they turned to me and a cadre of friends for help. I had virtually unlimited access to U.S. Capitol venues for our numerous ministry functions. Our pro-life gatherings, news conferences, panel discussions, Bible studies, and prayer services often took place in conference rooms, hearing rooms, and auditoriums within the Capitol complex. We held the keys to the kingdom.

21

9/11

When Anna graduated from Grove City College in May 2001, she immediately went to work at Feminists for Life in Washington, D.C., an anti-abortion organization unlike any I knew. Run by women, they weren't mired in shutting down clinics and challenging laws like the organizations with which I had been involved. Instead, they were focused on the practical realities of helping mothers cope with unexpected pregnancies. They rejected the one-size-fits-all approach espoused by the predominantly male leaders on my end of the movement, and provided resources, support, and guidance appropriate to a woman's age and life stage. To avoid the long drive to and from our Manassas home, Anna moved into one of the overnight rooms in our Capitol Hill row house in mid-August.

A month later, I was in our organization's Virginia administrative offices near our Manassas home, when my secretary rushed in to tell me she had just heard about a plane crashing into a New York skyscraper. We turned on the small television in the front office and huddled around watching as a second plane hit in New York, another slammed into the Pentagon, and still another hijacked flight was unaccounted-for. If it was still in the air, officials were speculating its likely target was the U.S. Capitol. My daughter was a block away.

I rushed back to my desk and called Anna's cell phone. She answered sleepily and I told her to get out of the building and drive east to leave the city. My anxiety and the urgency must have made me sound crazy, but this was a matter of life and death—her death. If the plane missed the Capitol by just a few degrees, it would destroy the building where my daughter was just waking up. The specter of loss, of her violent death, was terrifying in its imminence. Anna kept trying to interrupt me and I became more vehement. Finally, she managed to break through and ask what direction was east. Under other circumstances, I would have laughed, but the best I could do was take a deep breath, try to sound slightly less frantic, and give her directions. She crossed the border into Maryland as police closed roads behind her. Capitol Hill was completely cordoned off for weeks. With Anna safely ensconced in a hotel, and Matthew accounted for at school, in Philadelphia Cheryl and I spent the rest of the day as most of America and the world did: watching countless reruns of buildings crumbling; hellish scenes in New York, in Pennsylvania, and at the Pentagon; victims and family members incoherently asking about wives or husbands, and others pleading for missing parents or children.

My community was generally predisposed to the apocalyptic narrative of the End Times, so it had its own way of assimilating what had happened. There was some talk about God's punishment, about this being the prelude to far greater catastrophes for a sinful world. Jerry Falwell uttered what some of us, including me, believed back then when he told Pat Robertson on *The 700 Club,* "The abortionists have got to bear some of the burden for this because God will not be mocked." Pat nodded approvingly. "And when we destroy 40 million little innocent babies, we make God mad," he continued. "I believe that the pagans, and the abortionists, and the feminists, and the gays and the lesbians, the ACLU, and the people for the American Way, all of them have tried to secularize America. I point the finger in their face and say, 'You helped make this happen.'" I cringed as I listened, but I couldn't disagree.

Could this be the price for our immorality? Had Bill Clinton invited God's wrath upon us by appointing gay public officials? I knew enough not to express these thoughts out loud, but they were all part of the conversation out of the public eye. Eventually, Falwell apologized, and I understood why. Rather than join the public battle over rhetoric, I turned my attention to figuring out how to cope with this changed world. Roadways were closed, we could not access our facility on Capitol Hill, there would be no mail delivery—which cut us off from our main revenue supply—and most forms of public transportation were either not functioning or had greatly reduced service.

President Bush had designated Friday, September 14, as a National Day of Prayer, so Paul and I organized a group of pastors from several denominations to join us in leading a service outside the Pentagon, opposite the crash site. We positioned ourselves along a ridge that overlooked the collapsed south wall. I had visited the building many times for my work, so I had clear memories of what the devastated site had looked like before an American Airlines Boeing 757 with sixty-four passengers and crew aboard slammed into it. The building was still smoking three days after the attack.

Our procession of Catholic, Evangelical, Orthodox, and Protestant priests and ministers walked down a knoll onto grounds where helicopters were landing and taking off and where streetlamps were strewn after being sheared off by the plane's underbelly. Dressed in our respective vestments—robes and stoles of various colors, dark suits and ties, clerical collars—we stood there, the smell of acrid smoke lingering. Weary emergency workers were still searching for the bodies of Pentagon employees in the charred debris. We knelt, recited the Lord's Prayer, and laid two hundred flowers in remembrance of the victims. Passersby, reporters, and military personnel stopped to join us. A journalist who was among them later told me, choking back tears, that he hadn't said a prayer since he was a child.

President Bush, in his address to Congress on September 15, provided the context for the catastrophe, explaining that al Qaeda, which practiced "a fringe form of Islamic extremism," had attacked us because they hated the freedoms guaranteed by our Constitution, the very essence of our identity as Americans. He employed potent and familiar language in his public remarks referring repeatedly to "evil." This was a morally unambiguous term, part of the theological nomenclature; it resonated in my community. We understood evil in a broader context: Abortion was evil. Homosexuality was evil. Communism was evil. And now, we believed, Muslims were evil, too.

A consensus quickly formed among evangelicals: our Judeo-Christian nation was defending itself against a global Islamic jihad, and Muslims had declared death to both America—especially Americans of the Cross—and Israel, God's land and chosen people. Many in my community believed that all Muslims hated Christians and were out to subjugate if not slaughter us, after which they would impose Sharia law on America by way of a satanic and tyrannical worldwide caliphate. It was a dire scenario that soon became an article of faith. As with much of what was asserted during those dire days, I struggled to find some approach that felt authentic to who I was and what I truly believed, but the shock of the event, and the rhetorical excesses, made it difficult.

Many of my colleagues spoke about 9/11 marking the beginning of the End Times. It was only the most recent iteration of a recurring theme of fear fueled by a combination of apocalyptic narratives and xenophobia that preoccupied most American evangelicals throughout the twentieth century. First it was the Bolsheviks who would be the army of the Antichrist and engage in battle with the forces of good to bring a cataclysmic end to civilization. Then it was Hitler and the Nazis. After their defeat, the Soviet Union took their place, and after that, China. The Bible told us that hostile armies would always come from the East. Al Qaeda fit the bill perfectly.

My colleagues and I reminded our people that Jesus said to his disciples, just as they looked to the sky to see what the weather would be, they should also look at the signs around them for the imminence of the End. This constant state of hypervigilance, which in certain times and places looks and behaves more like fear than faith, has always informed the emotional temperature of evangelicals, but it was heightened after 9/11. And it would stay that way. The timeless words of Matthew seemed especially relevant: "And you will hear of wars and rumors of wars. See that you are not alarmed, for this must take place, but the end is not yet. For nation will rise against nation, and kingdom against kingdom, and there will be famines and earthquakes in various places. All these are but the beginning of the birth pains." Though I was conflicted about overwrought interpretations of such passages, I couldn't argue with them.

I had outgrown my preoccupation with Last Days, but nonetheless, they constituted the centerpiece of evangelical teaching for generations. Could the swarm of locusts in the book of Revelation, which are released to torment the people of the earth, really refer to the Muslim masses? I was in turmoil about all this speculation, but my universe was filled with people who took them as gospel truth. I had known followers of Islam who were peaceful, loving, decent people, but I couldn't dismiss what had just been perpetrated in the name of Allah.

The 9/11 terrorist attacks and Bush's response dramatically shifted my Christian ethical orientation. For most of my life, I was either anti-war or highly suspicious of the moral justification for war. I admired military men and women and was proud to bear the name of one who gave his life while in service to our country, but I was skeptical of those in power and their use of military might to impose their will on the world. That doubt was only confirmed in the book of James, "From whence come wars and fightings among you? Come they not hence, even of your lusts that war in your members? Ye lust, and have not:

ye kill, and desire to have, and cannot obtain: ye fight and war, yet ye have not." In my early Christian years, war was nothing more than the macro manifestation of man's micro inner sinfulness. It may be a necessary evil, but it lacked moral justification. Or so I had believed. I held that position through the Reagan years and even when we embarked on the Gulf Wars. But all that had changed after 9/11.

I would often remember and find solace in Bush's address to the nation the night of the attacks. He asked for our prayers, then quoted Psalm 23:4: "Even though I walk through the valley of the shadow of death, I fear no evil, for You are with me." Too often I may have considered George Bush to be wishy-washy, but he wasn't now. And if I had any questions about the rightness or wrongness of military action, I didn't have any after his brief message to the American people. He gave voice to the surging emotions inside me. I wasn't just indignant about what had been done to thousands of innocent Americans, I was becoming enraged about it. For the first time I desired the death of a human being, Osama bin Laden. Not only did I cheer Bush's resolve and our military's bravery, I buttressed it with moral and theological support.

In many ways I had begun to see George Bush as a kind of divine oracle. Given the way the election had unfolded, our president had become not just another elected official but evidence that God had heard our prayers. The sanctioning of his election by the Supreme Court was personal; it affirmed me, my community, and the Christian worldview. Bush's ascendancy was typological of Christian ascendancy.

No one knew or appreciated just how much I was shaken by 9/11. I was haunted by the images, the tragedy, the vulnerability of us all. But mostly I could not stop thinking about my daughter sleeping peacefully in our office building when only the grace of God diverted that murderous airplane headed in her direction. When she was still in harm's way, I had vividly imagined her death: what it would have been like to try to recover her body, the unfathomable loss, the inability to make up for the mistakes I had made. As much as I suffered in thinking of this scenario, I was also grateful that, unlike so many others, we were spared. We had another chance. I resolved to be a better father to both my children. A better husband to Cheryl. A better Christian.

22

A Friend in the White House

By January 2002, Paul and I had distanced ourselves from the group that had once represented our mission, amplified our public persona, created lasting friendships, and led us into serious legal trouble. We remained friends with Randall and many of those in Operation Rescue with whom we had worked, but the organization itself had deteriorated during the Clinton presidency. There were lawsuits and arguments about who owned the name, what the strategies should be, and—most of all—who was in charge. The organization's decline seemed inevitable. In addition to the oversized egos of all the leaders, mine included, there was simply no plan for the next phase of the movement, especially after it ran out of volunteers who were willing to risk the severe fines, lengthy sentences, and judgments levied against them. All the energy, adrenaline, singular dedication, and vitriol that once defined Operation Rescue was gone.

Our exit did not mean abandoning the cause. Our efforts to end abortion continued in Washington by our pushing for legislation, preaching the "gospel of life" in churches, and commemorating all the victims of abortion during our yearly events in connection with the March for Life. A repeal of *Roe v. Wade* was impossible; Justice Antonin Scalia, the pro-life champion of the anti-*Roe* Rehnquist court, had told us so himself in a private meeting. But we knew incremental restrictions could also save the unborn and, over time, possibly make it so difficult for women to access the procedure, they would have no option but to choose life. So we decided to join the mainstream anti-abortion forces that set their sights on a more gradual and legislative approach to ending abortion in America. That meant focusing on the strategic targeting of abortion restrictions—from twenty-four-hour waiting periods and parental notification, to more substantial laws banning partial-birth abortion and acknowledging the legal personhood of the unborn.

There was a lot of competition in this arena. Many similar organizations to ours were lobbying Congress or working with the White House on policy, so Paul and I decided our ultimate goal would be to inform the consciences of those in the judicial branch. There were no pro-life groups directly approaching the judges and justices who shaped abortion law simply by their precedent-setting decisions. We knew we were stuck with members of the federal bench—they were appointed for life—so why not convert them while in office? In 2003 we created the National Pro-Life Action Center, securing headquarters just one door north of our Faith and Action offices, putting this center of pro-life advocacy right at the nerve center of judicial activism. The new location became a beehive of activity as we invited several other large-scale pro-life advocacy organizations to move their Washington operations into our facility, allowing us to share personnel, resources, and expertise.

The trauma of 9/11 was quickly being superseded by the deployment of troops and concerns about security, but domestic issues remained at the top of the list of priorities for religious conservatives. That made those same issues important to the Bush White House and the Congress. As Paul ramped up engagement with the judiciary, our Faith and Action team continued its work with those other two branches.

The ban on partial-birth abortion was again introduced in the Senate, this time by our good friend Pennsylvania senator Rick Santorum, and passed in March 2003. The House cleared a similar measure in June, and after minor differences were resolved between the two bills, it was ready for Mr. Bush's signature by the end of October. The signing ceremony took place not in the White House or the Rose Garden but in a large auditorium of the massive Ronald Reagan Building. As I looked at the crowd, it seemed as if all the most important conservatives and evangelicals were there. President Bush knew exactly how to frame this momentous event. "The right to life cannot be granted or decreed by government, because it does not come from the government," he said. "It comes from the Creator of life." Bush was the most loyal and accessible president evangelicals had ever had. We had worked and prayed with such intensity for over eight years to put a stop to this barbaric and evil practice, at last we could feel that we were making real progress toward its demise.

Paul and I knew that in order to widen the breadth of pro-life support in the country, we would need to broaden our agenda. Being pro-life didn't end at birth but spread across life's continuum. We found the perfect example of this in the case of Terri Schiavo, who had suffered a heart attack in her St. Petersburg, Florida, home in 1990 and, ever since, had lived in what doctors called a "persistent vegetative state." For eight years her husband sought treatments that might bring her back to some state of awareness. Finally concluding there was no hope, he went to court to have her feeding tube removed, insisting his wife would not have wanted her life prolonged by artificial means.

Terri's devout Catholic parents vehemently disagreed and claimed their daughter would never have wanted to be a victim of euthanasia. It would be wrong to deprive her of nourishment when she was still manifestly alive, they argued. Litigation dragged on for seven years, and when a county judge ordered Terri's feeding tube removed, the Schiavo family hired Randall Terry to mobilize his pro-life network to stop the courts from interfering.

Paul and I worked intensely behind the scenes to move legislation in Congress to preserve the life of this young woman. The issue was not just the feeding tube but judicial overreach, the same problem we encountered during our pro-life demonstrations. We had long pointed to judges acting as super-legislators, reinterpreting and misapplying law, as the core problem in America. In many sermons, I had decried judges—especially on the federal level—as vestiges of the monarchy America broke from in the War of Independence. Our own attorney general, John Ashcroft, had reminded the American people that the early patriots emphatically cried, "We have no king but Jesus!" Federal judges were like fickle princes making and nullifying law with a single stroke of the pen.

What we called the fight against judicial overreach had become an article of faith for those of us in the religious right. These wicked judges were behind everything bad in America: they had ordered prayer and Bible reading out of public schools, yanked the Ten Commandments out of courthouses and state capitol buildings, and erased the immorality from homosexual relations. By now we had teamed up with Richard Land, the head of policy for the Southern Baptist convention, who announced, "We're seeing this in case after case, with homosexual marriage, with abortion, with the Terri Schiavo case. Are we going to have a government of the people, by the people and for the people? Or a government of the judges, by the judges and for the judges?"

Paul begged our friends in Congress to act, arguing there was no time like the present—and no case like Terri's—that could both advance the cause of life and limit the out-of-control judiciary. Two Republican leaders in the House negotiated a bill to protect Terri from what one lawmaker described as a "merciless directive" from a state judge. The bill passed and President Bush signed it at one in the morning. But all our efforts finally failed in 2005, when the courts insisted again that the feeding tube be removed. I went to Pinellas Park, where Terri was in hospice care, to lead a prayer vigil within view of where, we believed, Terri was being starved to death. She died on March 31.

I was outside the facility and when the news of her passing was announced, I fell to my face on the ground and cried out to God for mercy, a photo of which would appear on the front page of the *Washington Post*. But my feelings were more complicated than what was captured in that image. I wanted to truly inhabit the family's sphere of loss and fragile hope that something could have been done. But more than that, my major concern was that this was a unique opportunity to galvanize the attention of those who may have been on the margins in protecting the lives of unborn babies. They would care about Terri and by extension be brought fully to our cause, I thought. If I was sad that day, I was also satisfied that we might have moved the needle for life further than ever before. Terri's death was tragic, for sure, but there was something bigger at stake. While I was busy decrying the depersonalization of the unborn, I'm afraid I was doing that very thing by exploiting the situation of this tragically damaged woman.

★★★

Once back in Washington, I continued to distribute the Ten Commandments on Capitol Hill, but I was frustrated I had still not gotten them into the White House. There would be no president as receptive as George Bush, I thought; I just needed the right opportunity to propose it to him. We may have been seen as a constituent group important to him, but we hadn't yet made our mark with these stone tablets on the inside of his White House. Our chance presented itself when Cheryl and I were invited by two of our supporters to join them at a reception where the honored guests would be the president and first lady.

We arrived early for the dinner and soon found ourselves standing next to the president and Mrs. Bush for a photo. We engaged them in small talk, but knowing I had only a few minutes, I seized the opportunity and told the president that the National Clergy Council wanted to send a delegation to present him with a framed sculpture of the Ten Commandments for display in the Executive Mansion. He looked surprised, as if I had broken a rule by turning a social conversation into a business proposition, but then, without a moment's hesitation, he said, "Accepted!"

When the president's special assistant, Tim Goeglein, called to tell me the president would likely not attend the ceremony but wanted it to be scheduled, I replied with undisguised annoyance. Plain and simple, I was offended. We had done a lot to help George Bush; the least he could do was duck into a room for a quick handoff of our plaques. That I was incredulous that the president of the United States had better things to do was a testament to how inflated my self-regard had become by then. Nonetheless, I accepted the proposed date and asked some major donors, the officers of our National Clergy Council, and several handpicked pastors and leaders of well-known ministries to join me in presenting the president with the sacred tablets.

The ceremony was set to take place in the ornate Treaty Room of the Eisenhower Executive Office Building, immediately adjacent to the White House, where the Office of Public Liaison was located. I stood to the side of the Secret Service security clearance desk while two uniformed officers checked the ID for each of the fifty members of our delegation against a computer database. After they had passed through a metal detector, they were instructed to wait for me on the other side of a set of turnstiles. I had wanted to be sure everyone got through, and I was the last to be screened.

The officer scrolled casually to my name, then, with a look of alarm, stared up at me and back down at her screen. Turning to her partner at the desk, she drew his attention to her monitor and pointed at my name. The other officer rapidly nodded his head, apparently confirming the cause for her concern. I looked at my delegation on the other side of the security detail and shrugged my shoulders, reading this as a momentary inconvenience.

I was wrong.

She told me that there was a flag next to my name that meant I could never, under any circumstances, gain access to the White House. Tim Goeglein immediately tried to argue on my behalf, but there was no point. I had to leave the premises. I learned several weeks later, the Secret Service had placed the flag next to my name because of my involvement in the episode with the aborted baby at the 1992 Democratic National Convention. My "flag" would eventually be lifted, but only after a Herculean effort, my own Operation Enduring Freedom, which included internal advocacy from the White House and calls from several well-placed friends to White House counsel Alberto Gonzales.

The years of the Bush presidency passed as a kind of dream of achievement and influence. Having a friend in the White House emboldened me on every front. I now walked through the halls of Congress with an air of entitlement. I had earned my place. I mingled with Supreme Court justices, and more than one reached out to me for a private moment. I had penetrated the opaque federal judiciary, and sitting judges and their staff attended my regular prayer groups and Bible studies. I trusted our friends in public office and took pleasure in assisting them to achieve their goals as they assisted me in achieving mine. And yet this time of achievement also had its darker sides: the sacred became confused with the political; my own ambitions and arrogance contrasted with the claims of Christ on me for humility, kindness, and generosity. While I was contrite at the altar, when in the political arena I was thrilled at being a part of the modern-day blood sport. In these turbulent waters, Jesus would come to me, offering his hand and leading me toward a different path.

Part III

My Third Conversion

"Peter had to leave the ship and risk his life on the sea, in order to learn both his own weakness and the almighty power of his Lord. If Peter had not taken the risk, he would never have learnt the meaning of faith."

—DIETRICH BONHOEFFER,
THE COST OF DISCIPLESHIP

23

Amish Grace

By the mid-2000s I was on the road three Sundays out of almost every month, preaching in small-town pulpits anywhere from Florida to Alaska, Arizona to New Hampshire. Occasionally I'd slip across the northern border to conservative-friendly Canadian towns to regale congregations with stories of what a missionary does in the scandalous capital of their neighbor nation to the south. These stops almost always meant increased financial support for my work, but these congregations also relied on me to be their eyes and ears in the immoral swamp that was Washington. It worked both ways for me. Visiting folks in real-world America gave me a sense of the worries and preoccupations, the fears, the hopes, and the prayers of the people who faithfully sent me their $10, $20, $100, so I could do the work God called me to do. I never wanted to lose contact with these down-home evangelical Christians whose perception of politicians was a bracing contrast to my sometimes insulated life in the world known as "inside the Beltway." These visits were my opportunity to listen to and understand the priorities and the concerns of those who lived in what they were sure the liberals called "the fly-over states." This was most of America, populated by people who wanted their voices heard during more than election years.

A frequent stop on these weekend itineraries was bucolic Lancaster County, Pennsylvania, the Bible Belt of the Northeast, famous for its concentration of Old Order Amish and their horses and buggies.

My time there always offered me an antidote to my frenetic, frantic, and combative Washington world. Over a twenty-year period, I had recruited many supporters, pastors, and even volunteers from the Lancaster area, just a two-hour drive from my ministry headquarters.

On October 3, 2006, I was in my office when I got an urgent call from one of those longtime Lancaster donors, Glenn Eshelman. His voice was shaking as he told me five Amish girls had just been murdered in a schoolhouse down the road from him. The perpetrator was the son of a woman who worked for his company. The milk delivery truck driver had stormed into a one-room schoolhouse, ordered the boys out, and lined up the remaining ten girls—then, systematically shot them. Five survived, five did not. The gunman then shot himself.

I told my secretary to cancel my appointments for the day, and I jumped into my car and drove to Lancaster County. As I turned off the highway, the beautiful countryside was drenched with rain. My mind reeled at the thought of an act of such horrific violence happening in a place so serene and seemingly untouched by modern problems.

In contrast to the simplicity of their Amish neighbors, Glenn and his wife, Shirley, had created a state-of-the-art, two-thousand-seat theater called Sight & Sound Auditorium that produced live musicals based exclusively on Bible stories. Since the auditorium opened in 1991, more than a million people had bought tickets to see their shows. I arrived at the vast complex, usually a site of wonder and happiness, now the central location for those to mourn and try to come to terms with this innocence-shattering experience. Hundreds of Glenn's employees, most of whom knew somebody tied to the tragedy, gathered in the giant auditorium, many weeping on each other's shoulders. I offered words of consolation, then invited the grieving assembly to bow their heads and pray for the loved ones of the girls, the comfort of their families, the healing of survivors, and the family of Charles Roberts, the man who had single-handedly created this immense sorrow. I thought of my own encounters with this version of tragedy: the lasting effect of the suicide of my mother's first husband; the murders of two Capitol Hill police officers in 1998 who were shot when I was in the building; and the murders of Drs. Gunn and Slepian. It seemed to me that gun violence wasn't just a social problem; it could be a spiritual and theological one. I wondered if our community might be too cavalier about lethal firepower.

Glenn took me to the home of Terri Roberts, the killer's mother and his employee. Marie, the shooter's widow, and their three children had taken refuge there from the media storm. Marie had been at a prayer meeting when her husband was in the schoolhouse. When she returned home, she found four suicide notes he had written to her and the children. Her husband had called her from inside the schoolhouse, in a panic, to say he was angry with God because their own baby daughter had died despite their prayers. Marie called 911, but police were already at the scene.

Marie sat, pale and unable to speak. As it grew dark, there was a knock at the door: Amish elders, representatives from the community that had just been grievously injured by the loss of five beautiful children, stood outside. Terri's husband, Chuck, welcomed them in and tried to express his sorrow and contrition. They had come, the eldest member said, to share their love and forgiveness, assuring Chuck, Terri, and Marie that the community understood it wasn't their fault, and they forgave them. Chuck, a retired police officer, broke down sobbing and one of the elders took him into his arms and held him.

I had never seen such pure Christlike love and caring in my life— the nobility of these grieving men, still reaching out with compassion to the parents and wife of the person who had perpetrated such a heinous crime. I carried away with me that day a greater reverence for the miracle of God's grace and the power of forgiveness. It took me back to an earlier time, when Jesus' words more directly informed my conscience: "Blessed are the merciful . . ."

When I left Lancaster after attending the funerals for some of the girls, I realized that, rather than having done the Eshelmans a favor, they had given me an extraordinary gift. This was one of many moments when I stepped out of my familiar world and encountered Christ among us, in simplicity and humility. I spent so much of my time enmeshed in power politics that too often the balance between my Christian ministry and sheer ambition was tilted to a dangerous degree. I returned to Washington humbled by the compassion and mercy I had witnessed. The working of God's healing grace was demonstrated directly in the midst of this unfathomable tragedy by those who would have the most reason to turn their backs in despair. I contrasted this with the way I had felt during Matthew's and Cheryl's illnesses all those years ago, and realized even now that I would have a long way to go to approach the goodness of what I had seen in the Amish of Lancaster. I needed to find that level of grace.

I wish I could say I took those lessons to my mission field on Capitol Hill, but the compassion and Christlike care amidst the suffering in a little community in Lancaster County didn't translate easily to where I spent my time—in a cauldron of often manufactured conflict meant to score points for one side or the other. Democrats and Republicans, progressives and conservatives just didn't share the same sensibilities as the Amish. Sadly, or cynically, I could only justify my return to bare-knuckle partisan behavior by convincing myself Washington was "different," that the innocence of the Amish would be trampled by the folks who populated my mission field. Lancaster did cause a stirring in my heart, though: I couldn't forget the forgiveness, the acceptance, the human understanding and divine grace, the esteem of one human being for another, and I longed for it to be part of my own spiritual experience. My faith had in too many ways become something other than Christlike. Instead of being a conduit of unmerited favor and kindness, as I had learned Christianity should be long ago at Elim Bible Institute, mine was now a cudgel for beating ideological opponents into submission. I began to consider just how much politics had corrupted my faith and marred my Christian witness.

24

Family Journeys

After the election of George Bush in 2000, Paul had been keeping closer company with the Catholics who had played such an important role in our pro-life work. I suspected my brother was thinking of "crossing the Tiber," the expression for people who move from other forms of Christianity to Roman Catholicism; but when he accompanied Pope John Paul II as a Protestant observer during the pontiff's pilgrimage to Bethlehem, I saw it was inevitable. Paul's approach to living his faith always seemed more rigid than mine. He was drawn to the discipline, the hierarchy, and the strict liturgy of the Catholic Church. That was fine with me theologically. After all, Paul and I had both been influenced by Catholic spirituality at the very beginning of our Christian experience, but it made me terribly nervous for other reasons. When he transferred his clergy faculties to the Reformed Episcopal Church, a longtime and conservative splinter from the liberal Episcopal denomination, it was simply a first step toward taking advantage of a pathway for married Anglican ministers to become Catholic priests.

My anxieties about this transition were tied only to the fact that I had spent the last ten years building a network of fundamentalist-leaning supporters, both individuals and churches, whose attitudes toward "papists" ranged from cool to hostile. Catholics were seen by many evangelicals as being prisoners of the pope in Rome, obsessed with complicated ceremonies at the cost of a personal relationship with Jesus. Some bridges had been built in the pro-life arena, but the suspicion toward this church was deep and stubborn.

Paul's embrace of Catholicism would spell trouble with our biggest donors, who considered it a false religion that would eventually become an agent of the Antichrist to dominate the world. In a phone conversation, I asked him to reconsider taking a leap that would alienate many who had supported us for years, but he dismissed my concerns, arguing that the fundamentalists never fully backed the pro-life movement, and I was giving them undeserved deference. I was so angry, I hung up on him. I hoped he could just quietly disappear into the Catholic world, but that's not what happened.

In 2005, Paul formally entered the Catholic Church as a layman for a transitional period, before he could be ordained a deacon and subsequently, by special papal dispensation, a married priest with eight children. In an hour-long interview on the Eternal Word Television Network, Paul told his story of how he came to realize the Catholic Church was the true church of Christ and the bishop of Rome the true successor to Saint Peter. I was besieged by phone calls, emails, and letters from distressed financial backers, some of them furious and others in tears. They felt Paul had not only apostatized from the faith, he had betrayed them after they had given our organizations their money. Even our mentor, Pastor Tommy Reid, called to express his complete befuddlement. Many of our pastor friends felt Paul had put them in a terrible spot, because they had led many former Catholics to evangelical conversion.

I wasn't wedded to the narrow doctrinal concerns of my fundamentalist friends, for which they playfully scolded me, but I did think Paul's move was a strategic blunder. It caused a deep rift between us that set us toward separation. I began to understand more fully my father's reaction when he faced our conversion so many years before. This was my flesh and blood, my twin brother, defiantly repudiating what we had been and what we had built over nearly a lifetime. It was not just a professional affront to me, it was a personal one. Paul's move was a statement that the Christian faith of our supporters—and my Christian faith—were both deficient, much as my father must have thought when we considered his Jewish faith and the faith of his family deficient. I was supremely insulted.

Paul's conversion came at a time when we had enormous reach in the Christian community, so his actions jeopardized an otherwise hugely successful enterprise. By 2006 the parent ministry Paul and I had established in 1982 and its newer affiliates—Faith and Action in the Nation's Capital, the National Pro-Life Action Center, and the National Clergy Council—had tens of thousands of supporters spread across all fifty states, and even a few substantial backers in foreign countries. Our ever-expanding universe of churches routinely sent to Washington hundreds of pastors, who joined me in making Ten Commandments presentations and in developing and executing plans to advance our moral agenda on a national scale.

My role in other organizations was expanding as well. One in particular, the Institute on Religion and Public Policy, caught my attention with its effective track record of bringing an unlikely mix of religious leaders to the same table to tackle deeply entrenched conflicts between cultures and civilizations. The founding president of the IRPP, Joseph Grieboski, viewed religion as a little-used but effective tool for international diplomacy, an idea that aligned with my own about the efficacy of politics and religion working hand in hand. I was honored to join its board, but when Joe asked me to serve on a delegation to examine religious freedom issues in the North African Islamic nation of Morocco and to work toward an ongoing dialogue between religious leaders there and evangelical representatives from the U.S., I was more than a bit unnerved.

In the years following the 9/11 attacks, I joined many Americans in being afraid and mistrustful of Muslims. The hijackers had taken so many lives while invoking the name of their deity. It seemed clear to me then that Islam not only approved of such violence but that the Koran obligated adherents to undertake terrorist jihad against nonbelievers, especially Jews and Christians. Now I was being asked to visit a Muslim country, and it seemed a terrible idea. After all, the other members of the delegation wouldn't be conspicuous the way that I felt I was with my more Semitic appearance and Jewish last name. Plus, I possessed an Israeli-stamped passport. Was I really expected to risk martyrdom in Casablanca?

With great trepidation, and after a lot of pressure, I finally acquiesced. Our nine-member team flew through Paris to Morocco's royal capital of Rabat. To my surprise, from the moment we stepped out of the plane, we were treated with the warmest hospitality I had experienced in over twenty years of international travel to more than forty countries. Our Muslim hosts were kind, respectful toward other faiths, and open-minded. In a five-day whirlwind itinerary, we met with the prime minister, regional governors, and representatives of various nongovernmental organizations, including the U.N., as well as Jewish and Christian clerics. At times our commission strongly criticized the Moroccan government for its limitations on religious freedom, such as its laws against conversion and proselytizing—cornerstones of my evangelical faith—and at other times commended them for their expansive policies on religious worship relative to other Muslim countries.

The visit was such a success, I returned several times over the next few years and developed a warm friendship with the Moroccan ambassador to the U.S., Aziz Mekouar, an extraordinarily gifted, Westernized man raised in Portugal and married to an Italian-Catholic woman. I began to see my wariness of Muslims as unfounded and replaced it with an appreciation for the surprising similarities between American evangelicalism and Moroccan Islam. Both emphasized prayer and reasonable modesty in dress and behavior and shared a predilection toward assimilation without compromising religious convictions. They, too, respected the sanctity of the unborn and disdained homosexuality, two beliefs I held strongly then. I also witnessed the power of human-to-human contact and the wonders it can do to foster friendship, opening hearts and minds to new ideas. My Moroccan experience lowered my Christian defenses.

In fact, many of my other highly cultivated defenses were in the process of being dismantled at that time. Cheryl had become more deeply involved in therapy, and together we went to couples' sessions. For the first time I was examining closely my behavior: how it had dominated our lives in ways that worked against intimacy with Cheryl, and how it had alienated me in many ways from my children.

Over time, Cheryl was drawn to working as a psychotherapist and began attending workshops. One in Seattle was with Dr. Dan Allender, a prominent Christian therapist, author, and founder of what was then called Mars Hill Graduate School. Allender had created a community in Seattle that incorporated Christian spirituality with psychological healing. Cheryl wanted me to benefit from what she was learning under his tutelage, but I was hesitant. Dr. Dan Allender's avant-garde methods and sometimes provocative style challenged my sensibilities. In many ways he represented an emerging form of evangelicalism that my universe viewed with great suspicion. It was big on blending what I thought of back then as pop psychology with theology—a noxious mix—and it was soft on social issues like abortion and homosexuality. It also tended to favor the Palestinians over the Israelis when it came to the conflicts in the Middle East, rendering them an anathema to my hyper-Zionist brand of evangelicalism.

One day I asked Cheryl, by then my wife of thirty years, if she could do anything at all to make herself truly happy, what it would be. Without hesitating, she said she would like to study at Mars Hill with Allender. I surprised both of us when I told her she should—that we were at a place in our lives when we could do such a crazy thing. Allender's operation would never be my first choice for anything, but I was at a place where I felt a great debt of gratitude to my life partner; she had put up with my drama for so long, and I really wanted to do something for her now. I explained I would need to remain in Washington, but we could figure out a way to live bicoastally; it could even be an adventure for us. We had never done things conventionally, so her plan to go off to grad school on the other side of the country seemed tame in comparison to some of my antics.

With a joy she should have known at a much earlier stage in her life, Cheryl applied to Mars Hill and was accepted in the counseling psychology program. She was elated and eagerly mapped an exit plan from her job as an occupational therapist with the school district. We went on several scouting missions to Seattle, figuring out how we would live simultaneously on two ends of the continent. To balance the budget, we'd rent out our home in Manassas for the three years it would take for Cheryl to complete her degree. I planned on going west about every six weeks and staying for various stretches of time, and she would return east on holidays, for the summer, and during other school breaks.

We were both excited about our crazy midlife escapade, even as I knew that if it had been complicated for me to explain Cheryl attending college to some of my supporters, this situation might be impossible. But something was shifting for me—another turning. What would have set me off into a hive of anxiety five years before—the specter of her independence, her higher education, our separation—no longer bothered me. In fact, I found it all rather exhilarating. By this point I was more secure. Maybe it was the result of my spiritual exercises, maybe therapy, maybe just age and greater maturity, or probably a combination of all of them, but it was a good time in my life and in Cheryl's. We had worked hard to resolve some big issues between us.

And for once, probably for the first time in our marriage, I was letting her take the lead, perhaps for the first time in our marriage. In the end, it would require a little more than a year for us to get our act—and money—together and get her out to Seattle. But first, there was a president to elect.

25

Obama and Hope

I first opposed the candidacy of Barack Obama during his 2004 Senate race when my good friend former assistant secretary of state Alan Keyes ran against him. Despite being a resident of Maryland, Alan had answered a distress signal from Illinois Republican Party officials, who couldn't drum up anyone to run against the young, charismatic state lawmaker. A senatorial campaign in which both candidates from the major parties were African-American made it unique, but on policy, Obama and Keyes were diametric opposites: Alan supported the war in Iraq and believed Saddam Hussein was involved with 9/11; Obama opposed it and argued there was no connection. Alan said gay marriage was invalid morally and biologically—gay couples could not procreate; Obama believed homosexual couples should have the same rights as heterosexuals. Alan believed parents, not schools, should be responsible for educating children on the facts of life; Obama argued that schools should be involved. For Alan, the Illinois election was about transcendent moral principles: marriage and the sanctity of life. Obama seemed to me to resort to a predictable liberal platform of seeking the values we have in common and avoiding moral crusades.

Alan's bold and unapologetic challenge to the pro-death, leftist-liberal, "statist" establishment—now embodied in a fellow man of color, but with a foreign last name—made him a hero in my world then but a sideshow for mainstream voters. In the end, Alan was trounced by the young star. For me, Obama as a Senate candidate and later as a presidential hopeful was two-dimensional. He was pro-choice, pro-gay marriage, and against nearly everything that was important to me.

Senator Obama issued a statement acknowledging the differences of opinion about abortion but saying he hoped for unity "to honor the entirety of Christ's teachings by working to eradicate the scourge of AIDS, poverty and other challenges we all can agree must be met . . . It is that spirit which has allowed me to work together—and pray together—with some of my conservative colleagues in the Senate to make progress on a range of key issues facing America." At that time it was jarring for me to hear Barack Obama preach about the "entirety of Christ's teachings." Even though he used our language so fluently, I was sure it was insincere. I even dispatched a staff member to Chicago to visit the Obama family church, Trinity United Church of Christ, to check out his controversial pastor, Jeremiah Wright, whose leftist liberation theology was apparent in his preaching. I got all the data I needed to label Obama a heretic.

In 2008, without having served one entire term in the Senate, Obama announced he would challenge Hillary Clinton for the Democratic presidential nomination. I went on *Nightline* and stated my reasons for opposing him. Put simply, I said, he represented political positions inimical to God's moral will. I helped the National Pro-Life Religious Council compose a thick briefing book for our allies and friends to use as talking points against the "Obamanation." I realized we were up against a strong contender, however, when I tested the material on my own daughter. Sheepishly, Anna told me she and her friends all planned to vote for him.

Admittedly, our Republican candidate, John McCain, did not exactly inspire trust and enthusiasm within my community. I met with his advisors several times and came away wholly unimpressed, especially by their attitude on religion, which ranged from indifference to more indifference. Mitt Romney—the virtuous and deeply religious Massachusetts former governor—was my candidate. It had taken me a bit of time to make peace with his Mormon faith—which, in evangelical circles, had always been considered false and cultic—but I came to see how much we agreed on core moral tenets. I also liked him personally.

I traveled the country with Romney's campaign, sometimes visiting several small towns in a single day. I experienced a mind-boggling, full-immersion tutorial in presidential politics: the Herculean demands, the constant reactivity and vigilance, the relentless monotony of one small gathering over cake and coffee after another—each one a make-or-break donor and voter opportunity. It was exhausting enough to participate for just a few weeks; it was unimaginable for months and months. But Romney just couldn't best his rivals, and on February 7, 2008, I walked with the governor on his way to the podium at the annual Conservative Political Action Conference in Washington, where he ended his bid.

I quickly divided my remaining time between supporting McCain and blocking Obama from becoming the next president. Backing McCain was excruciating. His "straight talk" personality was, at best, curmudgeonly and often rude and peremptory. He clearly had no interest in the concerns of evangelicals, although his supporters, major donors, and advisors reached out and tried to persuade me he would be a great president—and not only because his opponent was so clearly unqualified. The title of his memoir, *Faith of My Fathers*, from his time as a POW in Vietnam, gave McCain's campaign the opportunity to cast him as religious man, but I thought it phony and cynical. He had also cleverly moved his church attendance from the liberal Episcopal Church of his upbringing to a Baptist congregation in order to telegraph to evangelical voters that he was one of us—at least marginally. I saw through the hoax, but it worked. Both improved his lot with my folks.

The night before the senator announced his running mate at a rally, one of his advisors called and told me to get to Dayton, because McCain was going to reveal that his vice presidential pick was Alaska governor Sarah Palin. When Palin entered the race, evangelicals breathed a sigh of relief. We already knew she had spent her teen years in an Assemblies of God church, was involved with the well-known and much-celebrated Fellowship of Christian Athletes, and as an adult attended an independent Bible Church, quintessentially evangelical. She was also solid on all the moral issues we worried McCain had no vested interest in, particularly abortion.

More than fifteen thousand people, myself among them, watched McCain introduce the governor as "a running mate who can best help me shake up Washington." The crowd went crazy. Sarah's husband, Todd, stood next to her, cradling their four-month-old baby boy, Trig, who has Down syndrome. When so many justified abortion due to abnormalities, I thought of families like the Palins for whom such a child is one of God's great gifts. I appreciated the emotional cost of the Palins' loving care, and it impressed me greatly.

After remarks by the two candidates, the McCain campaign invited me to the stage with other strategically selected supporters. I congratulated Senator McCain, telling him he made a brilliant choice and that millions of others would feel the same way. Suddenly this ticket was not just the lesser of two evils but the promise of something special. There was a great deal of talk among my peers about how the prospect of an evangelical vice president with a visible faith and clear moral compass could ease the pain of a less-than-perfect president.

The dramatic backdrop of the country's financial crisis added to the tremendous sense of insecurity my community felt about the future of our country. Small-town churches that I visited on those three Sundays out of four, were grappling with economic forces beyond anyone's comprehension. How could retirement investments have just disappeared?

How could the rock-solid value of homes, the brick-and-mortar se-curity that generations relied on, evaporate? What had happened to American leadership? In all my regular churches, ones I would see at least annually—in Illinois, Kansas, Pennsylvania, upstate New York, Alabama, and Oklahoma—people told me over and over how anxious they were about the state of the world and of humanity, what their chil-dren and grandchildren would inherit, especially as they were engulfed by the financial crisis and the specter of Barack Hussein Obama, whom they believed was a crypto-Muslim, running for president. These typi-cal generational worries had escalated into crippling anxiety over the prospect of impending eschatological catastrophes, religious perse-cution, Armageddon-scale warfare, and the emergence of a terrifying Antichrist. If the supposed Muslim Democratic candidate succeeded, it seemed that Christian America was doomed.

These voters were the consumers of Fox News, Rush Limbaugh, the Drudge Report, and an array of conservative religious broadcasters who diligently alerted my constituents, hour by hour, to the endless onslaught of dangers to our personal safety, to the welfare of our chil-dren and grandchildren, to the peace and security of our country, to our freedom to worship God, educate our children in the Bible, and pray in public. Obama's liberal social scheming and secret intention to institute Sharia as the law of the land would undermine all the prog-ress we had made in the Bush years. But we were powerless to stop his momentum, and Obama was eventually elected the president of the United States.

On the morning after the election, sitting in my office on Capitol Hill, I fielded messages and phone calls that ranged from grim politi-cal despair to real paranoia. A longtime pastor and close friend called to announce that we had just elected the first Marxist president. Then came the steady stream of other calls: about Obama's birth certificate, his Muslim religion, his shadowy background, his possible identity as the Antichrist—or at least *an* Antichrist. "He's going to destroy this country," one of my biggest financial backers lamented, going on to tell me Islam would now become the national religion and, in order to survive, we'd be paying a special tax as ransom to jihadists. While I understood why they were afraid, I never bought completely into the most extreme of their fears. I knew Obama had had two Muslim fathers, but I also knew they had been nonreligious revolutionaries—the opposite of jihadis. I also knew by now that, while Obama's Christianity was woefully deficient, he was a Christian—probably in name only, but he couldn't join a church and remain Muslim.

As I sat recovering from the wave of frantic phone messages, a more welcome call came in from a friend, Reverend Kenneth Barney of the New Antioch Baptist Church in Randallstown, Maryland. Ken was the pastor of one of the most significant black churches in the metropolitan D.C. area, and someone I had known and admired for years. He delivered the keynote address at one of our National Memorials for the Pre-Born, and he had even traveled with me to Morocco. I was always conscious that our politics were at odds, but we always agreed completely on the paramount moral issues.

After a brief exchange of pleasantries, Ken got to the point and correctly observed that it was likely not a good day for me. I acknowledged he was right. Then he solemnly pronounced that it was a great day for him. Given that we had similar views on abortion, on same-sex marriage, on the need for more, not less, public acknowledgment of God, this confused me. He continued to oppose Obama's take on these things, he carefully explained, but then went on to say why he was celebrating.

He told me that all his life he had been instructed that when in the presence of a white man, he was to look at the floor because he was not his equal. His children and grandchildren grew up in different times, but still, they knew some parts of their dreams would never come true.

Now, for the first time in their lives, their father and their grandfather could stand straight up and look white men in the eye as equals.

"That's why I'm celebrating today," he said, slowly and deliberately, in his rich baritone voice. "Today I am as much of a man as you are. I know you can appreciate that, my friend."

I was speechless. I never dreamed Ken and I did anything but look each other in the eye, but that morning I began to understand the monumental significance of Obama's victory for so many people of color. Until that conversation, I believed that because of my experience with anti-Semitism, I was racially sensitive. As a kid, I had been called a "kike." When I visited some congregations, there would be the occasional dig about Jews and money. In the South, I was once introduced in the pulpit by a pastor as his "favorite Jew boy." Still, the marginalization I had felt because of my Jewish heritage was mild compared to the crippling dehumanization that Ken and his entire people had experienced. This was a long-overdue validation of their very humanity.

Ken's words humbled me, and I told him so. From that conversation, the two-dimensional, dichotomized Republican-versus-Democrat, conservative-versus-liberal presidency would slowly become something far more complex and multifaceted to me. I had to face the reality that I had violated a core evangelical tenet—in John 3:16—that God so loved the *whole* world and *every* person who has ever lived, and that is why "he gave his only begotten Son." In all my work, culminating in my visceral reaction to Barack Obama, I had self-righteously questioned whether God could *really* love liberals like Barack Obama, Bill and Hillary Clinton, and countless others who opposed us, because their political beliefs appeared so patently hostile to God's moral will.

As I sat prayerfully ruminating, I came to the conclusion that, of course God loved all these people. Transient earthly concerns did not negate the fact that they were all wonders of his creation. But even if I could come to terms with the enormity of this realization, it was and would continue to be a solitary experience. The people around me had no interest in exploring, much less bridging, this gap between what we said we believed as Christians and what we practiced. Soul-searching was for navel-gazing liberals. God wasn't interested in our looking inward but in our looking outward, to the crazy world around us that was spinning out of control. I returned to Psalm 139, a favorite of pro-lifers because of its reference to the child in the womb, and reexamined what it had come to mean for me. Its ending now seemed personal: "Search me, O God, and know my heart: try me, and know my thoughts: And see if there be any wicked way in me . . ."

26

My Pilgrimage

I n the summer of 2009, my father had just turned eighty and was battling the last stage of the cancer that would end his days on earth. That July 21, days before my dad died, my brother asked him if he wanted to be baptized, and he answered yes. Dad had always acknowledged the existence of God, but he had his own theories about who, or more precisely what, God was and how human beings benefited from faith. For all the years we discussed religion, for Dad, Jesus Christ was one of those advanced humans in contact with higher dimensions of consciousness but emphatically *not* the promised Jewish messiah. The rest of the family—our mother and sisters—all came to Christian faith at various points of their lives, not because Paul and I set out to convert them, but through their own unique experiences surrounding the work we did. But Dad had held out until nearly the end. His baptism came not really as a result of an earnest pursuit of Christian conversion, but more as an accession to my brother's gentle cajoling. Dad was, ironically, highly risk averse. He liked to have a plan B for everything: he had had that Reform rabbi in the wings to take Mom through a quick and easy Jewish conversion to make peace with the family; he had carried a penknife in his pocket so he could cut himself from a seat belt if he crashed and there was a fire in the car; he had slept with a flashlight by his side in case he needed to lead an emergency evacuation of the family in the middle of the night. Paul proposed baptism in the same way. Why not be safe? If it was meaningless, there would be no harm done; but if it was not, what joy awaited him. Dad agreed and ritually affirmed his belief in the saving grace of Jesus Christ.

I believe Dad's baptism brought him a measure of peace in his final hours, but I cannot know for sure. He was never verbal after that moment. Only my sister Kathy and I were present in Mom and Dad's room at the nursing home when he took his last breath. He may have just been baptized, but we knew he would have wanted to be buried as a Jew. We all agreed, and Paul arranged for an Orthodox rabbi to conduct a traditional Jewish graveside service. I could never have predicted just how much I'd miss him and our lifelong conversation on every subject imaginable.

A few weeks later, Cheryl and I packed up the contents of our house and set out on a momentous road trip from Manassas to Seattle in our Toyota SUV, which was packed to the ceiling. We had to get Cheryl settled before classes began at what would become the Seattle School of Theology and Psychology but was known then as Mars Hill Graduate School. In three years she would emerge with a counseling degree and be qualified to provide others the help we had so benefited from ourselves. We hauled boxes of cookware and books up to the fourth floor of the apartment building overlooking Elliott Bay, a stunning stretch of Puget Sound and one of the most spectacular inland bodies of water in the United States. On a clear day her view was of a framed cerulean plain flecked with brilliant white sails and in the distance the snowcapped Olympic Mountains.

I had known Cheryl for thirty-six years and had rarely seen her this happy, a fact that brought me great joy. As a fifty-one-year-old graduate student, in her jeans and New Balance sneakers, with her backpack filled with books and a laptop, she was radiant. For her, every day at Mars Hill that first year would be a bounty of revelations, insights, moments of self-discovery, and intellectual, emotional, and spiritual stimulation. She would share them with me in long nightly phone conversations.

At first it was her exploration of "mystery," that place of uncertainty and unknowing that makes room for God. Then I heard about how the divine can be seen and experienced through human emotion, sexuality, the body, and community. These were strange and even uncomfortable concepts for me. Oddly, for all our evangelical denunciations of modernity and secular science, we were amazingly formulaic and demanding of empirical evidence for anything in the spiritual realm. This ethereal stuff Cheryl was talking about was far from where fundamentalist-leaning—even charismatic—Christians parked our faith.

By the time we got to the really big subject in our conversations, I was somewhat prepared. That came one night when Cheryl told me about a fellow student of hers, an openly "gay evangelical"—until then, an oxymoron in our lexicon—and how he was beginning to change her mind not only about gay people but about how to read Bible passages we had always seen as nonnegotiable condemnations of homosexuality. It was scary to venture out with her on such a dangerous exploration of new ideas, but by that point I knew this was a journey we would take together.

As if telling me about gay Christians weren't enough, there was more. She had begun reading the controversial early-twentieth-century "neo-orthodox" theologian Karl Barth—persona non grata in our world, because he refused to say the Bible was infallible—and she was beginning to see there was a large and accepting strain of evangelicalism outside our hyper-conservative community. Would we venture toward that world? I wasn't sure, but again could feel more open to the possibility than I had ever imagined possible.

Meanwhile, I was living in a tiny basement apartment in one of our ministry buildings across the street from the Supreme Court. For thirty years Cheryl and I had lived in two thousand square feet or more. Now, together, our new residences—mine in D.C., hers in Seattle—were less than half of that. Capitol Hill was a beehive of activity during weekdays, but at night and on weekends it could be a ghost town. As I settled into my little hovel, I felt seriously lonely and even depressed. Cheryl had been my constant companion for thirty-five of my fifty-one years. I had moved from my parents' home, where I shared a bedroom with my twin brother, to the Teen Challenge center and its cadre of residents and staff, to homes with Cheryl. I had never lived alone.

Slowly, I got used to my new routine, my melancholy eased and gave way to a kind of contentedness as I grew accustomed to my living situation, and I even began to like the newfound freedom of not having to report back to anyone. I came to accept and even to enjoy my solitude, but Cheryl, a born introvert, was way ahead of me in finding her contentment. Paradoxically, living the twenty-something life in our early fifties would help us both mature: in the therapeutic language that Cheryl was mastering, we were both separating and individuating so that we would return to each other as much more complete human beings.

We cobbled together a modus vivendi in which I would go west at least once a month, staying for two or three days, often including preaching engagements along the West Coast. When Cheryl could, she came back east. A few major donors complained about this unconventional arrangement, and some suspected we were concealing our path to divorce. One went to the bother of flying from Chicago to Seattle for a fatherly talk with me, telling me that Cheryl needed to withdraw from school and get back home where she belonged. He insisted our arrangement was not God's will. I thanked him for his good advice and told him, as I knew I would have to, that I'd take it under prayerful advisement. But the fact was that Cheryl's happiness and our new separate and joint discoveries were proof enough that we were exactly where we both belonged.

On one trip to Seattle, I drove south to Tacoma to visit my alma mater, Faith Evangelical Seminary, a small graduate school where I had completed my master's degree a dozen years earlier. When I poked my head in the administration building, I was delighted to discover that Dr. Michael J. Adams, the dean who had been so helpful to me in the past, had become the seminary's president. He asked why I wasn't in their doctoral program. When I told him I couldn't afford it, he responded, feigning offense, "Who said *anything* about money?" Part of my envy of Cheryl's earlier educational pursuits had been my sense of longing to advance my own intellectual life. A secret dream had been to complete a doctorate and join some of my ministerial colleagues as someone with the precious "Doctor" instead of just "Reverend" preceding my name. Dr. Adams was giving me that chance.

I felt a bit past my academic prime, but with Cheryl's encouragement I signed up and started immediately. The program would be a "Doctor of Ministry in Strategic Leadership," a professional degree that stressed concrete implementation of research conclusions. It was an opportunity to consolidate what I had lived and learned in real-life Washington about the intersection between church and state. The program required thirty-six credits of course work and a dissertation, a total of about three years—coincidentally, or providentially, the same length of time of Cheryl's program.

The arrangement was propitious, but on a practical level I had to figure out how to make it work with my day job at Faith and Action, remaining fully engaged with my ministry on Capitol Hill while devoting the time I needed to successfully complete such a demanding program. I sandwiched in the weeklong intensive courses, which ran from morning until night, over five-day periods. I enrolled in classes on "Integrity, Communication, and Decision Making" and "Missional Thought and Theology," and luxuriated in reading, studying, and talking about all of it with Cheryl. For the first time in our marriage, our professional worlds were intersecting and complementing one another. She was studying psychology from a theologically progressive evangelical perspective, while I was studying theology from an evangelically conservative perspective. It made for very interesting and mutually enriching exchanges.

My faculty advisor was Gary Waldron, a smart, well-traveled, easygoing guy about my age with a PhD from the University of South Carolina. His field was applied theology and missions, and he had worked for years in China with Billy Graham's son Ned. When it came time to pick my dissertation topic, Gary began the conversation in a surprising way by asking me who I wanted to be most like. (Jesus was not an option.) Without hesitating, I responded: Dietrich Bonhoeffer, the German theologian most famous for his description of the gospel as "costly grace."

I knew only the basics about the man behind that seemingly contradictory phrase: he bravely stood up to Nazis and boldly challenged Adolf Hitler. He had written a book that was a rare classic for both liberal and conservative Christians, *The Cost of Discipleship*, a guidebook for living according to Jesus' Sermon on the Mount. I had devoured it as a young believer. I admired Bonhoeffer's courage—to challenge the zeitgeist and suffer martyrdom. Initially, evangelicals had embraced Bonhoeffer's call to serious Christian commitment, but they soon grew wary of a liberally trained German intellectual, and he fell out of favor for nearly half a century. Then evangelical intellectual Eric Metaxas, a kind of twenty-first-century successor to Francis Schaeffer, published a new biography, *Bonhoeffer: Pastor, Martyr, Prophet, Spy*, essentially claiming the great figure as one of us. After that, Bonhoeffer was brought back into the evangelical fold.

The German martyr who had first caught my attention soon after I became a Christian was again present in my consciousness. Shortly after my experience with the Amish, I reread the first sentences of that seminal work, recently retitled simply *Discipleship*: "Cheap grace is the mortal enemy of our Church. Our struggle today is for costly grace." Even without knowing the full context, those words defined my early Christian life. In the first days of my faith journey, Bonhoeffer had reinforced what I was already learning: that I needed to be devoted singularly to God and live by virtuous practices based in the Beatitudes. This was the message that first drew me and was the motivation for my work with the junkies at Teen Challenge, with the *pepenadores* in the Mexican dumps, and with Hearts for the Homeless in Buffalo. This was the essence, for me, of what it meant to be a Christian. Or at least it had been.

I would need considerable help gaining mastery over the works of this genius, a man who had completed his second dissertation by age twenty-four. His brilliance was often impenetrable, but I found my guide in Peter Frick, a lanky, bearded Canadian academic from St. Paul's University College at the University of Waterloo, Ontario. Peter was one of only a few to work on translating the complete collection of Bonhoeffer's books, correspondence, lecture notes, and sermons. In email correspondence, he agreed to oversee my work. Soon after, when I was reading the newsletter from the International Bonhoeffer Society, a scholarly organization that preserves his legacy, I saw an announcement for a study tour of Bonhoeffer's life and ministry, hosted by Professor Frick himself. When I told Cheryl about it, she urged me to go.

My trip to Germany was scheduled for May 2010, but in late March that year a crisis erupted in Morocco. Twenty Christian workers, mostly German but including a few Americans, were accused of trying to convert Muslim children to Christianity. Under Moroccan law,

Christians could worship without restriction, but it was illegal to teach, proselytize, or in any way encourage citizens from the Muslim majority to change their religion. These Christian missionaries had been quickly deported, but the outrage among evangelicals in the U.S. was swift and their complaints to Congress threatened newly signed trade agreements that stood to benefit the Moroccan economy.

The Tom Lantos Human Rights Commission—established in memory of this U.S. congressman from California who was also a Holocaust survivor—reached out to me in my role as the president of the National Clergy Council and as someone who had developed deep ties to Morocco. We decided our best option would be to send a delegation of evangelical ministers to work with the Moroccan government to defuse the situation. Inflammatory words and statements could jeopardize the thousands of Christians who lived and worked peacefully in the kingdom. It took some time to convince players on both sides of the Atlantic to agree to negotiations, but by late April, I had put together a group of four other council members and we flew to Rabat.

Bellicose rhetoric from some members of Congress who welcomed a good brawl over religious liberty—especially with a Muslim majority country—didn't make things easy. When I suggested the best way to resolve the expulsion of the Christian workers was to sit down quietly with Moroccan authorities and work out a compromise, I was defying the approach my conservative friends favored when dealing with such assaults on religious freedom. As always, they wanted blood. There was talk of sanctions and other punitive measures. Republican congressman Joe Pitts of Pennsylvania, with whom I had shared many a speaking platform, practically declared war on me for fraternizing with the enemy. Things didn't get any better when we reached a fragile agreement after endless haggling with representatives from the Moroccan ministry of foreign affairs, allowing some of those expelled workers to return to the country.

The delegation headed back to the U.S., but I went on to Berlin for my Bonhoeffer tour. When I landed, I was already exhausted by what I had been through in Morocco. I was about to embark on a study of one of the greatest religious figures of the last century, but I was reeling from the intensity of the negotiations. I wondered if it had been a mistake to try to tackle two demanding experiences back-to-back. But then one of the other participants on the tour reminded me that Bonhoeffer had taken a study tour of his own across North Africa and that we would see his photographs from Morocco during our visit to the Staatsbibliothek zu Berlin, the largest research library in Germany. Suddenly the timing of a trip to Morocco before plunging into Bonhoeffer's life seemed not to be a separate event at all but an important part of a complex man's complicated life.

Bonhoeffer presented a formidable challenge to German liberal theology, but he was far from the theological conservative American evangelicals had initially embraced when they first learned of his martyrdom in the late forties. Over the subsequent decades, they came to reject him because he did not embrace biblical inerrancy or individual salvation, instead favoring the concept of a living, dynamic revelation of God's will in contrast to something static. He also subscribed to the notion of a communal redemption instead of a singular, individual experience. Worse still, he tended toward a universalism that suggested all people go to heaven, whether they believed in Jesus or not—something evangelicals could not abide. Despite my great admiration for Bonhoeffer himself, now that I was in Germany, about to spend the next ten days fully focused on him alone, I became acutely aware of the ideological differences I had with him. I began wondering why I had wanted to go on this trip at all. What was my purpose?

Bonhoeffer was championed by the left-liberal side of Christianity, and that was evident in the Mennonite, or Anabaptist, religious orientation of our two hosts. Anabaptists represent a pacifist wing of

Protestantism and generally eschew violence in all forms and on all levels, including the prosecution of war. Most Mennonites would be conscientious objectors, something many of my evangelical colleagues would consider cowardly. Peter and his colleague Professor A. James Reimer, of Conrad Grebel University College and the Toronto School of Theology, teamed up for this project. Peter had been born in Germany and studied at Tübingen, where Bonhoeffer had lectured. Jim grew up in a German-speaking Mennonite community in Canada's prairie province of Manitoba. For those ten days, these two "peaceniks" would be my spiritual directors. For many of my supporters back home, I was consorting with the enemy.

Notwithstanding all my internal conflicts, everywhere we visited, I found another reason to admire Bonhoeffer more, and began to note the dramatic contrast between his actions and the choices I had made in my own life and work. Although Bonhoeffer never had a family of his own, he was devoted to his parents and siblings. I could identify with the special bond he had with his twin sister, Sabina. He cherished the frequent family recitals held in the Bonhoeffer family home in the Grunewald neighborhood of Berlin. On those occasions, nearly every member either played an instrument or sang. Even during the direst periods of the war, he would joyfully direct the family ensemble, and did so until his imprisonment made it impossible. He corresponded regularly with his mother and father and stopped only when he was prohibited from doing so by his Nazi captors. When we visited the family estate at Marienburger Allee 43, the intimacy of the civilized surroundings evoked a place where a loving and united family had lived. If Bonhoeffer had maintained his family as a top priority while contending with Nazis, what was my excuse for not doing so for so long? During those years that had slipped by when my children were growing up, my attention had been turned elsewhere. Why didn't I realize then what Bonhoeffer intuitively understood?

As we drove through the grounds where Bonhoeffer had been imprisoned, Jim talked about the extraordinary deference and even kindness this unusual prisoner had shown to the guards, a quality that so touched them, they became Bonhoeffer's advocates by sneaking out letters and other communiqués to family members and church officials. Bonhoeffer's treatment of his mortal enemies was in stark, almost embarrassing contrast to my community's approach to our ideological foes: our unwillingness to even consider compromise. How was it that I had bought into the idea that the only way to be with your opponents is in conflict? What had I missed in my ministry formation that this long-dead German theologian had learned himself and later taught to the young seminarians under his charge? I'd been on the trip for only a few days, but already these questions I was asking of myself portended a huge change on the horizon.

When we reached Zingst, on the southern shore of the Baltic Sea, we sat in the sand on the beach where Bonhoeffer brought his seminary students for lessons. I could almost see his bespectacled form, cross-legged, a forearm and hand articulated, motioning his listeners through the Beatitudes. I thought about how he helped his students become consummate shepherds of souls who loved their charges, even when those charges raised their arms in the Hitler salute.

Each day we would read, listen, and talk about the life and work of this admittedly imperfect, brilliant, but sometimes obtuse young man who dared to take the words of Jesus in the Sermon on the Mount literally and then apply them to a period of unprecedented evil in human history. As we walked through the yards at Auschwitz and Buchenwald, I could barely remain standing. We were there for all the obvious reasons, but also because Bonhoeffer had learned of these places of horror before most Germans knew of them as a result of his work as a spy for the Allies. I could hear the echo of my father's observation, as Paul and I looked at his scrapbook, that the Nazi treatment of Jews was the ultimate example of "man's inhumanity to man." This was where some of the emaciated bodies were photographed. This was where numbers were tattooed on the arms of my distant family members. All the while, Bonhoeffer was in the background, praying, preaching, helping, plotting. He continued as a faithful Christ-follower when I probably would have given up.

On the last night that our study group was together, as we gathered to reflect on our experience, Peter read to us from a collection of Bonhoeffer's poems and other writings that he had curated and translated. "Every Christian needs spiritual direction," he said, and began to read:

> Costly grace
> is the hidden treasure in the field,
> is the costly pearl,
> is Christ's sovereignty, is the call of Jesus Christ.
> Costly grace
> is the gospel that must be sought again and again,
> the gift which has to be asked for,
> the door at which one has to knock.
> It is costly because it calls to discipleship;
> It is grace because it calls to follow Jesus Christ.
> It is costly because it costs people their lives;
> it is grace because it thereby makes them live.
> It is costly because it condemns sin;
> It is grace because it justifies the sinner.
> Above all,
> grace is costly,
> because it was costly to God,
> because it cost God
> the life of God's Son.

Peter closed the book; we sat in silence. I have made many pilgrimages in my life. I have walked through Jerusalem in the steps of Jesus. My two-thousand-mile FaithWalk to Mexico in 1988 was a pilgrimage focused on works of mercy. At Easter, every year for the last decade, I had carried a large cross around Capitol Hill, marking the stations in the Passion Week of Christ. And yet nothing I'd done had affected me like this. During that quiet moment, thinking of Bonhoeffer's costly grace, to quote Wesley, the father of modern evangelicalism, "My heart was strangely warmed." Dietrich Bonhoeffer became my posthumous mentor. As the apostle Paul adjured the Christians at Corinth, "Be imitators of me, as I am of Christ," I would follow this martyred German pastor as he followed Christ, as he understood Christ, as he communicated Christ.

It was like being born again—again.

27
Reentry

When I returned to Washington, D.C., in June, I had to reacquaint myself with the life I had led for the last twenty-five years. It now seemed unalterably changed. Each encounter with a lawmaker, an evangelical ally, a lobbyist, became an invitation to do things differently. The "we"-versus-"them" dichotomy that drove everything for me—from fund-raising to evangelizing—no longer applied. Reading Bonhoeffer and walking through his life—and death—had introduced me to so much, including his concept of our shared humanity. He helped me to see that we are all in this together—religious, nonreligious, Christian, Jewish, Muslim, or whatever other religious identity we adhere to—we are all creations of the same Creator. There is no "we" versus "them" because we are *all* "we."

I began to see that the world was not divided between simply pro-life or pro-choice people: we were all pro-life, to one degree or another, and we were all pro-choice, to one degree or another. I knew plenty of people who championed the right of an unborn child to be born and yet who thought helping the kids in the Mexican garbage dumps somehow hurt Americans. I was also coming to know plenty of people who chose to abort children because they knew they couldn't give them good lives—or because they feared, rightly or wrongly, that a pregnancy threatened their own lives in some way. Whether I agreed with any of these people or not wasn't the point. What Bonhoeffer taught me was that Jesus fully affirmed the humanity of everyone he encountered.

This new insight opened all kinds of possibilities. Could it be that evangelicals like me might find points of agreement with Barack Obama and points of disagreement with George Bush? Could we face the possibility that people in the Democratic Party lived out some Christian values the Republican Party had yet to discover? Could we find common ground with Muslims that perhaps we did not share with some of our own fellow Christians? And if God could use me in His work to help others, riddled as I was with sin, and filled with faults, couldn't He use anyone in His work? These were dangerous questions that challenged the most basic premises of the way we had organized the world.

I was working through some of them when, in September, I got a call from Pat Mahoney about a former missionary's plans for a "Burn a Koran" day to commemorate 9/11. Anti-Muslim rhetoric had been increasing in evangelical circles and online, including on a website that was gaining popularity: Breitbart News. Randall Terry announced he would stand in front of the White House on the anniversary of September 11 and tear pages from the Koran; and Baptist pastor Terry Jones, of the ironically named Dove World Outreach Center in Gainesville, Florida, announced he would create his own "Ground Zero Mosque" by burning a tower of Korans. This would be his way of defying and insulting the Muslims he perceived to have celebrated the terror attacks of 2001. As the hours ticked on, publicity surrounding Jones was increasing and his intended conflagration was becoming more and more dangerous.

Pat and I were deeply distressed about Jones's plans, and we had already decided to denounce him publicly, when a State Department official called to ask if there was anything I could do to get this guy to back down. The worldwide consequences, both to the diplomatic progress made between the U.S. and various Muslim-majority countries, and to humanitarian aid workers in places like Pakistan, could be devastating. My own concerns centered as much on the fragile relationships between ancient Christian communities and their Muslim neighbors in places like Iraq as on the welfare of expatriate Christian workers ministering in sensitive areas.

Pat and I decided to go to Gainesville and directly appeal to Pastor Jones. On September 9, I called the Dove World Outreach Center to explore the possibility of a meeting. I was told that if Pat and I came, the pastor might see us—if he had time—but there would be no guarantees. We arrived on the tenth and were met at the front door of the church by armed volunteers, one with a rifle and two with handguns strapped on their belts. It was my first real glimpse of passionate evangelicalism intertwined so grotesquely with extreme nationalism. The black-garbed, armed security assumed a paramilitary stance. They seemed unsure of whether to let us in. Finally, a woman stepped to the door, pointed to me, and said, "Just you." I turned to Pat, confused, but followed their directions to enter. "I'll be waiting out here," Pat said, adding his typically mordant humor by saying, "If you survive." Given how I was struggling just to control my anxiety, I couldn't even manage a smile.

Once inside the church, armed escorts led me through hallways bedecked with American flags and other patriotic symbols. I was taken into Jones's office, where two more armed guards stood at attention. I was seated silently at a desk, facing a wooden nameplate with "Pastor Terry" carved into it. Several minutes passed before a side door to the office popped open and Pastor Jones, with his graying mustache, wrinkled T-shirt, and shorts, sat down, plopped a large revolver on the metal desk, and asked with a tinge of sarcasm, "Brother, what do you want here?"

I thought of Bonhoeffer and summoned within me the will to respect this man and hope that he might return the sentiment before things went awry. I explained that I had come because his intended actions would place many of our fellow Christians in grave danger; that it would set back decades of work by missionaries around the world, certainly closing off Muslims from ever listening to the gospel. I tried to appeal to the Christian within him, who should have wanted to convert those who could still be saved. He said very little, shook his head disapprovingly, then abruptly stood up, took his gun, thanked me for visiting, and muttered that he would pray about it. His bodyguards then led me out of the building. Was this a resolution? I couldn't be sure. But I somehow felt that of all the things that could have happened—of all the reactions that could have escalated the already difficult situation—this at least left the door open a crack for a peaceful resolution.

The story about this preacher and his plans to set Korans on fire had attracted a great deal of media attention, so Pat and I held a news conference on the front lawn of the church, a few paces from where the pyre was to be built. I told reporters I was hopeful the pastor would do the right thing and call off his dangerous stunt, but my meeting with him had been inconclusive. Then we headed for the airport to return home. On the way, we heard the news Jones had "suspended" his plans to burn the Korans the next morning, but, given his strange and unpredictable personality, we didn't trust him. I called to ask Jones to surrender to me the 225 Korans he had collected as a show of good faith. To my surprise, he agreed. Because I had to be back in D.C. for meetings the next day, Pat remained to claim the books from Jones and take them into safekeeping. As I headed for my gate at the airport, Pat rented a car; he later filled it with the holy books and drove them to a UPS Store, where they were packed and shipped to our ministry center in Washington.

In my office display cabinet, I have the small paperback Koran that topped the pile to be burned that day. Scrawled angrily in permanent black marker across its cover and along its edge are the words "Burn

This Book!" I often glance at it. It is almost as if the book cover itself contains a straight trajectory from my father's World War II scrapbook to the experience I had in Germany studying Bonhoeffer, right up to my encounter with Pastor Jones. Burning books had historically been the actions of fascists and thugs, and to see a sacred text with that hateful message, written under the orders of a man purporting to be a follower of Christ, was chilling. It brought to mind the ominous events that presaged the Nazi atrocities, and that they could, indeed, happen on our own shores. Even though Jones and his planned Koran burning proved one of only a few such incidents, the warning was clear: no nation, no culture, no people is immune to such extreme acts of contempt by one group for another. "Man's inhumanity to man" could happen at any time and in any place. That book in my display case would be a reminder to me of the importance of the sentiment that is fittingly inscribed at the entrance of the National Archives in Washington: "Eternal vigilance is the price of liberty."

$$\star\star\star$$

By the fall of 2010, I was watching a big realignment in the evangelical world. My longtime patron, D. James Kennedy, as well as Jerry Falwell and Paul Weyrich, had all passed away; Chuck Colson would die within two years of Obama taking office. Jim Dobson would step down from Focus on the Family, and Beverly LaHaye was no longer at Concerned Women for America. All around me, during Obama's first years, people were lamenting that we might have lost the war for traditional values.

Although I was going through a personal and very private philosophical realignment, my job was still to champion the issues that remained at the center of evangelical social concerns: ending abortion, preventing the legalization of gay marriage, and protecting the right of churches and religious organizations to remain insulated from government intrusion. The 2010 midterm elections and rise of the Tea Party proved there was still a robust and effective group of voters who cared about these things. Tea Partiers were overwhelmingly white evangelical Protestants and most of them fully supported the Christian conservative movement. In other words, they were a huge group of potential allies to our cause. Because I didn't know what else to do, I reached out and established strong relationships with them.

As all this change in the evangelical landscape was happening, I had to continue with my studies. I had a dissertation to write and my time was running out. During a visit to Toronto to address the Canadian chapter of the Evangelical Church Alliance, Peter met up with me to discuss my progress. He was an academic good cop/bad cop all in one, asking bluntly if I intended to master mid-twentieth-century German. If not, Peter cautioned, I couldn't write on Bonhoeffer.

I was crushed. I knew Peter was right, but I didn't know what other subject I could tackle so late in the process. I wanted to master Bonhoeffer as best I could and fully incorporate his insights into my own work. I knew my ministry, along with scores of other much larger and influential groups, was flirting with a kind of Christian nationalism that portended the collapse of our theological integrity and the disappearance of the human compassion that once characterized evangelicalism. From the founding of Harvard and Yale to the abolitionist movement and the humanitarian work of the Salvation Army, evangelicals once contributed energetically to the betterment of society. Since the 1980s, though, our message had become overwhelmingly political and more narrow and self-interested, the opposite of the gospel's.

My disappointing conversation with Peter about my dissertation left me stumped. If not Bonhoeffer, then what? Peter, fortunately, offered a compelling alternative. What if I looked at what made Bonhoeffer what he was—specifically what was happening in the German churches at the time? I understood his idea immediately. This was a manageable undertaking that intersected with my concerns over the nationalist drift among our evangelical churches. I took his advice and turned the direction of my research to what is known as "the German Church Crisis."

I did a whirlwind tour of the country to meet with experts on German churches during the Nazi era. One of them was United Methodist minister Steve Martin—not the comedian but a filmmaker—who had produced a series of short documentaries on the *Kirchenkampf*, or struggle of the churches during Nazism. I noted that the official state-sanctioned denomination of the period was the *Evangelische Kirche*, or "Evangelical Church." It wasn't exactly what "evangelical" was in the United States, but very close. Many of the churches that were part of my network shared strong and deep common roots with the German churches of the Reformation.

It was out of the *Evangelische Kirche* that another, ultraconservative, racialized, and highly politicized movement grew, the *Deutsche Christen*, or "German Christians." I dove deep into this part of evangelical history and was appalled by what I found: one of the most famous of evangelical theologians of that day was Paul Althaus, a man who celebrated Hitler's rise to power as "a gift and miracle from God." A pastoral letter read from all the evangelical churches of Bavaria included this encomium for the new Nazi government: "With thanks and joy the church perceives how the new state protects against blasphemy, represses immorality, upholds discipline and orderliness with a stronger hand. It calls for fear of God, holds marriage holy, wants to know that youth are spiritually educated, and it brings the role of the fathers once again into honor . . ."

Sitting at a table in the musty basement library at Faith Seminary in Tacoma, I pored over documents from the era, deeply disturbed by their familiar ring. The American evangelical churches had never endorsed anything as ghastly as the mass-murderous Nazi regime, but there was a thread running through its story that had a recognizable color and texture. As I pulled on that thread, it led to a conclusion: the American churches I had kept company with shared a common genetic disease with the German evangelical churches of the 1930s. We, like our forebears, had traded the supreme lordship of Jesus Christ for the demigods of political and social potentates. For the Germans, that demigod was Adolf Hitler and his henchmen, including the despicable Bishop Ludwig Müller, who gave Hitler all the religious cover he needed. For Americans, the same Faustian pact had been consummated with any number of political personalities, and most certainly with the Republican Party. We also had our Müllers who provided a spiritual veneer for the party and its leadership, making it more palatable to the pastors in our pulpits.

This was not the conclusion I had expected to reach in my doctoral work. I had set out to simply examine a brave and moral spiritual leader who dared to challenge one of the most dangerously anti-Christian and anti-human political juggernauts in history. Instead, I had located the troubled heart of my own church and my own party. As I read more on the German crisis and consulted with a wide variety of experts on the history of evangelicalism, Christian ethics, and the politicization of American churches, I developed an informal thesis: American evangelicals were on the brink of a moral disaster, as our pastors and other leaders lacked the theological tools to protect them from being cynically exploited by politically motivated actors.

The similarity with the Nazification of the German evangelical churches—and specifically its pastors—was breathtaking. I had already been in churches where the American flag had replaced the cross as the most prominent symbol in the sanctuary, something eerily reminiscent of when the German Christians draped their altars with their patriotic symbol, the swastika. In other churches, I had heard patriotic songs being sung in place of biblically themed worship choruses and theologically rich hymns, and even one where the pastor told me he was careful to always preach in a "Ronald Reagan suit" with crisply pressed shirts and Ronald Reagan cuff links. "He was always my role model," the pastor explained. I remember thinking, *Shouldn't our role model be Jesus?*

Admittedly, these were exaggerated manifestations of the problem. It mostly showed itself in subtle ways—in the idea that a Christian could only be Republican, or that tax increases violated the commandment against stealing. The kernel of the problem was that evangelicals were no longer deriving their value system from the Bible, historic Christian teaching, evangelical doctrine, or, most importantly, the words and actions of Jesus Christ, but instead from the pronouncements of political personalities and a particular political party. The cornerstone of evangelical belief had always been one's personal profession of Jesus Christ as Lord: "If you confess with your mouth that Jesus is Lord and believe in your heart that God raised him from the dead, you will be saved." To make Jesus the Lord of one's life means to make him the last word on whatever you believe and how you are to practice that belief. Our folks had gotten this all muddled with our allegiance to political platforms. The German Christians had traded Jesus Christ for Adolf Hitler and the church for the Nazi Party; we had done something similar with Ronald Reagan and the Republican Party. The consequences were different, but the error was the same.

After discussing my unwelcome revelation with my advisors, I took a leave of absence from Faith and Action and went to Seattle to write my dissertation, entitled "Bulwark Against Political Idolatry: The Necessity of a Theology of Church and State for American Evangelical Pastors." I asserted that American evangelicals were vulnerable to committing the egregious sins of idolatry, substituting, to use Bonhoefferian terms, the penultimate for the ultimate. German evangelical churches committed the sin when they accepted the Nazi Party and

Adolf Hitler and their guiding values of "blood and soil," or race and patriotism. These were the vehicles with which to interpret and understand their religion and their moral, ethical, and social standards. The result was a near-complete politicization of Christianity in Germany. Instead of being, as Karl Barth called the church, "the conscience of the state," the German church had become the tool of the state, helping to pave the way for the moral catastrophe that was both the war and the Holocaust. In my work, I pointed to a similar danger of demoralization in the incremental politicization of American evangelicalism that I had both witnessed and enabled for nearly thirty years.

When my committee accepted my work and granted my doctorate, I was relieved to learn they wouldn't be publishing my dissertation on any of the academic databases. I had written it as honestly as I have ever written anything in my life, but I was terrified my critique of my own community would be perceived as a career-ending act of betrayal. I may have had a better understanding of my people, but I was still afraid of them. They held enormous power over my life—financial, political, and emotional. As further proof of how far we had drifted from the gospel of grace and forgiveness, our community had a history of punishing political defectors, and my dissertation could be perceived as evidence that I was one. I could expect financial backers to pull away, pastors to stop inviting me to preach in their pulpits, and old allies to shun me.

Cheryl's and my shared time of study was drawing to a close, and the intellectual, emotional, and even religious changes we each had experienced over those three years were momentous. As a married couple, we were closer than ever; our vows had been joyfully renewed by the experience. I fell in love with Cheryl all over again—and in a new way. For the first time since the early years of our marriage, I really saw—and appreciated—her not only as equal to me in many of the most important things, but in still other ways, such as how she exceeded my abilities—especially academically and in emotional intelligence. I no longer found these qualities about Cheryl threatening. Thirty-five years into our marriage, we were finding a new way of being with one another. It was exciting. Still, as we had changed together, I wondered how I would function in my old circumstances. Would I be attempting to fit into a wardrobe I had long ago outgrown?

In the summer of 2012, after Cheryl received her master's degree, we returned to Washington, D.C., just in time for me to dive into another presidential campaign, this time for Mitt Romney, who had secured the nomination. In my own mind and heart, I had to recalibrate my approach to politics. Instead of demanding that Romney adopt the entirety of our evangelical suite of social policy demands as well as our religious jargon, as I had the first time around with him, I encouraged him to be authentic, and I wanted my people to judge him on that basis. This campaign was also a time for me to help my community mature to the point where they could honor his religious beliefs instead of demanding that he embrace ours. I campaigned for him, but even before the primaries began, in December 2011, I wrote a letter to Christians in Iowa that signaled how much I had changed. I urged them to reconsider religious beliefs as the most important factor in their choice of a 2012 presidential candidate: "We should pick our candidates for president in the same way we pick our doctors—on their skills, experience, reputation, and approach to our problems." I went so far as to say, "Evangelical doctrine is not a litmus test" of whether a candidate will be a successful and effective president.

It may not have changed many minds, but for me, this was the first step into a new era.

28

Guns

In late spring of 2013, only a few months after the horrific murder of twenty schoolchildren and six adults at Sandy Hook Elementary School in Newtown, Connecticut, I received an email from Katharine Rhodes Henderson, a seminary president in New York. She was ordained a Presbyterian minister, but Katharine may as well have been from the other end of the religious galaxy. Her institution, Auburn Seminary, was known in my community as one of the furthest to the left in the Christian world; in fact, most of my colleagues would not have considered Auburn to be even remotely Christian because it had no specific "statement of faith," much less a distinctly Christian one. Instead, the school's statement on "Mission, Vision, and Values" said nothing about the Bible, Jesus Christ, the Resurrection, or heaven and hell but did employ words and phrases like "multi-faith," "justice," "dignity and humanity," and, worst of all, "well-being of the planet." These were all taboo terms in the religious right— code words for a new regime that was at least pagan if not satanic in origin.

Katharine knew about my work and had originally reached out to me as part of her school's ongoing mission to build bridges of understanding between groups that were otherwise alienated from each other—another suspicious activity in my old universe. When we had first met, I officially represented a camp that was both estranged from and hostile to her progressive community. A few years before that, I never would have accepted her invitation, but after my doctoral work and subsequent reorientation in my understanding of the gospel, I was as interested in listening to her as she was in listening to me. When we had met at my office in March 2013, she and I had gotten along well and discovered a common language of faith. In this latest email, she asked if I would speak with a friend of hers, a documentary filmmaker named Abigail Disney, who was exploring the role of guns in evangelical culture and focusing on the question: "How can one be pro-life, yet also pro-gun?" Disney and her producer were in Washington, and Katharine hoped I could meet up with them for a short conversation.

Happy to cooperate with what I thought was one of Katharine's projects, I arranged to meet Ms. Disney and her colleague at Union Station, the city's main rail depot. As I walked the few blocks from our offices, I passed many places that held special memories for me. The corner where we had gathered in the freezing cold before January's March for Life marking the fortieth anniversary of *Roe v. Wade*. The spot where I began my annual pilgrimage during Holy Week, when I carried the cross near the Capitol at Easter. The Bible Reading Marathon that took place on the west steps of the Capitol Building. For ninety continuous hours, every word of the Bible was read aloud until we reached the end of the book of Revelation. It had become a fixture and reference point in my life and work.

Once at Union Station, I approached the café to see two women sitting at a table, sipping wine. The vague apprehension I had while walking over, which I kept at bay by recalling happy memories, got the better of me. *Why on earth did I accept this invitation?* Prominent evangelicals had been ousted from their leadership positions for far less egregious associations with the left. I thought of one with whom I had worked extensively over the years. He had lost his job at the National Association of Evangelicals only because he said on the radio he was open to the idea of civil unions for gay couples. My career could be in jeopardy if I spent any time with associates of the Auburn Theological Seminary. I resolved that I would chat briefly, then politely extricate myself from what could easily be seen by my supporters as a dangerous dalliance with leftist operatives.

After exchanging the usual pleasantries, "Abby," as she insisted I call her, said she wanted to avoid all the topics we would inevitably disagree on and instead, make a conscious choice to inhabit the spaces we did share. I wasn't sure what those spaces were, but her suggestion loosened me up a bit. We exchanged personal information. I told her about Grand Island, my twin brother, Paul, and our Jewish background; that I had married Cheryl when we were only eighteen, and we had a son and a daughter. She told me about her husband, Pierre, and their four children. Her producer, Kathy Hughes, did the same. We were at least successfully convivial.

Abby's famous last name went right over my head. It wasn't until we were halfway through the discussion that it dawned on me that Disney wasn't a garden-variety family name. I hesitated before asking. If she was surprised I was the only person on the planet who hadn't googled her before a meeting, she didn't show it. Yes, she acknowledged, she was from *that* family. Walt was her great-uncle, and Roy, Walt's brother and her grandfather, had been the business mastermind of the Disney entertainment empire. This was a woman with filmmaking in her genes and, no doubt, the resources to bring them to reality. My hesitation mounted as I realized that, unlike so many filmmakers with big plans, the odds were in favor that this film would actually be made.

After we'd established some rapport, Abby and Kathy finally raised the issue that had brought us together. They began by showing me data on the astonishing number of firearms owned by people identifying themselves as evangelical Christians. They described the close connection between my community and the National Rifle Association, America's biggest and most powerful gun rights lobby. Among religious groups, evangelicals were shown to be the most resistant to gun control legislation and also the most likely to have access to fire-arms. She pointed to our overwhelming support of the new "Stand Your Ground" state laws that allowed anyone who felt threatened to pursue and shoot someone they perceived to be a threat. Abby raised the question of how any evangelical could square that with a belief in the sanctity of human life. While I knew many of our people were hunters and sports shooters, I had never owned a gun and had never really considered how much the popular gun culture had insinuated itself into our religious ethos. In all my years of being involved in our evangelical community—even in the leadership of it—the arming up of Christians had just not been a concern for me. Second Amendment rights seemed to be a given. It was in the Constitution, and that was good enough for me.

Abby wanted to meet and try to engage me, because she didn't want her project to be just another earnest film that liberals would cherish and conservatives would dismiss. She wanted to get into the heart and mind and, perhaps, even soul of an evangelical Christian and explore the issue from that perspective. But I wasn't sure I was the right person. After all, I didn't grow up with guns, and at the Teen Challenge house for recovering addicts, the presence of a firearm always meant serious trouble. In other words, I wasn't a gun advocate. I was cautious and indifferent. At the same time, at least in theory, I defended everyone's right to self-defense, even if it meant using a lethal weapon.

My preoccupation was with what I considered more urgent prob-lems in our society, and gun ownership seemed to be a given. It was an unalienable right for Americans. Aligned as I was with the Repub-licans, I had come to support Second Amendment rights as part of the package. Lately, though, I had experienced a creeping discomfort with what appeared to be my community's growing infatuation with deadly force. Not knowing what to do about it, I left it alone. After staying with

Abby and Kathy longer than I had planned, I apologized for having a busy schedule and announced I would have to go. As far as her invitation to talk about the gun issue on camera, I remained adamantly noncommittal and ironically thanked her for setting me up for a night of lost sleep. There was so much at stake for me personally and professionally that I could have easily chalked this up to another never-to-be-repeated chance meeting. And yet part of me wondered whether I didn't owe it to myself to think harder about the issue in light of my recent philosophical and theological insights. As I walked back to my office, I literally shook my head, seeing how much this fit into my re-evaluation of what it meant to be pro-life. It was also consummately Bonhoefferian with its intersection of faith and ethics. It was also dangerous.

Later that evening, I googled Abigail Disney and was shocked. As a wealthy philanthropist, she had heavily funded causes I had spent a lifetime opposing—especially abortion rights. Most of my community would consider her an enemy. Yet I couldn't ignore the timing of her appearance in my life. I had just finished an exhaustive study of a church gone damningly wrong and had been looking at the life of a minister who courageously took on his community's moral failure at the price of his own life. I had learned from Bonhoeffer the importance of treating my opponent decently and respectfully. Abby had raised profound moral and theological questions I found difficult to reconcile in my own heart and soul. This project would require me to move beyond the realm of political gamesmanship, it was true, but I wondered if all my recent work—academically, spiritually, even in my marriage and family life—might have been preparation for taking on another important cause.

I grappled with formulating my own position on Christians and gun control, but my mind kept returning to the fact that this was an issue that could likely rupture most, if not all, of my most important personal and professional relationships. Gun rights were part and parcel of social policy that had been assembled by a coalition of conservative forces over almost forty years. To publicly question the Second Amendment could more quickly lead to my being branded a traitor than if I questioned a core article of Christian faith. The right to bear arms was not some idiosyncratic aspect of one community, like, say, speaking in tongues, but a massive organizing principle in the entire Republican worldview, including that of my religious wing. To cooperate with Abby would mean associating myself with an issue that was impossible to separate from the sort of person they neither liked nor trusted. Guns could be the cause of my professional suicide.

On the other hand, I dreaded that cooperating with Abby would expose me to being constantly judged by her and her peers. Viewed by them the way they seemed to view most evangelicals: as dolts, benighted ignoramuses. Even if I did decide to work with her, I couldn't shake my concern that I would be treated badly—patronized at best or viewed with contempt. We evangelicals had a long history of feeling defensive about the way we were perceived by educated liberals. Even Cheryl warned me to be very cautious. She had seen me misrepresented by the liberal media in the past, and those wounds remained fresh. I broached the subject with trusted colleagues from the pro-life movement who were adamant in warning me against exploring the relationship between evangelical culture and guns. "Take that one on and kiss your ministry good-bye," one of them said. And yet, I knew that fundamentally I shared Abby's concern about the basic contradiction between our community's commitment to the sanctity of life and our love of guns.

Abby not only typified everything I had fought against as an evangelical, but the film she was planning to make would remind people of who I had once been: the activist with the babies in New York, the guy denouncing gays—moments I now wanted to forget. I just couldn't relive all of that. Each of those episodes in my life reminded me that I had lost the true north of the gospel in favor of playing to expectations and following a script written by someone else. I had to own my internal conflict. If I had really prayed, if I had listened to the still-small voice within me, perhaps I wouldn't have done half of it, I thought. I was in absolute turmoil. One moment I wanted to forget ever having met Katharine and Abby, and the next moment I thought maybe this was the opportunity to break from the script again.

Abby persisted and I delayed. For five weeks I struggled and prayed and could not stop thinking about the intersection of gun violence with my life: Dr. Gunn and Dr. Slepian, the five Amish girls, and the twenty children at Newtown, shot while I was just a few train stops away in Yonkers, preparing to preach—even Mom's first husband and his gun suicide in the attic. My sisters still suffered from that trauma. Each tragic event, with the same thread running through them, a firearm, now seemed to demand a response.

Slowly and inexorably, I realized it was time for me to take a big risk. If this wasn't worth it, I didn't know what was. "Peter had to leave the ship and risk his life on the sea," Bonhoeffer wrote in *The Cost of Discipleship,* "in order to learn both his own weakness and the almighty power of his Lord. If Peter had not taken the risk, he would never have learned the meaning of faith." I had always identified with Peter, the most flawed of the disciples, always questioning and yet fully human in his agonies. Indeed, it was because of Peter's very humanity that Christ offered him the stewardship of his church. I needed to explore more deeply the unsettling pairing between God and guns. The crisis in morality and ethics seemed clear, but the theological connection was just out of reach.

The next time Abby called, I surprised her by telling her I would work with her. There was a deep moral failing at the center of my community, I explained, and I couldn't pretend I didn't see it. To assuage my deepest fears, I offered one caveat: I reserved the right to back out at any time. What I didn't say to her was that I also planned to couch everything I said on camera in a way I could later disavow. She agreed to my stipulated terms, and planned our first on-camera interview for September 17.

Then, on September 16, a lone gunman opened fire at the Washington Navy Yard. It was a shocking episode of violence on a scale almost unthinkable inside a military complex. That complex also happened to be within sight of my living room window. When I heard what had happened, I grabbed my prayer stole and my Bible and went to the gates of the Navy yard, knelt, and prayed. The issue suddenly went from theoretical to concrete. If I had needed some proof that my decision to work on this issue was the right one, I found it in the deaths of twelve people and the wounding of three others on that day. The next morning I headed to New York, where I met up with Abby's film crew and we began.

A few weeks into filming, Abby introduced me to another person she planned to include in the story. Lucy McBath had lost her teenage son and only child, Jordan Davis, when he was gunned down in front of a convenience store in Florida by a man who insisted he needed to "stand his ground" and defend himself in what he perceived to be a "life-threatening circumstance." That circumstance? Four unarmed African-American boys playing loud music in a car.

Lucy was also a born-again Christian, which placed her squarely in the evangelical universe. Her grief consumed her, and yet she never became bitter or lost her faith in God. Instead she saw her loss as God's call to a personal crusade to end gun violence by addressing the inflammatory Stand Your Ground laws that were being instituted in more and more states. Lucy wasn't a theologian—she was a laywoman, a faithful member of her Pentecostal church—but she possessed sophisticated spiritual insight. Her faith alone would have been enough to embolden my own journey.

During one of our many conversations, captured on film, she got to the crux of the problem when she said to me, "We have replaced God with our guns." Lucy's insightful comment connected directly to the thesis of my dissertation on the danger of political idolatry. Had we, as Americans—and, more specifically, as Christians—begun to idolize guns in their power to save us from perceived threats to our lives—or, worse, our way of life? Were we trusting in *objects* to protect us as we capitulated to our imaginary fears?

One modern translation renders the second of the Ten Commandments as "You shall not make for yourself an image in the form of anything in heaven above or on the earth beneath or in the waters below. You shall not bow down to them or worship them." As I reflected on this, I thought how a gun is something designed by a human being and sometimes even hand-tooled, at least to some degree, and when we entrust our lives to it, we essentially look to those handcrafted instruments to save us—in effect, bowing down and worshipping them. By venerating the Second Amendment, we evangelicals were in danger of violating the Second Commandment.

The more I thought and prayed about this, the more I consulted the theological literature on the sin of idolatry, the more convinced I became that the wholesale embrace of the gun culture indicated that our moral failure in this area was also a theological emergency for the evangelical church. If we couldn't correct this serious error, it would inevitably nullify our claim to belief in the sanctity of human life and strip us of all moral credibility; not only that, but our community's infatuation with firearms would leave us living contrary to the core tenets of our Christian faith—essentially making us apostates.

This was no longer a theoretical exercise for me. Instead, this theological emergency demanded my full attention—and that of my fellow clergy. Unlike the Catholic or Orthodox churches, evangelicals have no universal hierarchy to offer a top-down instruction when it comes to practice and belief. At best, we come to conclusions on theological questions by consensus. Doctrinal and dogmatic conflicts must be handled on a denomination-by-denomination, congregation-by-congregation, and, in many ways, person-by-person basis.

What gave me hope was that by framing the issue in theological terms, I could help my community at least understand the problem. Using the Ten Commandments and the teaching of Christ would no doubt help others to come on board with my newfound mission. I began to think about how to talk to my peers about this issue, and Abby wanted to capture those conversations on film. I decided to start with my closest circle of pro-life cohorts.

On a hot July day in 2015, I sat down with three of my most trusted confidants to talk about guns while Abby's cameras rolled. Troy Newman had successfully rebuilt Operation Rescue and now ran its headquarters in Wichita, Kansas. I was startled to learn he kept a cache of weapons in his home, his office, and in his truck. My old friend Pat Mahoney was the head of the Christian Defense Coalition and an unqualified pacifist who hated guns and saw no use for them. Allen Church was moderator of the oldest line of evangelical Presbyterians in the U.S. and advocated for Christians to arm themselves to check the power of the state.

We had formed our own little discussion group, four middle-aged men who had grown up together in the fight for life and Christian values in our country. Over lunch in an Irish pub called the Dubliner, I told the men I wanted to talk about a pretty tough subject. I began by reminding them of all the pro-life work we had done together for decades. I then asked if they would share their thoughts about a question that had troubled me: Is deadly force consistent with our pro-life position? I wanted a brutally honest treatment of this subject on film.

Troy answered immediately. "I think it absolutely is, Rob. People of conscience and people of faith have responsible gun ownership to protect innocent human life. More so than their own life. And we need to have people in our congregations armed." Troy then described the scenario in which someone walks into a crowded church, perhaps a former parishioner who had come unglued, and pulls out a gun, threatening to take out the whole congregation. If there were not someone else with a weapon, it would be mass homicide, because the only thing that stops a bad guy with a gun is a good guy with a gun.

I may not have been surprised by what he said, but the speed with which the conversation simultaneously escalated and degenerated took me by surprise.

"You're living in a delusional fantasyland that you've created for yourself in the ivory towers of Washington," Troy snapped. "You don't live in the real world."

I had to work on controlling my temper. "Look, Troy, if you want to hurl that kind of accusation, I could easily say you're living in a delusional world where the good guys know where to fire and how to fire and they win every time. That's not the way it happens in a violent confrontation when bullets are flying. Drawing the bead and firing the silver bullet and ending the melee and everything comes back to peace and quiet—that just does not comport with reality."

"Don't own one, okay, Rob?" Troy retorted. "You're afraid of guns, you leave them to other people. I'm not afraid of guns."

"You know one of the reasons that I'm afraid of them?" I asked. "Because I don't trust *myself* in the moment of crisis when I'm awash in adrenaline. I do not trust *my* judgment, and I'm amazed at how much you trust yours. I'm amazed by that, Troy."

Pat and Allen both offered energetic arguments on either side of the debate. We spoke for almost two hours and ate very little. By the time we left, we had replicated the intransigence of the gun debate in the country. None of us had changed our minds, but I had a much better appreciation for what I was in for as I waded deeper into this quagmire. If four old friends who agreed on some of the other most volatile social issues in the country could not find common ground on this one, how could any question about guns be resolved?

My vision had been permanently altered around this issue. The more I attempted to discuss it with those around me, the clearer it became that this was a more serious divide than I had ever imagined, particularly between the generations. When I spoke to middle-aged and older evangelical Christians, they expressed the same opinions I had heard from Troy and Allen at that table in the Dubliner. But younger people sided more with my point of view, or the pacifism of Pat, and they were relieved that someone was finally addressing this problem. Many pastors under the age of forty viewed the obsession with the Second Amendment as being inconsistent with the deepest Christian ethical principles. I had worried about losing my old connections—which would happen—but in this work, I was able to build a bridge to the next generation.

In one discussion with young evangelicals, a college student stood up, crying. She described the Sunday school class of her youth, which required children to go to target practice after the lesson for the sole purpose of self-defense—in other words, to learn how to kill human beings. She could never understand how that fit into her Christian belief system. Young evangelicals remained solidly pro-life, but they had a more nuanced understanding about abortion as well as about gay, lesbian, and transgender people. They actually had LGBTQ friends, they knew them intimately, and they realized they shouldn't be turned into caricatures or political pawns. They were also unafraid to question the presuppositions, dogmatism, and taboos of our community. They yearned for open and unrestricted exploration of all these critical subjects. They weren't interested in fighting ideological opponents and they rejected what they perceived as my generation's dismissal of our common humanity. This was the kind of integration of the Beatitudes in real life I had craved. My spiritual journey, my academic work, and my experience with Cheryl and my family were all beginning to harmonize. But the gap between the community that had defined and supported me and who I was was widening. I worried that the differences would be irreconcilable.

Throughout the rest of 2014, work on the film became a big part of my life as Abby's crew followed me around the country, to churches, conferences, pro-life leadership meetings, even to a shooting range, where I actually fired a variety of weapons. I felt both the thrill of having so much power in my hands and the fear of what these weapons could do if I pointed them in the wrong direction. That was especially true with the AR-15, the semiautomatic long gun often referred to as an "assault-style weapon." It reminded me very much of the military M16, romanticized during the Vietnam War. I remember as a young boy being enthralled with the images of soldiers in the jungles with that handsome, seemingly all-powerful weapon, barrel extended upward, the gun's stock propped on the inside of the elbow and hand confidently wrapped around its grip. In those days, the weapon seemed magical to me, but as I took it in my hands at the range, I felt something very different about it. This was the weapon that had been turned on those children, mostly six-year-olds, at Sandy Hook Elementary School. This was the gun that the chaplains, who were among the first responders, told me literally blew apart those small bodies, dismembering and disfiguring them. It was no longer magical in my mind but monstrous.

The crew and I also went to an NRA convention and I threaded my way through the massive crowd, looking at the immense amounts of firepower in the vast exhibit hall: new weapons, bullets, sighting devices, rifles, handguns, new gear for carrying concealed pistols, holsters, munitions that a small army would envy. Billy Graham's son, Reverend Franklin Graham, offered the opening prayer. "Our country is in trouble," he said. "Father, we know there's a lot of people in this country that would like to register guns and take 'em away."

The most difficult part of this stage of my new work on the gun issue was interacting with the people who were most likely to passively
reject my message. I had always enjoyed spirited debates and had had
plenty in my pro-life activist days, but quiet, unspoken rejection was
harder for me to deal with. I'd rather have someone engage me in a
disagreement than silently write me off. As I planned my first sermons
and public statements on the spiritual crises surrounding Christians
and guns, another terrible mass shooting episode took away the luxury
of having time to formulate just the right words.

In May of 2014, as I sat back for the first time in months to simply contemplate how I would convey my new ideas in sermonic form,
twenty-two-year-old Elliot Rodger went on a shooting rampage at the
University of California, Santa Barbara, killing six people and injuring
fourteen others. I called the father of Chris Michael-Martinez, one of
the victims who died. This was the first time I would speak to a loved
one of a gun violence victim in real time. His grief was raw, his rage
consuming. Mr. Martinez, a lawyer, demanded to know "where the
hell the clergy are on this matter?" I needed an answer for this man. I
would have to be more public, and on a much quicker timetable than I
had imagined. I decided this was the time to do it. My office put out a
press release announcing I would go to California to talk about evangelicals and the issue of gun violence in the wake of another tragedy.

The people on my staff who handle media approached this press
event as we had all the others, sending out the release to the scores
of reporters on our contact list, making advance phone calls to local
leaders, issuing invitations to colleagues to join me in making statements. We could always rely on a certain contingent of conservative
and pro-life news agencies to cover our activities. They almost never
disappointed us.

On the plane to California, I polished my remarks and tried to
imagine myself in Mr. Martinez's place, grieving for my son, Matthew.

I couldn't imagine the pain. When I reached Isla Vista, I presented my first public statement on the problem of gun violence, attached my name to this issue, and spoke about my concerns. I assumed it would make some headlines, at least in the always reliable Christian media outlets. "We are in crisis in America," I said. "And saying and doing nothing in the wake of this kind of horror and loss is not right or good. I am here today to challenge my fellow clergy. To step forward now and speak their hearts and minds on this subject. To courageously offer clear spiritual, moral, and ethical guidance on this life-and-death matter. The time for the clergy to be brave is now. There is no more time to wait, no more time to be silent. May God help us."

There were no reporters, no cameras, no satellite dishes; there was no coverage. One person was there: a passerby with a cell phone. He took a few pictures and left. This was going to be a lonely road.

29

The Armor of Light

By October of 2014, my decades-long public battles with my ideological foes was giving way to something new. Tackling the question of evangelicals and gun control had forced me to rethink my previous approach of sustaining and escalating conflict for the sake of scoring points. Instead, I had become more interested in seeing how a bone of contention in the public arena might give me an opportunity to be more reflective and, yes, even more Christlike in my personal life. Such a circumstance presented itself in Houston when the city elected Annise Parker, the first openly lesbian mayor of a major American city.

The shifting discussion surrounding gay rights in Houston had garnered attention first in May 2014, when the city council passed the Houston Equal Rights Ordinance (HERO), radically expanding legal protections for LGBTQ people. The most controversial part of the measure permitted transgender people to file a discrimination complaint if they could not access a gender-appropriate bathroom in any of the city's public businesses. The ordinance exempted religious organizations, but nonetheless, those organizations mobilized for war, decrying the "bathroom bill," warning that young girls would be at risk of predators masquerading as transgender women.

Several local mega-church pastors were key players in gathering signatures to force a ballot initiative in the fall, but the city attorney disqualified most of those signatures and said the requisite 17,269 had not been achieved. Church leaders sued the city, insisting they had counted 50,000 signatures and complained that the administration had been motivated by a hidden political agenda. The city attorney responded with subpoenas for the pastors' sermons. In the words of the mayor's chief policy officer, "Using the pulpit to do political organizing . . . is not protected speech. Our tax-exempt status depends on a bright line between the world of politics and the world of religion, even as that bright line is often blurred."

Pastors across the country immediately condemned the subpoenas, arguing that long-standing protections of unimpeded exercise of religion were in danger if the actions taken against the Houston pastors became a precedent. The stakes for church leaders thus grew much higher than a question of LGBTQ rights in Houston. My colleagues and I felt the mayor had overreached, threatening the unique and privileged nature of pastoral communications. A bitter confrontation was not going to help anyone's cause, but lots of the groups I had worked with over the years exploited the Houston uproar to gain attention and fund-raising dollars. As the court case between the pastors and the city continued, several of my past acquaintances—Senator Ted Cruz's evangelist father, Rafael Cruz, and Tony Perkins of the Family Research Council—weighed in heavily on the debate. Perkins, with whom I had shared many speaking circuits over the years, told Fox News commentator Todd Starnes, "Pastors need to step forward and challenge this across the country. I'd like to see literally thousands of pastors after they read this story begin to challenge government authorities—to dare them to come into their churches and demand their sermons."

This was the latest version of the kind of fear- and anger-generating vehicle we had all long employed to galvanize our constituents, increase donor response, and score valuable points against our political opponents. I could no longer count the number of strategy sessions in which I was asked to identify which elements of an illustrative story were the most terrifying, offensive, or even obscene and would thereby inspire the most vehement and lucrative reactions. Mitigating and nuanced factors were deliberately ignored or exposed as ruses meant to dupe the inattentive multitudes. I had come to deeply regret my involvement in this kind of activity, realizing it was itself a serious breach of Christian ethics, not to mention a violation of the gospel itself. Jesus never deliberately exploited people's fears and prejudices for his own gain. In fact, he rebuked the religious leaders of his day for doing just that. For the most prominent figures in American evangelicalism, winning political and ideological contests had become far more important than winning lost souls. It was all abjectly cynical and on full display in Houston.

While I was deeply distressed and disheartened by this kind of agenda-driven behavior, I was also just as deeply troubled, even alarmed, by the intrusion of government authority into the pulpit, the sanctuary, and the pastor's study. A subpoena for not just sermons but private "notes" made by the pastors could violate confidential counseling, which would undermine the mutual trust at the heart of a pastor's relationships with congregants. This issue needed to be urgently addressed and resolved, or, we surmised, other government entities might also attempt to breach those traditional limits.

I recruited five other clergy from around the country to travel to Houston to hold a news conference in front of City Hall. We had no other agenda except to publicly ask the mayor to voluntarily withdraw her demand for these documents in the interest of preserving both the unique relationship of pastor and parishioners, as well as the First Amendment rights of church leaders. We would make it clear that HERO, which all the members of my delegation opposed, should be left to the citizens of Houston to resolve. We had agreed that our responsibility was to present ourselves in humility and Christlike love, only appealing to Mayor Parker to do the right thing, showing her all the deference her elected office deserved.

After a prayer service on the plaza leading to the front door of City Hall, our spokesman publicly asked the mayor for a personal meeting. Her chief of staff offered to organize it. Later that afternoon we found ourselves in her sprawling office suite, far away from the cameras and reporters who had covered our earlier event. Over the years I've learned that physical presence can be as important as words when it comes to communicating with the opposition. When I was in North Africa facilitating a dialogue between American evangelical representatives and regional Islamic leaders, I found that bowing in just the right way, placing my hand over my heart, and looking down instead of at or over my audiences, conveyed a message of humility, engagement, and honest curiosity I just couldn't get across verbally. My Moroccan hosts were astounded by the unexpectedly positive reception I got from a potentially hostile group and credited it to the way I averted my eyes and moved my body so as not to appear confrontational.

In Mayor Parker's office, conscious of the lesson I had learned in Morocco, I sat in a way that communicated my effort to seek her understanding. We were not there to denounce her, as so many others had. On his national television show, speaking about the Houston crisis, former Arkansas governor and Fox News commentator Mike Huckabee had used the words "intolerant despot" and said the mayor was guilty of "hate-filled Gestapo-like tactics." All that poison was in the room when I began by assuring Mayor Parker we had no political goals and weren't there to discuss the HERO bill. Our focus was our deeply held concern over the sacrosanct nature of pastoral communications.

A Harvard-educated scholar, Russian Orthodox priest, and moral philosophy professor we had brought with us explained the historically unique status of the clerical role and the bond between a pastor and his flock. I expressed our concern that violating the confidentiality of the pastor's relationship with his or her flock could unintentionally lead to similar actions, and maybe worse, across the country, putting in peril this timeless and universal bond between the people in the pews and the men and women God had given to them to shepherd them. For this reason alone, we hoped she would withdraw her subpoenas, we told her. The mayor sat looking at us pensively as we spoke, glancing occasionally at her staff. It felt as if the ice had melted and we were relatives trying to settle a family matter rather than activists on two sides of a political divide engaged in a bitter war to best the other. The mayor told us she appreciated our visit, especially the tone we had struck and the points we had made. I asked if she would mind if one of our members offered a prayer. She welcomed it and for a few moments we prayed together.

Our objective had been met; now it was up to her. As two of her staff members escorted us from the building, cameras and microphones were pushed in our faces from the elevator to the sidewalk. In one interview after another, our delegates thanked and even praised the mayor for her hospitality, her attentiveness, and her sincerity in considering our argument. This had been a rare moment for my side, a breakthrough really, when we found we could be conciliatory and congenial even with a seemingly extreme ideological opponent. In a group exercise, we had found what Abraham Lincoln had referred to as "the better angels of our nature." We knew, of course, that, in the end, the mayor and her political advisors would make their decision with a view toward what best served their political priorities, but there had been nothing jaded or cynical about our interaction.

Not everyone agreed with us, especially some Houston megachurch pastors. When I arrived back at my hotel room, I returned an urgent call from Reverend David Welch of the Texas Pastor Council. In a tense voice, he asked if I could join some area pastors that evening to discuss our meeting with Mayor Parker. After thirty-five years of ordained ministry, visits to thousands of churches, and encounters with innumerable pastors, I could tell when I was being set up. Even though I suspected something sinister in his tone, I felt it was my obligation to accept his invitation. There is a certain ethic among evangelical ministers that all due consideration be given to the opinions of local pastors. I felt I owed that to the Pastor Council. Two members of my delegation, both longtime friends and confidants, would join me.

That evening we arrived at the giant Grace Community Church, a complex the size of a Walmart. I had never heard about its founding pastor, Steve Riggle, but everybody else we met in Houston seemed to know him. Once inside, I was escorted to a conference room where several area ministers sat around a large table. Riggle sat at the head, obviously to chair the meeting. His jaw and shoulders instantly communicated to me his displeasure. He demanded to know what I was doing in his town, as if I had neglected to seek his permission to visit. I explained we had asked the mayor to withdraw the subpoenas. He became more agitated, castigating me for parachuting into Houston, pretending I could remedy the situation, and then getting credit for it when I didn't know what I was doing. Reverend Welch asserted Mayor Parker had been their "enemy" since she had been elected. He snapped some papers he held—presumably his sermons or other notes that could be subpoenaed—saying he could go to jail because of what they contained. He accused my team of being carpetbaggers coming in from high-and-mighty Washington to mess with their business.

It was clear what was going on. I could see that they were using every trick in the book to intimidate us, drive us out of town, force us to apologize—even backtrack—for our actions because this conflict had been a bonanza for the churches. But I was not going to follow his script. I feigned amazement that everyone around the table wasn't pleased after hearing the late-breaking news that the mayor was likely to withdraw her subpoenas the next morning. Instead, Riggle charged, my group had robbed them of a powerful weapon they had planned to use to take down this mayor and her godless administration. If the conflict were to be resolved, they would be left without any leverage and would be forced into a mutual nonaggression treaty they had no intention of ratifying, robbing them of an extremely effective recruitment and, I was sure, a fund-raising tool.

I did my best to assure Riggle that the point of our meeting with Mayor Parker had nothing to do with the nature of HERO, but to no avail. He angrily told me it was time to get on the next plane out of Texas. If the subject and potential consequences of our encounter had not been so serious, I would have burst out laughing at Riggle's Marshal Dillon–like pronouncement that it was time for me to "git back on my horse and git outta town." Over the next few minutes the meeting degenerated into something between a roast and an inquisition. As I got up to leave, Riggle warned that we should not show up with the mayor in front of any cameras. I had no idea what he thought he was going to do to me if we did appear with her, but the three of us nonetheless decided to respect this demand. Again, it was incumbent on us to do everything we could to show deference to local church leadership; something Riggle was never going to do for the mayor, despite the Bible's admonition to "Let every person be subject to the governing authorities."

It had been a demoralizing experience. The three of us knew we had represented the gospel well, and because we had made a good case for the mayor to relent, she was likely to do so. This was great news not only for every pastor in Houston but for every religious leader throughout the country. But we had also denied Riggle his most effective promotional tool for his weekend rally and we had short-circuited his fund-raising plan. Taking the threat of the subpoenas off the table would be like denying oxygen to a fire, and it seemed Riggle's group didn't care much about the implications of the subpoenas beyond the political and financial advantages it gave them.

Less than twenty-four hours after we had met, the mayor's chief of staff called to confirm she would withdraw the subpoenas. He asked if we wanted to stand with her when she announced her decision, but we respectfully declined: to appear would have been too provocative, only exacerbating the tension with Riggle and the other pastors. In her statement, Mayor Parker described our meeting: "They came without political agendas, without hate in their hearts and without any desire to debate the merits of the HERO. They simply wanted to express their passionate and very sincere concerns about the subpoenas."

In my hotel room, I sat in front of the television as the rest of the story played on the news, but I was lost in a new feeling very deep inside of me. I had known it in the past, but I hadn't felt it in decades. It was the connection with another soul—another human being—across a great gulf, across a seemingly insurmountable divide. It was also the cessation of a long and drawn-out conflict that I had spent most of my adult years stoking. In its absence, I felt peace. It made me think of a Bible verse I hadn't preached about for years: "The peace of God, which surpasses all understanding, will guard your hearts and your minds in Christ Jesus."

★★★

The next month Abby and her film crew followed me to a benefit event for the Freedom Center, an organization established by conservative writer David Horowitz. "Restoration Weekend" at the tony Breakers Resort in Palm Beach promised to be a who's who of movement leadership, and I was to deliver the opening prayer. Abby's plan was to film my invocation and scan the crowd as a way of showing my stature in this community. Horowitz, a former liberal, described his organization in ways that were a call to arms for conservative isolationism, even xenophobia. The Freedom Center was committed "to the defense of free societies whose moral, cultural and economic foundations are under attack by enemies both secular and religious, at home and abroad."

This was certainly not Abby's crowd, and by now I had plenty of my own misgivings about them, too. I had been part of so many similar events over the years that I had almost become desensitized to the harsh, contemptuous, and narrow-minded messaging at these types of gatherings. But this time my perception was different. With Abby as a kind of external reference point, I was able to see these people and hear their speeches in a new way. Texas congressman Louie Gohmert was there; I knew him back in Washington as involved with the bipartisan House Prayer Caucus, but here he was the valiant crusader against what he called climate-change propagandists—something I couldn't relate to. Michele Bachmann was a specialist on the economy, particularly the benefits of eliminating the minimum wage. And Texas governor Rick Perry was warming up for another presidential run. I looked around and wondered if I agreed with anything any of these people stood for anymore.

When it came time for me to deliver the blessing, I stood on the stage and waited for silence. I began by reading Psalm 15, which begins, "O Lord, who shall sojourn in your tent? Who shall dwell on your holy hill?" I then invited the room to bow their heads with me:

> God, whose name and nature is true, help us always to act in truth—to love truth more than we love our own spin on it. Thank you for those in this room who are lovers of truth and who act on it at great personal risk, who have paid the price for their convictions . . . Keep us mindful of those who are deprived of the good life, especially those who suffer because of tyranny, dictatorship, corruption, and violence. Help us to help them. I ask these things in the name of the One who is the Way, *the Truth*, and the Life. Amen.

"Amen," the crowd responded, before breaking into conversation and tucking into the salad. I socialized with those around me even though I was beginning to feel like a stranger among them. The speeches were filled with glib disparaging remarks about those with whom we differed on matters of race or religion or politics. Our enemies were ridiculed, but I had come to know some of them as decent, even God-loving people. The star of the program, the acerbic and often crude Ann Coulter, rounded up her usual list of liberal suspects and shot them down with remarks so coarse, I shuddered.

The Breakers was a reckoning for me. I couldn't ignore that so many of my evangelical peers were violating God's commandments for how we are to live—that the whole thing had become ideology and entertainment. This was my Paul-on-the-road-to-Damascus moment. Doing what is right is, like grace, costly. But there was no longer any other option than to speak the truth in my heart. Soon the documentary would be distributed and my differences with members of my community, the people who were sitting in the banquet room at the Breakers, would move from private concerns to public ones. I had been pleased to receive this invitation, but it would be my finale on the conservative stage—and not a grand one.

After most people had exited the room, and the staff was cleaning up the post-gala mess, Abby and I found each other. She had eventually taken refuge in the ladies' room when the venom became too much for her liberal sensibilities to bear. We talked for a long time about why the event was so upsetting. Abby remembered her southern mother and grandmother being flagrantly, unapologetically racist. She described the agonies of her own childlike inability to talk back to them, to speak the truth. I shared with her the struggle I felt in discerning if I was on the right side, God's side, of the political and religious chasm. I told her that the event had brought to the surface the uncomfortable possibility that many of my comrades in arms, my funders and allies—those with whom I had created an important life—were agents of hate and discord. Fear was a profound motivator for evangelicals. We carried a vestigial memory of being the little ramshackle clapboard church from across the tracks whose congregation couldn't pay its minister. We collectively carried a chip on our shoulders for being marginalized. Fear and revenge were far from the teachings of Christ, but we had practiced them so often in recent years. How had we gotten to this point?

A few days later, after we had returned to our normal lives, Abby called me. I was surprised to hear a tremor in her voice. She assured me that nothing was wrong, but she needed to tell me something that could jeopardize our collaboration. We had become close friends, and this meant she could no longer keep an important personal experience from me—even if that meant I would choose not to work with her any longer. When Abby was twenty-one years old, she told me, she had gotten pregnant and—not knowing what to do, and unable to tell her mother—she had an abortion.

I had dreaded the conversation we were having but somehow knew that it was inevitable; at some point in my life a close friend who was a woman had suffered, and I would have to face my own attitude and behavior toward others like her—not in a theoretical way, as an activist, but as a friend. I had a very strong conviction about the innate value of every human life but needed to fully understand and appreciate Abby's decision: how she made it and why she felt she had to. She asked me what I would have done in her situation. I thought long and hard about it and faced my true self—not the public persona most people knew. I searched my heart of hearts, then answered her candidly.

"I think I would have had the abortion," I told her. I have talked with many women who have regretted their abortions. I have comforted and counseled women who were afraid of being pregnant but then decided to go through with the pregnancy. But in none of these hundreds, maybe thousands, of conversations over the years has anyone ever asked me what I would have done as an unmarried twenty-one-year-old woman. In making all sorts of imaginative leaps in time and gender, I had a shocking but authentic moment of reckoning.

By characterizing women who had made this choice as a specific type of sinner—our movement labeled them "post-abortive women"—I was perpetrating exactly what I had spent much of my adult life decrying: the dehumanizing of others. The label diminished them and made them less threatening, less relevant to the discussion, easier to dismiss. To fully recognize the suffering of others, to feel Christlike compassion for human failing, was to recognize my own capacity for failure—for sin—and to put my head at the same level as Abby's at the foot of the cross. It was essential for embracing and being grateful for the redemptive grace of God.

Several months later, Cheryl, Matthew, and I sat in Abby's midtown Manhattan apartment, waiting to get our first look at the film that was the result of two of the most difficult and eventful years I had spent in Christian ministry. Abby had taken the name of her documentary, *The Armor of Light*, from a verse in the book of Romans: "The night is far gone; the day is at hand. So then let us cast off the works of darkness and put on the armor of light." The film officially chronicled my examination of evangelicals and our infatuation with guns, but for me the project had been much more personal.

Ever since I completed my doctoral work on the grave problem of political idolatry, I had carried my revelations of the moral failings of my community in the frustrated recesses of my own heart. I feared that by going public I would lose the relationships and organization I had spent most of my life building. But this film would soon be shown at festivals, in theaters, and in a prime-time television broadcast. There was no going back. My stomach was in knots, but there was some modicum of relief in knowing I would no longer be imprisoned in my own frustrated conscience.

Somebody cut the lights and the large screen on the living room wall glowed. The next thing I saw was old news footage from my Buffalo days. There was the younger Rob Schenck in a clerical collar, with the requisite oversized nineties hair and glasses. I held in my hands Baby Tia. There I was, being dragged by police on the day I was arrested for creating a "physically offensive situation." It was just the beginning of ninety minutes of my deep and personal journey of faith, beginning at little Emmanuel Church, to when I confused submission to Christ with political fealty, to my pursuit of redemption in the rediscovery of Bonhoeffer and his concept of costly grace.

As I watched the film, my emotions ranged from fear to exhilaration. There would be a price to pay for airing my dirty laundry and that of my Christian family—I knew that—but there was no way to sugarcoat our surrender to political interests, to our fears, to our baser instincts. I wanted to lift the cloak of secrecy that allowed this disease in our collective soul to spread and threaten the future of American evangelicalism. We would need to deal with this deep moral failing or it would be the end of us. We faced a spiritual crisis that, depending on what we did with it, could either be our destruction or our salvation.

Over the previous five years, I had learned that the path to spiritual and emotional health, and healthy interpersonal relationships, involved integrating the public and the private, and living authentically. For too long I had suppressed my concerns about our church teachings, practices, and attitude toward outsiders while publicly giving my supporters and colleagues what they wanted to hear. Living this way had threatened not only my personal and spiritual well-being but my family and my marriage. It presented both a real and a symbolic danger. In contrast, *The Armor of Light* was a brutally honest, unvarnished peek at what was really going on: in me, in my community, in our country. I had taken big risks in not concealing or evading any of it, but it felt now that the reward would compensate for any losses I might experience.

When the film ended, I looked over at Cheryl to see her reaction. She reached out and squeezed my hand, and I knew that whatever might happen outside that room, I would be fine because we were together. Just as meaningfully, Matthew stepped up from the couch and put his hands on my shoulders, giving me a squeeze of approval. He had the most serene look of relief I had seen on his face in a long, long time.

After the release of *The Armor of Light* at New York's Tribeca Film Festival, I traveled the country for screenings at other festivals, at colleges and universities, and in churches. I felt I was doing the work God had called me to do, and I became closer to Cheryl, Anna, and Matthew, who, for the first time in decades, commended me for exhibiting moral courage. Standing up for what I truly believed, without apology and despite the costs, gave me new beginnings in love and life and ministry. I needed to reassess how I was doing my work in Washington. My new model of ministry could not be directed by the expectations, demands, and threats of those whose agenda was to divide people and punish perceived opponents. My new approach would be an attempt to share the transcendent gospel of God's love and the model of Jesus—God in human flesh—with all, bar none.

Bonhoeffer wrote a letter to the pastors he had trained during the worst years of the Nazi horrors, men who were eventually scattered all over war-torn Germany. Some were placed on the front lines of battle as part of Hitler's design to rid his Reich of troublesome clerics. "Who stands fast?" Bonhoeffer asked. "Only the one whose final standard is not his reason, his principles, his conscience, his freedom, his virtue, but who is ready to sacrifice all this when he is called to obedient and responsible action in faith and in exclusive allegiance to God—the responsible man, who tries to make his whole life an answer to the question and call of God." Bonhoeffer's words challenged me to take the ultimate risk. I needed to live by a conscience informed only by the still-small voice of God in my heart, even if it flew in the face of every convention I've ever known. Perhaps especially if it did.

By July 2015, Abby and I had become a kind of traveling road show, visiting churches, student groups, and community organizations all over the country. Sometimes there were hundreds of people there, on other occasions maybe twenty or thirty. But each one was important in its own way. Some venues were familiar to me—mega churches, Christian colleges—but others, like Harvard and Yale, felt like going into enemy territory. I was still experiencing a residual animosity toward these institutions that had for so long been the bastions of everything hostile to the religious right. In the moment, I was having the time of my life, finally engaging in the frank, unedited public conversation about faith, morality, and humanity I had seen in Bonhoeffer's vast personal correspondence with his family, friends, and colleagues. In those letters I read of his most private fears, feelings of failure and loneliness, his guilt, his modest pleasures and frustrated longings. In a word, Bonhoeffer was genuine. I had once envied such transparency and authenticity, but I was now practicing it, and I found it liberating.

A few days before one of these road trips, I was included in a conference call with Troy Newman, the head of Operation Rescue, and David Deleiden, a young pro-life activist who had rented space in our offices. Paul was much more involved in this community than I was, but I still maintained a close friendship with Pat Mahoney and even Troy, who had triumphed over Randall Terry in taking control of Operation Rescue. I was still respected as an advisor to the movement, albeit by this time an unofficial one, and I had no reason yet to decline the invitation to join this conversation. Besides, ending relationships of any kind has never come easy to me. I've always valued long friendships, even simply collegial relationships, and I wanted to do everything I could to preserve even the ones in a movement I could no longer unequivocally endorse.

By the time of this teleconference, the wing of the pro-life movement that Operation Rescue had once epitomized had become somewhat more sedate, working on legislative efforts to curtail abortion, exposing subpar practices at clinics, and pushing for prosecution of abusive practitioners—but it was no longer the central focus of pro-life activism. The subject of this call was going to put it once more in the spotlight. I don't remember all the participants on the line, but my own board member, Father Frank Pavone of Priests for Life, chaired the discussion, while Troy and David delivered the big news: David had been working underground, pretending to be a researcher, and had clandestinely recorded Planned Parenthood officials on video apparently negotiating the sale of "baby body parts." Troy and David were triumphant. They explained their video images and crystal-clear audio showed two of Planned Parenthood's top medical personnel haggling over the price of fetal organs and tissue—their sale is illegal—and admitting to altering the abortion procedure to better preserve fetal specimens.

We were assured the video was solid gold, 100 percent legitimate, and could do enormous damage to Planned Parenthood and its abortion business. Father Frank briefed the participants on how these videos would buttress the call for Congress to cut off public funding for Planned Parenthood and other similar groups. The conversation shed light on another aspect of the pro-life movement that had been so much a part of my life and how much I had changed in relation to it. I continued to believe that every human life, no matter how big or how small, how dependent or independent, is of equal value in the eyes of God and should be in the eyes of fellow human beings. I don't think the termination of a human life should ever be done cavalierly—whether by abortion, by withdrawal of medical life support, or by execution. Society and even government should do all that it can to reinforce the value of human life at every stage of existence. But I no longer believed that this extremely difficult, extremely complex, and extremely sensitive subject could be handled as if it were two-dimensional—and most certainly not by politicians. It was not made up of zeroes and ones, and should not be a tool for political advantage. If David had captured a "Gotcha!" moment, at what cost did it come? I wasn't sure what it meant for me then. What I did know was that I no longer had a taste for this kind of sensational activism.

The videos were as earthshaking as they had hoped, and the criticism of Planned Parenthood was swift and harsh. When the news broke, Abby and I and a few others were at an art gallery in Richmond screening *The Armor of Light* with a vivacious group of young evangelicals, just the sort who always responded positively to our work. Abby was preoccupied by the Deleiden story and the damage it was doing to an organization she cared deeply about, but even more so the danger it presented to her friend, Planned Parenthood's president, Cecile Richards. After the screening, we went to dinner with our host and Pat Mahoney. Abby was on edge as headlines about the videos accusing Planned Parenthood of trading in baby body parts dominated the news. She seethed as she registered her feelings with Pat, who appealed to her to set up a meeting with Cecile Richards so they could talk about it amicably. Abby was not going to do that, because she wrongly blamed Pat for aiding and abetting a conspiracy that put her friend in mortal danger. (He had nothing to do with the videos.) I watched her grow quieter as the night wore on, and only later found myself on the receiving end as she vented her fury about what my friends were doing to her friend. After we parted, she texted me.

"Rob, I can't contain my rage here," she wrote. "As religious people, you claim moral high ground, and still you perpetuate these false impressions that can cause so much destruction for decent people. This was a horrible thing to do. I know what an extraordinarily brave and decent human being Cecile Richards is, and I don't need anyone to prove that to me. People are going to die because of these tapes. There will be blood on your hands."

Blood on my hands. I was much too familiar with that feeling—I experienced it after the Slepian murder. Of course, I knew what Abby meant and why she felt that way, but I was conflicted. What if this was an indication that some on her side, in her movement, had grown callous about human life? Was she open to that possibility? These were people I had been deeply bonded to over decades, just as she was bonded to her friend Cecile Richards. So much of this was personal, and I would need to address that dimension of the problem.

One of the greatest faults in the movement that I had been a part of for so long was our inability to appreciate others and empathize with them. We were sure anyone who allowed for abortion under virtually any circumstances—or permitted experimentation on the remains of the aborted for any reason at all—was evil, self-serving, morally bankrupt, and motivated only by financial gain. There just couldn't be—and never would be—any other rationale for such abhorrent behavior. But the stark dichotomy that had worked so well for building a movement no longer comported with my understanding of reality. Human experience was too intricate; human lives were too varied; human conscience was too unknown.

A few days after the tense table encounter between Abby and Pat, when the effects of the videos were still reverberating in the national conversation, she and I appeared at the Aspen Ideas Festival for a screening. "Aspen," whether the place was shorthand for convocations of the intelligentsia, or for skiing by the rich and famous, existed in an alternate universe for me. My people would have regarded those gathered at the Ideas Festival as archenemies from the left. Being at Aspen was as much of a leap for me as it had been for Abby to go to the fundraiser at the Breakers, but not as big a leap as it would have been two years prior. I had lost some friends and associates in the past couple of years as I traveled with Abby and her crew to address gun violence, but new people had entered my life as I tackled the seismic question of political idolatry not only in our churches but in myself. In one of the first events at the festival, handpicked presenters are asked to take the microphone and speak for two minutes on a "Big Idea" that could change the world. It was like speed-dating for Mensa members; even the surgeon general of the United States was restricted to two minutes. I felt as if this might be the most important talk I would give in my thirty-five years of preaching.

The Aspen literature described me as an "anti-abortion activist and fixture on the political far right," identities that would not appeal to this audience. My nervousness reminded me of my early days of preaching. When it was my turn, I grabbed my speech and raced to the podium. It had been a long time since I needed to take a heart-calming deep breath, but I did, and then began:

> *I am Rob Schenck, and I'm featured in Abigail Disney's film* The Armor of Light. *My Big Idea is really a very small one, but with BIG potential to improve our psychological, social, relational, and community health: launch a micro movement called My Neighbor, Myself, an INTENTIONAL, INDIVIDUAL LIFESTYLE focused on each of us as individuals—privately, quietly, almost unnoticeably— identifying just one person, one couple, one family—and the key is that they are as different from you, as opposite of you, as they can be.*
>
> *And that you and I work very hard, with determination, over time, over years, decades if necessary, to learn about that person, that couple, that family—from them, as your only source of knowledge about them, to spend time with them, to invite them into your life—and to be present in theirs; to suspend presuppositions, prejudice, and contempt toward them; to listen to them more than you talk to them—and to be thankful for them.*

If you're a person of faith, pray for them, or, if not, wish them well in every way and commit to stick with them until it's no longer possible to do so, or until they dismiss you from their lives. The idea will transform you for the better—and it may transform them for the better—and either one can transform everything for the better!

This idea is about loving your neighbor as yourself, and there's nothing on this earth closer to the love of God. As each of us does our little bit to become more relationally healthy, it will make the world we inhabit a healthier place—in a very BIG WAY. That's my very little, very doable Big Idea.

30

Donald Trump and the Moral Collapse of American Evangelicalism

I first met Donald Trump when he was a guest at Pat Robertson's eightieth birthday party in March 2010. Trump had been working the back rooms of evangelical politics for a year, and at Pat's banquet he seized the moment to pompously perform, even audition, for a ballroom full of evangelical leaders. I really couldn't make sense of Trump's being there, except that he and Pat were both members of the billionaires' club. The New York real estate magnate touted his Christian background and professed his love for his childhood pastor, the celebrity cleric Norman Vincent Peale, who wrote the 1952 motivational manual *Power of Positive Thinking*. (Trump clearly didn't know evangelicals had long rejected Peale as an apostate.) On a large screen, the reality show star displayed a photo of his teenage self with his church confirmation class. Another blunder: evangelicals don't do "confirmation." Finally, he held up a Bible with his name embossed on the cover, telling his audience his mother gave it to him and he had cherished it all his life. None of the pages appeared to be dog-eared, the sure sign of an avid Bible reader. Except for the news that Trump had been trounced in a straw poll the next year at CPAC, the annual conservative confab, he remained largely unnoticed at my end of the conservative Christian universe. He was, at best, a barker in a political sideshow. No one I knew took him seriously—most certainly not as any kind of religious man.

After *The Armor of Light* was released in April 2015, I spent an enormous amount of my time promoting it and talking about guns in the evangelical community. It had become a new crusade for me, but not one that replaced all my other work with Faith and Action, which continued unabated. I still supervised the training and deployment of short-term missionaries to work among top elected and appointed officials; I manned the back room at the National Prayer Breakfast; I presided at the opening of the National Bible Reading Marathon; I led prayers in front of the Supreme Court building on the National Day of Prayer; and I always read the gospel account of Christmas during our Live Nativity, when we paraded exotic animals and amateur actors in period costume between the Capitol and the Supreme Court to stage a reenactment of Jesus' birth at Bethlehem.

After eight years of Obama, my people were pining for a Republican presidential victory in the 2016 election. The field was crowded in the early months, and Jeb Bush was my choice to lead our country. I had met him a few times and found him very different from his brother. Meeting behind closed doors, I was impressed with what I read as his humble disposition, his candid critique of his own brother's presidency, and his facility in Spanish. I knew he had lived through his daughter's opioid addiction and recovery, and it seemed to both temper him and leave him sensitive to the suffering of others. Of course, like most Americans, I could never have imagined what would finally happen in the primaries.

The playboy and reality TV star who would become the Republican Party's 2016 nominee for president posed a terrible dilemma for me. I did not want Hillary Clinton to be president. I had too many issues with her and her party. At the same time, I thought Donald Trump appealed to the very worst impulses within the conservative and Christian worlds. If Hillary was a throwback to an old liberal statism that had not advanced much in terms of its ethical moorings, Trump represented a new brand of amorality and nativism that was just as threatening— perhaps more so. Trump's extravagant promises to evangelicals did nothing to assuage my concerns. I was aware of many leading Christian figures who, like me, vowed never to vote for Trump. Yet by the summer of 2016, you were either on the Trump train or you were a traitor. The logic was that we needed to elect a Republican at any cost, and my fellow evangelicals added a special urgency to this logic. I took the coward's way out of the dilemma and left the Republican Party.

For more than thirty years, people like me had prayed, worked, and repeatedly condemned nearly everything Donald Trump represented. The fact that, for most evangelicals, he now posed no problem at all was evidence of a crisis. In my estimation the Trump phenomenon foreshadowed not only the downfall of the old guard of American evangelicalism but perhaps the collapse of it altogether. It was hardly surprising that in poll after poll, interview after interview, many respondents would describe our support of Trump as unprincipled and cynical. We were seen as so craven, we were willing to pander to a demagogue in order to reclaim lost political clout.

Back in the Operation Rescue days, my colleagues and I considered the profligate Trump to be a one-man promotional operation for a hedonistic New York culture that needed abortion on demand as a safety net for their reckless lifestyles. And his relentless self-congratulation, his gilded airplanes, and his history as a casino mogul were the antithesis of not just middle-American values but of Christian virtues. In June of 2015, in an interview with CNN, Trump admitted it had never occurred to him to ask for God's forgiveness. When I heard that, I literally gasped. This was a living example of the man Jesus spoke of "who built his house on the sand. And the rain fell, and the floods came, and the winds blew and beat against that house, and it fell, and great was the fall of it."

Many political personalities in my community privately expressed to me their serious reservations about Trump but then publicly supported him. No one caused me more distress than Paul Ryan. I had come to know Paul fairly well since we first met some twenty years earlier when he was a young staffer for Kansas senator Sam Brownback, whom I would go on to befriend, attending many prayer gatherings and Bible studies at the senator's office. I saw Paul often over the next sixteen years he spent in the Congress, and I traveled with the Romney campaign when he was the vice presidential candidate.

The last time I had talked at length with Paul was in September 2015 when we sat next to each other at Mass during Pope Francis's visit to Washington. He expressed admiration for the new pope, especially Francis's emphasis on the gospel as what theologians and other religious scholars refer to as "God's encounter with the other"—if we are to be like the Son of God, we needed to reach out to those who are different from us. "He'll be good for the church—and for everybody," I remember Paul saying of the pontiff. We spoke about one of Paul's favorite subjects, moral theology. Sometimes I would bump into him in the dining room at the Capitol Hill Republican Club and he would have a priest or a theology professor with him. As we sat together at the Mass, I had a hopeful view of his possible rise to Speaker of the House, but the glow didn't last long. Once in office, Paul refused to take on the gun lobby. Then I watched his vacillating support of Trump give way into a generally positive and mildly-critical-when-necessary mode. Finally, Paul endorsed Trump. It was dispiriting to say the least.

Party loyalty, while distressing, was predictable, but what about the religious community? Trump's public comments about Christianity, religion, and even Holy Communion indicated he was utterly nonreligious, totally unfamiliar with the most rudimentary knowledge of the Bible, much less able to quote a chapter or a verse. Yet many of the people with whom I had served over the years—Jim Dobson, Tony Perkins, Gary Bauer, and others—provided Trump with evangelical affirmation. Dobson went so far as to describe him as a newly born-again "baby Christian." Presenting a consistent position to the world was essential for these leaders: they were not going to break with the likes of Senate Majority Leader Mitch McConnell, who reminded us repeatedly of the importance of a Trump victory to secure a conservative Supreme Court appointment. Rationalizing the choice became an important part of their role in the campaign.

My silence about Trump—worse, my criticism of him—would be noted and likely punished with ostracism, public censure, and more loss of financial and political support. I would be labeled disloyal and accused of being one of Hillary Clinton's secret minions. When dealing with nuanced and difficult conflicts within our community, we were quick to call out a defector, a traitor, or even an instrument of Satan. Maybe we've just learned as a species over the centuries that the only way to control our unruly bunch is to use communal intimidation. A month before the Republican National Convention, I tweeted, "I've met Trump. Warning 2 fellow evangelical leaders: No good choice this year is no reason to abandon core moral principles. Trump = danger." Many responses from other church leaders were hostile. Reacting to my warning in his own tweet, a pastor I had known for almost thirty years accused me of having been in D.C. too long: "Maybe upside will be money from the Clinton Foundation. SAD!"

Every time Mr. Trump would offer us another favor to seal the deal of our support—moving the embassy to Jerusalem, for example, or delivering a pro-life conservative to the Supreme Court—pastors and donors from all over the country called, emailed, and texted me to gush. In their minds it was reason enough to vote for him to eliminate the Johnson Amendment so we could endorse candidates from the pulpit. What about Merry Christmas? One of Trump's regular speeches included his assurance, "I told you about Christmas, and I guarantee you, if I become president, we're going to be saying Merry Christmas at every store . . . every store . . . every store . . . I'm saying Merry Christmas to whoever the hell wants to hear it." I asked a colleague who had jumped on the Trump bandwagon, "Is that why some of us went to prison: to say 'Merry Christmas'?"

Then came the ultimate gift to evangelicals, the pièce de résistance—Mike Pence. Mike was the governor of Indiana, a former congressman, and a tested evangelical. I had interacted with Mike throughout his twelve years in the House of Representatives and had given him the Ten Commandments Leadership Award. Needless to say, my people were thrilled with Trump's pick. When I raised questions about whether the rest of the Trump-Pence agenda would serve the country or even our members, they lost patience with me. The response was predictable: "Do you want Hillary?"

In comparison with my work on the gun issue, I thought withholding support for Trump would be easy, but now I found myself at odds with just about everyone with whom I had worked for decades—especially with an organization that had been a central part of my life and one for which I had been serving as chairman for three years. A minister generally leaves a denomination for only one of several extraordinary reasons. When I moved from Elim Fellowship to the Assemblies of God, I did so because I was required to. When I left the Assemblies of God, it was because I could no longer feel comfortable with its doctrinal requirement of speaking in tongues. Sometimes a minister is forced out due to a moral failing. But none of these were at play when I decided to leave the Evangelical Church Alliance.

I had been an ECA member since 1999, when I sought a spiritual home that was suitably broad but still conservative. I enjoyed my relationships with fellow members and closer friendships with our leadership team. There was great unanimity in our ranks: one party, the GOP; one philosophy, conservative; and one television network, Fox. These nonnegotiable twenty-first-century commandments became harder and harder for me to abide by, much less to promote. A month before the July 2016 semiannual board meeting of the Alliance, which took place on the opening day of the Republican National Convention, I resolved to resign my seat as its chairman and leave the organization altogether.

In addition to the confining ideological demands we placed on each other, we spent a lot of time and resources policing our members' personal behavior, especially having to do with our prohibition against alcohol. Most evangelical church bodies trace their roots to the nineteenth-century temperance movement, which campaigned against drinking and successfully brought about Prohibition. We were, as a Bible college instructor of mine once said, "majoring in the minors." Based on our strict policies regarding personal conduct, had Dietrich Bonhoeffer been among our clergy, I would have had to dismiss him because he was a smoker who also enjoyed an occasional brandy. It was difficult for me to sustain some of my important relationships with people for whom teetotaling had taken on a sacramental quality, especially given the fact it wasn't mandated by scripture in the first place. Strange as it seemed to me, this is where many of our members had found final consolation in their support of Trump: he may have been a vulgar womanizer, but he didn't drink. Did that really make him one of us? I asked myself.

It was our new political criteria for evaluating clergy that worried me most. The few members I knew to be Democrats were classified as morally suspicious. Was party affiliation a way of imputing that abortion wasn't murder? Or perhaps cloaking their approval of same-sex marriage? Or maybe they thought the federal government was better at taking care of people than the church? I was concerned this unofficial standard would be especially difficult for our African-American, Latino, and women members.

The breaking point with the Evangelical Church Alliance for me came after the Supreme Court's expansion of legal same-sex marriage reawakened a siege mentality among our leadership. The ECA board strengthened the wording of the policy prohibiting our members from solemnizing same-sex unions. When the terrible mass shooting by a self-proclaimed radical Islamic terrorist took the lives of forty-nine people at a gay nightclub in Orlando, Florida, I felt it was time at last for evangelicals to come to terms with our own attitudes toward the LGBTQ community. We could no longer glibly assert our tired adage, "Hate the sin but love the sinner." We would have to model more than tolerance for gays and lesbians; we needed to find authentic love and affirmation for them in their totality. This approach was anathema to the officers of the ECA. If I could not bring about change, then I needed to move on.

I had given the board advance notice of my intention to resign, so everyone was fully aware of what was coming. When I arrived at the Chicago hotel and met my fellow board members, our conversation was strained: everyone tried to ignore the elephant sitting patiently in the corner of the room. Following the meal, we moved to an adjacent conference area where I struck the gavel and called for the opening prayer. After the amen, I announced I would exercise the privilege of the chair to read my letter of resignation. I handed copies to the men around the table and, swallowing hard, began to read:

> My decision to resign falls in three areas of concern: my longtime unease with the implications of our rules about externals, particularly on alcohol and tobacco, but not for the more obvious reasons; my imminent plans to begin publicly speaking on what I see as the existence of a huge ethical failing in the evangelical support for a

Trump presidency, and what it suggests about us; and, finally, my
concern for the challenge that lies ahead in ministering to self-identified
LGBTQ persons.

By reading the letter aloud, I was essentially calling for a motion to accept my resignation, which was promptly offered. After a perfunctory second, I followed protocol and announced I would leave the room for the vote. I asked permission of the chair to say a personal good-bye to each of my fellows and give each a "holy hug." When we embraced, one of my longtime friends whispered, "Don't lose who you are."

And then it was over. I had never felt truer to myself, and yet I also felt more alone than I had for a long time. Deep personal and professional partnerships mean a lot to me. I'd been married to the same woman for thirty-eight years. There were churches whose pulpits I had routinely visited to see children born in them, grow into adults, and start their own families. I still had the same ministerial mentor I had when I was twenty. I had stayed in touch with people I knew in Bible college, and most of my best friends had been so for twenty-five and thirty years. My resignation meant a massive rupture in my life and an end to more friendships than the ones around that boardroom table. But, hard as it was, this was a necessary loss. As I drove the thirty-five miles back to the airport, I felt the same two emotions that I'd heard about from so many newly divorced couples: relief and remorse.

★★★

When I arrived in Cleveland for my tenth Republican National Convention, I wondered if this one would be like all the others—a kind of warm and happy reunion, a chance to meet friends, some of whom I saw only every four years. But there was nothing familiar about this convention: the delegates, the speakers, the role of the Republican establishment, and, obviously, the nominee were mostly strange to me. This no longer felt celebratory and familiar.

Outside the convention center I ran into former RNC chairman Michael Steele, a moderate, pro-life Catholic. Our paths usually crossed only at the annual Red Mass each October at Washington's St. Matthew's Cathedral, when members of the judicial branch, including most Supreme Court justices, attend church together the Sunday before the term begins. Michael and I had become regular nonjudicial guests and developed a warm friendship in that setting. But I could tell he wasn't his normal jovial self that day. I asked him about his feelings on the presumptive nominee, and he told me emphatically that Trump did not represent his corner of the party. He was about to say more, when Jim Garlow, pastor of an evangelical mega church in San Diego, approached us.

If Michael expressed ambivalence, Jim was all in, announcing happily that in Trump we had "God's man." Noting our skepticism, he acknowledged that his first choice was Ted Cruz, but assured us that God uses all sorts of people, even immoral men, invoking a reference to Cyrus I had heard many times in conversations about Trump. Cyrus was the sixth century B.C. megalomaniacal Persian emperor who became the go-to biblical justification for Trump among evangelicals. Even though Cyrus was a madman, he defeated the Babylonians who had held the Jews captive—thus, the prevailing interpretation went, God used flawed creatures for higher purposes. Jim's euphoric certainty that God was going to use Trump to do the work of the angels was an opinion reflected by every evangelical I would encounter at the convention.

Once inside the giant Quicken Loans Arena, I asked if there was a prayer room. All the conventions I had ever attended had such a designated space, but no one at the registration desk in Cleveland knew anything about a prayer room. When, finally, someone discovered a space in the adjacent ballpark for that purpose, I began holding services there, but no one came. Over the few days I was at the convention, the space became a kind of hermitage for me. I sat in that small prayer room, an island of peace amidst the convention's maelstrom—the chants of "Lock her up! Lock her up!" echoing in the distance. On the night Trump delivered his acceptance speech, he promised, "when I take the oath of office next year, I will restore law and order to our country." He went on to announce that he would "bring jobs back to Ohio," and bragged he had "the strong endorsement of the NRA." Then he thanked the evangelicals. The crowd cheered. I did not.

When I returned home, Cheryl saw how glum I was. In fact, being at the RNC in Cleveland had so vexed me that I decided to drive home instead of fly because I've always found long drives therapeutic. I needed time alone—with God, with my conscience, with my emotions. I was deeply, deeply troubled. After ten hours behind the wheel, alternating between carping, crying, and praying, I resolved that what I had been witness to in Cleveland was the final moral collapse of the politicized religion that had infected me and millions of others back in the eighties, when American evangelicals entered into their Faustian pact with Ronald Reagan's party. Nothing good could come of this badly diseased body. At home, I told Cheryl I could no longer toe the Republican or even the evangelical line when it came to our political choices. She shocked me when she said she didn't plan to, either; in fact, for the first time since Jimmy Carter in 1976, she would vote for the Democratic candidate, Hillary Clinton. Just a decade earlier, such an announcement would have had me thinking about divorce, but at this point I considered joining her.

Four days later I attended the Democratic National Convention in Philadelphia, and it stood in complete contrast to the previous week's dystopia. I still bristled when Cecile Richards of Planned Parenthood associated abortion with "reproductive rights," but not for the same reasons I had in the past. Now it was because I believed she knew abortion meant loss—of someone and something—and shouldn't be cheered. For the first time ever, I agreed with virtually everything else Richards said. She was not the only one. I never thought I would find such relief with liberals. If it wasn't their words, it was the optics. The stands in Cleveland had been a sea of white and mostly middle-aged people, but in Philadelphia, everywhere I looked reflected the gorgeous diversity of God's creation—every color, every ethnicity, every age, and as many women as men.

I was caught in a riptide of conflicted thoughts and emotions. I spent nearly all my ministry life depicting the Democrats as the party of death—and yet, in comparison to the Republicans in Cleveland, the optimism, dignity, and hope I saw in Philadelphia renewed my confidence in the human family. When I was with the Democrats for Life, I felt closer to their worldview than I did with what had become a strange Republican admixture of a pro-life religious ethic with a kind of godless Ayn Rand objectivism. Hillary Clinton had been formed religiously in Methodism, Wesley's "religion of the heart," and this was the Christianity present in that arena. I felt a surge of love for the people who surrounded me, and a fragile hope about the future. My whole world had turned upside down. When the towering Pentecostal preacher Dr. William Barber took to the podium, he announced, "I'm a theologically conservative, liberal, evangelical biblicist." In doing so, he articulated exactly what I thought Bonhoeffer to be, and what I hoped to become.

Just days before the election, our lawyer and friend Jay Sekulow asked if I would join him in Nashville to participate in a Facebook live video coverage of returns. On Election Day, I arrived at the studios of the American Center for Law and Justice, a sprawling industrial-style complex. In the thirty years I've known him, Jay has always been intense and driven, but that night he was uncharacteristically subdued.

Throughout the evening, the staff clustered around several large wall-mounted screens, watching various news outlets or staring into glowing monitors. My role was to offer intermittent commentary on the election results.

When Jay asked me who I thought would win, I provided the conventional wisdom in the days leading up to the election: that the race was a lock for Clinton. Around six p.m. Nashville time, as Jay paced the floor nervously, I received a text from a contact in Washington. It contained polling numbers from inside the Republican National Committee showing Hillary trouncing Trump. I was left gazing at my phone, adjusting to the reality of another Clinton presidency but one that, this time, I welcomed with relief. I voted in Washington, D.C., a secure Democratic victory, so I didn't cast my ballot for her. I felt as if I knew too much about the Clintons, and also knew that my vote for write-in candidate Evan McMullin would not swing the election. Like many Americans, if the Democratic nominee had been anyone else— Joe Biden, for instance—I would have switched parties.

Watching the returns, I chatted with some employees and other guests, and texted Cheryl. Then the numbers started coming in. A few states broke for Trump, followed by a few for Hillary. The next hour was a horse race and I was pulled into the studio for a few segments, during which I was so preoccupied by the vote tallies that I don't remember what I said. At nine o'clock the guests and crew huddled around the screens and went silent. Donald Trump was winning, but there were no cheers.

The Electoral College totals eventually turned toward Trump and stayed that way until Pennsylvania was called. When Trump was declared the winner, I was yanked back into the studio and spouted some meaningless jabber. I was stunned. I knew most of Jay's audience would be celebrating the unexpected victory, but like so many Americans that night, I was feeling sick. Trump's victory was the direct result of the evangelical sellout I had mourned after the Cleveland convention.

On the ride back to the hotel, I looked out the window and wondered what his win portended and how we might reclaim the moral core of our community. Before going to sleep I called home: Cheryl was anxious and incredulous, and my daughter was livid. A week later, the data would show that 81 percent of evangelicals had voted for Trump. I wasn't surprised. Many of our most generous supporters told me they wouldn't be helping our organization in the new year because they'd sent their money to Trump. One planned to attend the presidential inauguration; it would cost him $15,000.

As all this was unfolding for me, Paul was undergoing his own ordeal. He and I agreed that Donald Trump was a disaster for Christians, evangelical and Catholic, but the divisions in the Catholic community over Pope Francis and his invitation to members who had been ostracized— divorcees, gays, and lesbians—to come back to the Church had dominated Paul's time and sapped his energy. He decided it was time to make a clean break from his hybrid Catholic-evangelical project and work on his own. He would take the National Pro-Life Action Center in a new direction, rendering it autonomous in the process, and bring it in line with Catholic social teaching. It would become, for all intents and purposes, an entirely Catholic organization. For the first time in nearly forty years, we would no longer be paired in ministry.

31
Holy Week, 2017

Every few years, Easter and Passover—two great holidays of the Christian and Jewish traditions—occur over the same week. It's a fitting coincidence, because, as I have preached in countless sermons over the years, Jesus celebrated Passover in what became for Christians the Last Supper, sharing unleavened bread and wine with his disciples. The Easter journey replicates Christ's last week of earthly life, beginning with his triumphant entry into Jerusalem, the Last Supper and his washing of the disciples' feet on Holy Thursday, his crucifixion and death on Good Friday, and his glorious resurrection on Easter Sunday. Passover is an eight-day festival, divided into two parts, that also commemorates a holy journey: this one the Exodus—the emancipation of the Hebrew people from slavery in ancient Egypt.

The all-church council of Nicaea in 325 determined Easter would always fall on the first Sunday after the first full moon following the vernal equinox. Passover, on the other hand, would always start on the fifteenth day of the Hebrew month Nissan. In 2017, during the week of April 10, I began with a Palm Sunday service at a historic church in Oxford, England, while on a speaking engagement there. That afternoon I flew home and the next night, the first night of the Jewish feast, I went to Alexandria, Virginia, to observe the seder in the home of a Conservative rabbi. I would often celebrate Passover in church or at our ministry center, using it as an instructional tool for fellow evangelicals, but this was very different. My place at this Passover table emerged more from a budding friendship than from a professional affiliation.

Cheryl kept counseling hours on Monday nights, so I arrived alone at the front door of the home of Jack and Ann Moline. After heading a congregation for over twenty-five years, Jack took over the Interfaith Alliance, a nonprofit advocacy organization that was generally liberal in orientation but eager to bridge divides among people of faith. In the political sphere, we fell on opposite sides of the spectrum, and in years past I would never have accepted the invitation—not that I would have expected to receive it. But my hosts knew that my attitudes had changed a lot over recent years.

Every seder is unique, the host family's special gift to their guests. In true rabbinical fashion, Jack makes his seder a kind of teaching opportunity, expanding the lessons of the Exodus with an additional theme for discussion. This year their topic was the stranger, and the Molines sent around several questions that they wanted the guests to think about in anticipation of the conversation. When do you feel like a stranger? When do you feel at home? What does the stranger gain? What are our obligations to the strangers among us, and what are the limits of those obligations?

It was decided that the evening would be free of politics. Our thoughts should come from the heart, Jack said, not from the troubling headlines. His questions affected me deeply for many personal reasons, but also because I had received them while I was thinking about a sermon I would deliver later in the week, on Good Friday, at a large church in New Jersey. Jack's questions had inspired me to write about Jesus, who, as a man without a grave in which to be buried, was a stranger among his own. When I sat down at the Molines' table to ponder the questions at hand, I was already in this rabbi's debt.

I've identified as an evangelical Christian nearly three times longer than I identified as a Jew, but it didn't matter. I put on a yarmulke and immediately felt the comfort of belonging. Distant memories of seders gone by, with family and friends, came rushing back to me: the prayers, the Hebrew, the brisket, the giggles of children looking for the *afikomen*—the hidden part of the matzo broken at the beginning of the ceremony and retrieved at its conclusion—were all familiar. I heard the voice of my father telling me that, even in the camps, Jews found a way to conduct secret seders without food or wine, such was the importance of God's command: "You shall keep it as a feast to the Lord; throughout your generations, as a statute forever."

Jack emphasized one question that had become almost a fixation for me, "When have you felt like a stranger?" One guest, who had lived in China for many years, spoke about what it was like to always feel like an outsider, from not ever being able to master the language, to her physical appearance immediately setting her apart as "other." Someone else grew up in an immigrant home where her parents didn't teach her their native language, in many ways building a lifelong wall between them. I was lost in thought when my turn came. I had so much to say about this subject that editing it for a brief answer was a challenge.

I felt like a stranger, I said, when I could not reveal my true thoughts, express what I really believe, or tell people who I really am. I was thinking of the night I came home from the little Emmanuel Church, or the first time I realized my community had a gun problem, or my service on the ECA board, or my sense of not really belonging in the jam-packed arenas of either Cleveland or Philadelphia—or, most imminently, my evolving stand on the explosive issue of same-sex marriage. One place I didn't feel like a stranger was at Jack and Ann's table. I felt welcome.

After the main meal was served, a few of the participants spoke with me and thanked me for sharing my experiences. We got up to stretch our legs and talk with others out of range for table conversation. After Jack circulated through the room, he returned to sit by me. He mentioned he had watched *The Armor of Light* and was impressed with the film and my work on gun control advocacy. He then asked me if I had ever heard of a man named Garson Romalis. The name rang a bell, but I couldn't quite place it. He then told me the man's story. Romalis was a Canadian OB-GYN whose greatest joy in life was successfully delivering babies to bright and hopeful new parents. He considered bringing new life into the world a privilege that provided more fulfillment than nearly anything else he did. But as part of his job, he also performed abortions. As glorious as it was to bring life into the world, he had also seen the dire effects of illegal abortions as an intern in Chicago in the early sixties and became determined to offer safe and legal procedures in his practice.

When Canada legalized abortion in 1969, Romalis became one of the first providers in the province of British Columbia. His clinic was picketed regularly by the increasingly active pro-life movement in Canada. In November 1994, a sniper fired a bullet through the doors of his home kitchen; it lodged in his left thigh, severing an artery. He nearly bled to death and spent months in the hospital recovering. For security reasons, the family was forced to find a new home, where they lived with round-the-clock guards. Although Romalis would eventually continue practicing as a gynecologist, the injury left him so impaired that he couldn't stand for long periods of time. His days of delivering babies were over, but his days of performing abortions were not.

Six years later, another anti-abortion extremist ambushed Romalis in his clinic and stabbed him in the back. He again evaded death and recovered quickly, but his family begged him to take himself out of harm's way. This time he listened, and the women of Vancouver lost a beloved doctor. Of course, I had heard about this man—and the memories came rushing back. At the time of the first shooting, I had appeared on a daytime talk show in Toronto to discuss the case and do damage control for the pro-life movement, distancing us from the radicals who had become so dangerous and disruptive. I remembered it all vividly and told Jack.

"Garson was my cousin," Jack said.

The world froze for a moment. I was stunned. Jack wasn't blaming me, but I could not help but feel culpable. Jack had seen the old footage of me during the Spring of Life demonstrations in Buffalo. Jack's own family had been a casualty of the violence I had done so little to thwart. And now I was a guest at his home table.

He didn't ask me to take responsibility for those deaths or injuries, but he gave me another opportunity to see them for what they really were: not blips on a timeline, not so-called regrettable occurrences, but real people experiencing real suffering, with names, with hearts, with families. By sharing that story with me in the context of a Passover meal, an event that had been such a part of my childhood, I felt that my Jewish past and my evangelical present had been reconciled in a way that they never had been before. Jack left me feeling not guilty but forgiven—not condemned but understood—as a deeply flawed human being. But he also left me understanding better his side of this equation. Abby had started that process, and, with tact and care, Jack continued it. I was reminded of sitting in a pew at the beginning of another Holy Week, forty-three years earlier, in a Methodist church sanctuary, being bidden to the altar by the voice of a minister. This time that voice of invitation and forgiveness belonged to a rabbi.

Something had gone terribly wrong with American evangelicalism, or, perhaps, I thought, it had always been wrong and I was simply seeing the problem only now. Over the forty-three years I had been a Christian, the orientation of American evangelicals had shifted from what many theologians call the ultimate to the penultimate. We had descended from the high and heavenly calling in Christ to earthly politics, partisanship, and nativist rhetoric and behavior. We had traded a universal Savior for all people, all humanity, in all times, at all places, for a kind of tribal deity whose only interest was to preserve and protect a single group and their peculiar culture.

The next day I continued to work on my Good Friday sermon. I deliver most of my messages extemporaneously, without notes, fresh and in the moment. As an itinerant preacher, I've enjoyed the benefit of rarely being in front of the same congregation more than once a year, so I could repeat a message, perfecting it over time, until I was able to deliver it flawlessly, expanding themes congregations connect with or editing those they don't.

But this year I could take no chances, and wrote down every word. My focus was not going to be on the usual scene of Jesus on the Cross, the meaning of his death and suffering, or his Seven Last Words. Instead, I wanted to look at what happened afterward when a stranger, Joseph of Arimathea, donated his grave for Jesus, who didn't have a prearranged place of burial. Playing in the background was the controversy surrounding President Trump's travel bans that blocked certain people, mostly Muslims, from entering the United States. A few evangelical organizations had objected, but once again, their voices were drowned out by the hallelujah chorus of supporters. In Jesus' day, most people, especially Jews, had arranged where they would be laid to rest well in advance, and it was almost always in a family crypt of some kind. The fact that Jesus didn't make such arrangements was significant: it suggested not only that He may have been impoverished, but also that He was estranged from his community. A wanderer among his own.

Aren't we all?

This was the message I wanted to share on Good Friday with the people in New Jersey. During such difficult times, with a figure in the White House who had recently enacted a Muslim ban, I felt I had so much to say to those who wondered whether they would soon become pariahs, ejected from the country that had become their adopted home. Even members of Christian refugee communities, who, like my grandfather's family, had fled terrible persecution in their homelands, were vulnerable and afraid. I was beginning to feel closer to them. My suffering was far from theirs, but, I, too, had become a stranger in what had been, for me, a secure community for over forty years.

The sanctuary was packed. The momentous nature of Good Friday, the day that Christ died for our sins, often inspires even those who rarely go to church to attend. I came to the pulpit and began with a passage from Matthew. "As evening approached, there came a rich man from Arimathea, named Joseph, who had himself become a disciple of Jesus. Going to Pilate, he asked for Jesus' body, and Pilate ordered that it be given to him. Joseph took the body, wrapped it in a clean linen cloth, and placed it in his own new tomb that he had cut out of the rock."

I went on to talk about my Jewish background and the importance of burial in Jewish life. How the place of interment in ancient times was planned relatively early in life, which is what made Jesus' lack of a tomb particularly striking. Jesus came for the *outcast*, I told the congregation—and was one Himself. He was the *alien*—and He came for the alien. He was *homeless*—and He came for the homeless. He was a *foreigner*—and He came for the foreigner. Jesus, a man without a grave, a man dispossessed, a man alone, a man despised, a man on the outside.

I wasn't sure if this was resonating with a crowd that had been bombarded with messages about the threat of "radical Islamic terrorists" and the dangers of Syrian refugees. Had my sermon just alienated the very people I sought to comfort? Were they all Trump supporters and sensitive to the implicit criticism in my words? The congregation seemed paralyzed in silence for those fifteen minutes as I spoke about feeling lost or estranged, about being the black sheep in a family or a community. "If you're lost, you have a Savior," I concluded. "If you're orphaned, you have a Heavenly Father; if you're an alien, you have a country; if you're alone, you have friends." There was what I at first read as a tense silence. As I stepped back from the pulpit, I looked around the sanctuary, wondering if I had crossed a line. I glanced over at the pastor; he looked concerned.

Then someone began to clap.

Then someone else. Slowly, the entire congregation, one row after another, rose in their pews and delivered a long ovation. Even in the most demonstrative churches, Good Friday is generally subdued, but the people in that service were ebullient that day. I had never seen anything like it. The pastor bounded onto the altar and hugged me, thanking me under his breath. Then he turned to the congregation and said, "I promise you I won't put a sermon on a sermon, especially after that one." Another explosive round of applause followed. I can't know what was going on in the minds of those 1,200 people, but I hoped in that moment they saw and understood something about themselves and about all of us. We are all in the same boat; we need each other as much as we need God. There is no difference between me and the person next to me, in front of me, behind me. It doesn't matter who they are, where they came from, what they believe or don't believe, who they love or don't love. We are creations of God, every single one, from the best to the worst.

On Easter Sunday, I had no preaching assignment, so Cheryl and I attended services at a local church. I was awed by the power of the resurrected Christ's intersection with the reality of our everyday lives. During a very new reality in the United States under President Donald Trump, when many days seemed dark, the Resurrection provided comfort and hope in the knowledge that Jesus could not be relegated to the past or reserved for an idealized future. Through his resurrection, he is present here and now, in our immediate reality. For me, there is no more optimistic or enduring message on earth. Christ has risen. He is risen indeed.

★★★

In my travels, I have met many people who have shared with me their discomfort with the co-optation of Jesus' beautiful message by political forces. They know that something important has been lost but have no idea what to do about it. It has resulted in a restlessness and discontent that is emptying our churches. We've lost millions of young people because they do not see in our eyes or hear from our mouths the words or love of a Christ they know, deep in their souls, is the only source of human improvement. For them I hope to create and inhabit a new space in which conversations about the moral and spiritual content of our painfully human and social struggles are not acrimonious, contentious, hostile, and hateful but Christlike in love, in respect, and in honor of one another.

Once again, it would be my most unlikely benefactor, Abigail Disney, who would help me take this vision from concept to reality. With Cheryl beside me, Abby asked, "If you could do anything with your life at this stage, what would it be?" I was too shy to say what I was thinking, but Cheryl blurted out, "Honey, that would be your Bonhoeffer Institute." That was exactly how I had answered the question silently in my mind. Since the time in 2010 that I stood in the yard at the Flossenbürg concentration camp where Bonhoeffer was hanged, I harbored a dream of someday launching an institution that would apply his insights into ethics to social crises in our own time. "If that's it, Rob," Abby said matter-of-factly, "let's make it happen." With a generous start-up grant from Abby, followed by operational grants from other individuals and foundations, the Dietrich Bonhoeffer Institute was born. Its vision statement begins, "We settle for nothing less than a just society infused with collaboration and equity."

One of my favorite moments in the gospels is when Jesus told his disciples what would be the hallmark of a Christian, "By this shall all people know that you are my disciples, if you have love for one another." I long to return to that courageous kindness, to a spiritual simplicity based on that divine common denominator of love.

I can say three things about my spiritual journey: I was born again and professed Jesus Christ as my Lord and Savior. It was the beginning of something new, something hopeful, something beyond the limitations of our humanity. It led to a path filled with faith, hope, and love. But then I listened to a beguiling voice—mixed with others, of course, but it was not the voice of my Lord. This voice was determined not to lead souls to a savior but to capture them for a self-serving end. I was seduced by that voice, and it led me into that dark wood. I did some good in that place, but it was contaminated by ambition, hubris, and disregard for the other, the stranger. No longer were the addicts in the halfway house my flock. I surrendered too often to that same temptation and was blinded to the real work of caring for souls. To engage in the scrum of the debate, score a win, maneuver for domination, exercise influence, and leave it there, or worse, cloak it as gospel, is to do no good at all, but instead, to inflict great harm.

After a long period of preparation, like Jesus' forty days in the wilderness, or the apostle Paul's three years in the desert, I had reencountered Bonhoeffer, whom I thought I knew, but didn't. I reread his *Call to Discipleship*, and his other work, *Christ the Center*, and they recalibrated my spiritual compass. If I have lost friends in one community, I have found many others, and—secure in the love of my marriage, my family, and my Redeemer—I am on my way back to that original call and that critical center.

It is my hope and my prayer that others will join me in a place where we might try to discern the will of God, for each of us, no matter what church, what altar, what form of prayer leads us to salvation. What kind of world would it be if we returned to the curiosity and humility of the pilgrim? Where we tried to more fully understand and act on what the gospel says to us, to our communities, to our country, to the stranger?

As I emerged from my period of darkness, of succumbing to politics and power, I saw how expansive God's grace is and how universal his invitation is to it. I no longer believe you're excluded if you're homosexual, or if you've had an abortion, or if you perform them. I no longer believe Muslims are dangerous marauders, or that Democrats and liberals are apostates. I no longer believe Jesus is a Republican or that Ronald Reagan spoke for God and Jimmy Carter didn't. That gracious space is so vast, so much more complex, so much more beautifully mysterious than any of us could ever imagine.

I do believe we are better off when we listen more and talk less, and that especially includes our conversations with God. And I do believe we need to seek deeply and risk greatly to act courageously in obedience to the will of God as best as we can. My new journey is far more gratifying than a plane flight around the world, or a two-thousand-mile trek to Mexico, or a confident stroll through the corridors of political power. My destination is clear. I am on a journey to find the reality of God, every day, day after day, in this moment, in whomever I encounter.

"Cheap grace is the mortal enemy of our Church," Bonhoeffer wrote. I've also learned it's the mortal enemy of our politics, our self-perception, our identity. "Cheap grace is the grace we bestow on ourselves. Cheap grace is the preaching of forgiveness without requiring repentance, baptism without church discipline, Communion without confession," he wrote. "Cheap grace is grace without discipleship, grace without the cross, grace without Jesus Christ, living and incarnate." But then Bonhoeffer reassures us: "Our struggle today is for costly grace."

Of course it is a struggle. Of course it is costly. But how magnificent, how unearned, how surprising is that grace.

Acknowledgments

There are many people to thank after a more-than-two-year effort to produce this book, beginning with my family, who gave me emotional and practical support. For you, Cheryl, Anna, Matthew, Paul, Kathy, and Colleen, words are inadequate to express how much love and gratitude I have for your incomparable support. My agent, Stuart Krichevsky of Krichevsky Literary Agency, took a big risk on me, then kindly shepherded me through the process in every way, including improving the book with his numerous suggestions. Executive editor Luke Dempsey at HarperCollins drew the story out of me and encouraged me not only with his expert editorial guidance, but, more important, with his personal and passionate interest in the message I wanted to share. Luke's assistant, Sarah Haugen, kept everything moving forward, helping in so many ways. Marianne Szegedy-Maszak, an accomplished author in her own right, shaped the story, found words to capture even its most difficult parts, and ensured a product worthy of reading. I will always be in Marianne's debt. Finally, it was Abby Disney who first prompted me to write—then nudged me until I had unstoppable momentum. Abby is the angel behind this undertaking.

About the Author

Rob Schenck is a leading figure in American evangelicalism who has challenged the politicization of his religious community and its attitudes on guns, abortion, and homosexuality. An ordained minister, Rob holds degrees in Bible studies, theology, and church and state. During his decades-long ministry career, he has served as a missionary evangelist, a pastor, and a minister to top government officials in Washington, D.C. He is the founding president of the Dietrich Bonhoeffer Institute, dedicated to promoting ethical reflection and responsible action in public life and policy.